Policing Pleas

Policing Pleasure

Sex Work, Policy, and the State
in Global Perspective

Edited by Susan Dewey and Patty Kelly

NEW YORK UNIVERSITY PRESS
New York and London

NEW YORK UNIVERSITY PRESS
New York and London
www.nyupress.org

References to Internet websites (URLs) were accurate at the time of writing.
Neither the author nor New York University Press is responsible for URLs
that may have expired or changed since the manuscript was prepared.

Library of Congress Cataloging-in-Publication Data

Policing pleasure : sex work, policy, and the state in global perspective /
edited by Susan Dewey and Patty Kelly.
p. cm.
Includes bibliographical references and index.
ISBN 978-0-8147-8508-9 (cl : alk. paper)
ISBN 978-0-8147-8509-6 (pb : alk. paper)
ISBN 978-0-8147-8510-2 (ebook)
ISBN 978-0-8147-8511-9 (ebook)
1. Prostitution—Government policy. 2. Prostitution—Political aspects.
3. Prostitution. I. Dewey, Susan. II. Kelly, Patty, 1968–
HQ121.P65   2011
363.4'4—dc23   2011018457

New York University Press books are printed on acid-free paper,
and their binding materials are chosen for strength and durability.
We strive to use environmentally responsible suppliers and materials
to the greatest extent possible in publishing our books.

Manufactured in the United States of America

c   10 9 8 7 6 5 4 3 2 1
p   10 9 8 7 6 5 4 3 2 1

To all those who shared their stories with us

Contents

Acknowledgments

We are both exceedingly grateful to Jennifer Hammer, our editor at New York University (NYU) Press, whose wholehearted enthusiasm for the project energized and inspired us as we moved from a rather loosely structured book proposal to a polished final manuscript. Others at NYU Press were of tremendous assistance in bringing this project to fruition, including Assistant Editor Gabrielle Begue, Managing Editor Despina Gimbel, and Copyeditor Rita Bernhard. Two anonymous reviewers offered helpful feedback and constructive criticism that resulted in a more cohesive manuscript.

This volume initially drew its inspiration from our independent research on sex work and public policy, which has grown immeasurably as a result of our collaboration with the diverse set of international scholars whose work is featured in this volume. A great deal of this collaborative energy stemmed from interactions between some of this volume's contributors at two consecutive invited sessions at the Annual Meeting of the American Anthropological Association. The 2010 session "Gendered Migration and the Global Circulation of Trafficking Discourse," sponsored by the Association for Feminist Anthropology, was co-organized by Tiantian Zheng and Susan Dewey, and afforded the opportunity to receive feedback from Yasmina Katsulis, Denise Brennan, Svati Shah, Nandita Sharma, and Carole Vance. Discussions before and after our jointly organized 2009 panel session, "Moral Borders and the Boundaries of Labor: Culture and Commodified Sexualities in the Neoliberal Era," sponsored by the Society of Lesbian and Gay Anthropologists, helped enormously in strengthening our arguments about relationships between sex workers and the state.

In addition to these jointly experienced sources of inspiration, Susan wishes to thank Naomi Schneider at the University of California Press for bringing Patty into her life. It has been an honor to work with a scholar of her caliber. Susan also expresses her boundless gratitude to her colleagues in Gender and Women's Studies at the University of Wyoming, who are a source of constant support and precious friendship. She cannot imagine a more congenial group of coworkers than Cathy Connolly, Colleen Denney, Susie McKay, Danielle Pafunda, and Bonnie Zare. Thanks are also extended to her colleagues in International Studies at the University of Wyoming, particularly Jean Garrison. This project was also assisted immeasurably by the excellent work of Michael Goodyear in creating and maintaining a listserv for researchers interested in sex work and public policy.

Patty is incredibly grateful to Susan for her unbelievable diligence, patience, friendship, and motivation; without Susan, this project would not have happened. She also thanks her wonderful colleagues in the Department of Anthropology at George Washington University, her family, and Teresa Mascia, whose presence gave her the time to sit and write and think.

Introduction

Sex Work and the Politics of Public Policy

SUSAN DEWEY AND PATTY KELLY

When a woman is arrested for selling sex on the streets of Nairobi, the very first thing she does is pick up her mobile phone. She dials a number from a list of her colleagues, who will do what they can to earn sufficient bribe money to secure her release. As Chimaraoke Izugbara observes in this volume, participation in such information networks is critical to sex workers' survival in Nairobi. Sex workers, taxi drivers, and even night watchmen communicate via cell phone to help women navigate the dangerous streets of urban Kenya, securing clients while avoiding police harassment, arrest, and even worse fates. According to Kenyan sex worker Irene, "We have to watch out and act like sisters to each other. The one you help today will help you tomorrow." Once in custody, as twenty-five-year-old Melissa confirms, "you can't tell what they will do to you once the police have you with them." The list of indignities that sex workers suffer at the hands of law enforcement is long, and includes rape, physical and verbal abuse, illegal detention, and extortion. Such crimes against sex workers are perpetrated not only by police but also by clients who view them as easy prey. As twenty-three-year-old Comfort says, "People know they can get away with anything they do to you because they know you can't even go to the police."

Mónica sits waiting in the Anti-Venereal Medical Service of the legal, state-run brothel where she works in the southern Mexican city of Tuxtla Gutiérrez. She is surrounded by other women who also wait, clutching the Sanitary Control Cards that deem them registered with the city, disease-free, and able to work. When her turn comes, Mónica will receive a basic gynecological exam and any number of tests for illnesses ranging from simple bacterial vaginosis to HIV. Workers who test positive for any communicable infection are legally forbidden from exchanging sex for money until they are cured. Built in 1991, the Galactic Zone, as this particular brothel is called, is considered by municipal authorities a showplace for the successes of neoliberal[1] social policy in general and state-regulated prostitution in particular. The countless numbers of men and women who sell sex illegally in Tuxtla's streets and bars, driven to do so, in part, by the neoliberal economic policies that have resulted in ever increasing rural to urban migration and immiseration due to the widespread failure of subsistence farming, are viewed by city officials as sources of disease and chaos.

In contrast, the highly regulated workers of the Galactic Zone are, to many, symbols of modern progress. For many workers themselves, the testing and regulation they experience is both socially and personally beneficial; as Lorena puts it, "It's like a secretary with her typewriter. I've got to keep my machine clean." Yet political agendas, economic interests, and gender discrimination sometimes combine to create a dangerous situation in the brothel. In one particularly sobering example, four women immediately tested positive for HIV upon switching medical laboratories, thus casting doubts upon the efficacy of the state's claims to have improved public health via increased regulation.

In the Thai village that anthropologist Heather Montgomery calls Baan Nua, slightly more than half the boys and girls between the ages of six and fourteen work in prostitution. Unlike common media depictions of Thai child prostitutes as poor girls deceived into leaving their rural homes or sold by their struggling parents to brothels where they will be forced to have sex with countless foreign men, the young prostitutes of this coastal village on the edge of a larger tourist town live with their parents, who know what they do, and see themselves not as victims or even as prostitutes but as sons and daughters fulfilling obligations to their families. As one twelve year old who sells sex to foreign clients put it, "[That's] only my body, but this is my family." In addition, it is their engagement in occasional commercial sex that, ironically, allows these children some of the pleasures of childhood that would otherwise be unavailable to them, such as trips to arcades and theme parks.

As Montgomery argues in this volume, extradition laws passed in tourist-sending countries that help prosecute foreign men who purchase sex from children abroad were meaningless for the young sex workers of Baan Nua, as "neither the children nor their families [have] any interest in seeing their clients prosecuted. . . . In the absence of any social support or any form of welfare, these men [are] the only form of income and protection they [have], no matter how damaging that might seem to outsiders." Montgomery further argues that Thai legislation focusing on commercial sex with foreigners is a simplification that ignores the countless local residents who purchase sex from children, corrupt law enforcement, and the Thai government's informal promotion of sex tourism, or what the children of Baan Nua call "going out for fun with foreigners."

Vignettes drawn from the women of Nairobi's streets, the workers of the Galactic Zone, and the children of Baan Nua reveal the highly complex nature of commercial sexualities and the limits of policies and protections both local and global. The women, men, and children presented in the following pages are not simply criminals, victims, or even liberated individuals who shirk social norms, as some scholars, feminists, and activists might portray them. Indeed, recent ethnographic work[2] on commercial sexualities demonstrates the diverse and multidimensional nature of sex work, moving well beyond previous binary debates about structure versus agency and exploitation versus liberation.[3] The chapters in this volume provide ample evidence of the deficiencies inherent in subscribing to such polarized perspectives, which de-historicize, de-contextualize, and homogenize sex work, limiting our understanding of sexual labor and those who engage in it.

The ethnographic nature of the portraits in this volume richly illustrates the myriad ways in which discriminatory and counterproductive policies ranging from criminalization to forced medical testing to flawed legal protections coexist with discourses of agency presented by the workers themselves. As cultural anthropologists, we view the nuanced qualitative data collected through long-term fieldwork as essential to understanding commercial sexualities and forming effective policies to address them. Ethnography, the linchpin of anthropological research, gives readers the sense of "being there" (Bradburd 1998) by capturing the diversity of sex workers' experiences as well as the larger patterns of stigmatization, discrimination, and persecution that they face from Bahia, Brazil, to Dalian, China. The findings presented here make a strong case for using ethnographic work to inform more realistic and beneficial public policies.

The chapters in this volume also vividly illustrate how the pervasive global reach of neoliberal ideologies and practices permeates both public policy and the worldview of sex workers themselves, many of whom see sex work as part of their individual self-improvement strategies. In recent decades the implementation of neoliberal economic policies in many nations has resulted in a marked decline in subsistence agriculture, widening gaps between the rich and poor, increased economic migration, and the explosive growth of a highly gendered service sector. Many scholars have argued that the present phase of late capitalism results in the commodification of all things, especially domestic and other forms of service work (Basi 2009; Bernstein 2007a; Freeman 2000; Parreñas 2001; Spar 2006).

These factors combine to make sex work, whether organized or de facto, full-time or informal, an increasingly common way to survive in an unstable economy. Service-sector employment, including sex work, is one of the few available options many underprivileged individuals have to generate income. Work in the service sector often requires strict management of emotions and great discipline, and workers who perform it may consequently suffer self-estrangement and problems of identity (Hochschild 1983). This estrangement is equally evident in the fragmentation of community bonds as families struggle to survive at a time when neoliberal economic policies dramatically reduce social services and other state benefits. Such atomization is equally evident in the words and actions of individuals who, through sex work, view themselves as independent entrepreneurs rather than organized laborers.[4]

Despite these commonalities, this volume is not intended to recommend a universal policy on sex work. Indeed, as anthropologists, we stress the importance of cultural context and the continuing relevance of the local, even in an era of globalization. In heeding the call for sex work policy that is evidence-based rather than informed by cultural, moral, and other ideological values, as presented in chapter 2 by Michael Goodyear and Ronald Weitzer, this book provides concrete recommendations for improving policy across municipal, state, and national lines. In uniting these chapters, all based upon diverse geographical and cultural regions, we strive to answer two interrelated questions: What accounts for the striking parallels and patterns at work in the lives of individual sex workers in such a variety of divergent cultural contexts? And how, in turn, might ethnographies of the sexual labor of women, children, and men offer unique recommendations for improved public policy on sex work?

Public Policy Debates on Sex Work

In the interests of a holistic approach to the topic, the chapters in this volume define sex work as a continuum of behaviors involving the commodification of intimacy. The vast majority of studies presented here document the lives of marginalized individuals who engage in such behaviors as part of their strategies for survival or social mobility.[5] Their strategies generally involve the strategic use of sex or sexualized attention in exchange for money or something of value, and the highly nuanced and individual nature of these situations do not always lend themselves easily to clear-cut generalizations about sex work. Nonetheless, the ethnographic accounts presented here very effectively document an often sharp disconnect between policy and its practice.

It is certainly not our intention to portray the women, men, and children in this volume as unwitting sex workers whose poverty or innocence gives them a greater moral ground upon which to stand (as neither we nor our contributors believe that sex work is moral or immoral in and of itself). That the workers we write about are marginalized and that this arouses (intended or not) the sympathy of many readers and policy makers reflects many of the debates in the ensuing chapters on trafficking versus migration, morality, and beliefs about victimization that often inform faulty policy. Indeed, almost all the chapters demonstrate the nuanced ways in which prostitution policy impacts individuals differently based on class, race, ethnicity, citizenship, gender, and age.

From the legal brothels of the Netherlands to the illegal but very visible red light districts of urban India, public policy approaches to sex work are informed by shifting political climates and public perceptions of gender, health, and labor. Although these approaches vary cross-culturally, three broad categories emerge: legalization, criminalization, and decriminalization. This volume presents examples of the impact of legalized sex work in the Netherlands and in a state-run brothel in Mexico and discusses the consequences of criminalization in China, India, the United States, and South Africa, as well as the specific case of criminalization via municipal by-laws in Nairobi, Kenya. The impact of decriminalization is addressed in the context of New Zealand and in three very different Brazilian sites. Two chapters additionally address the problematic issue of age and the ability to consent in Thailand and South Africa, and another chapter raises unsettling questions about the rather unclear divisions between serial monogamy and sex work.

Where legal, sex work is often highly regulated by local or state authorities and generally requires that sex workers register with state authorities and have mandatory health screenings for HIV and other sexually transmitted illnesses. Women working in the legal brothels of rural Nevada are tested for gonorrhea, chlamydia, syphilis, and HIV before beginning work and then subsequently throughout their careers (Brents, Jackson, and Hausbeck 2009), whereas in urban Tijuana, Mexico, legal sex workers are given blood tests for some illnesses whereas other illnesses, such as syphilis, are screened for only visually (Katsulis 2008:99). In addition to medical management and bureaucratic oversight, legal sex work is often spatially regulated, as many countries confine legal sex work to bars, brothels, or particular districts with police oversight. Such areas are often far from private homes, businesses, and schools, and are characterized by the police and the public as places that tolerate sex work and other forms of "vice." Tellingly, such areas are called *zonas de tolerancia* (tolerance zones) throughout Spanish-speaking Latin America, and workers selling sex outside the boundaries of such zones, such as in a bar or on the street, may be subject to police harassment and arrest.

Though laws and policies surrounding sex work are generally shaped by those in positions of privilege, in certain nations, such as Brazil, sex workers themselves participate in designing national health-care policy (particularly with regard to HIV/AIDS) and social-service provisions. Proponents of legalized sex work believe that this approach protects the health and safety of sex workers and society while also providing valuable tax revenue for local and national governments. Approaches to criminalization vary from the threat of stoning in Iran (Tait and Hoseiny 2008: 17) to police tolerating its concentration in peripheral and low-income areas where residents, whether engaged in sex work or not, experience marginalization and economic distress. Decriminalization also varies in the degree of permissiveness and enforcement, varying from a low priority accorded to sex work–related offenses to its legal definition as work, with sex workers accorded the same rights, responsibilities, and protections as other workers.

Debates surrounding sex work can be said to suffer a particular sort of ailment involving "too much heat, not enough light" (Valverde 1987). The bitter polemics that have divided scholars, writers, journalists, sex workers, and activists have done little to improve public policy on sex work. As such, this volume hopes to dispel myth and moralizing by shining a bright light on a subject that is often, both figuratively and literally, confined to the darkest recesses. Debates around sex work can be divided into two primary camps: those who oppose all forms of sexual commerce because they view it as a threat to public health and morality as well as a form of violence against women[6] and those who recognize prostitution as an enduring reality. The latter group often takes either the position that state regulation minimizes the risks and dangers incurred by sex work or that participants in such activities should be free from government control, which they view as intrusive and even harmful.

Governments, organizations, and individuals that support anti–sex work legislation often contend that sex work is damaging to society at large and to women in particular. Those who take this position argue that sex work can never be considered legitimate employment, because it is always degrading, never freely chosen, and is characterized by extreme levels of exploitation. For those who believe that sexual labor is essentially a sexist and violent act, legalization represents governmental complicity and endorsement of gendered violence. States that illegalize certain or all aspects of sex work conceptualize sex work similarly, and Goodyear and Weitzer illustrate the impact of this policy in Sweden in chapter 2.

Institutions and individuals that recognize sex work as a pervasive and enduring (albeit problematic) institution maintain that criminalization does not effectively end sex work in its many forms but only removes it from public view, making it more dangerous for sex workers and society by raising the risk of violence, abuse, disease, and involvement by criminal elements. Feminist activists and organizations that support legalization or decriminalization insist that criminalizing sex work criminalizes sex workers, making them more vulnerable to social stigmatization, abuse, rape, and even murder. One of the central arguments for legalizing all forms of sex work is that, through government oversight, health risks for sex workers, clients, and society at large are reduced. Many institutions and individuals concerned with public health believe that medical testing, safe sex education, and condom distribution are effective means of preventing the transmission of sexually transmitted infections (STIs). As the ethnographic examples presented throughout this book clearly demonstrate, however, there is often a great difference between such discourse at the state level and its everyday practice by individuals.

Synopsis of Key Themes

The chapters that follow consistently reveal that sex work is itself inseparable from state actions and, indeed, is sometimes engendered by them. Much of the research presented in this volume offers strong evidence of how this intimate relationship between sex work and the state exists in all countries, albeit in divergent forms that alternately reject, accept, or tolerate the existence of sex work. Although state interest in regulating sex work is often couched in the rhetoric of public health, morality, or safety, the research presented here indicates that the relationship is in fact often much more complex for a variety of nuanced reasons. Chimaraoke Izugbara, for example, argues that sex work in Nairobi is inseparable from the postcolonial politics of Kenyan life, wherein economic difficulties and crises in neighboring African nations, pervasive rural-urban migration resulting in the growth of informal housing settlements, and crop failures have all contributed to greater numbers of women and men engaging in sex work. At the same time, however, the police actively benefit from this illegal activity in their capacity as state agents through the elaborate (and illicit) exchanges of bribes, women, and gifts between sex workers and police officers.

Even more troubling is that such a situation is hardly unique to Kenya, as Tiantian Zheng also notes this collusion between Chinese police and other state authorities with local officials and brothel managers. In such an uncertain atmosphere, where violence and extortion are the norm, sex workers are forced into a state of constant vigilance. This is particularly significant given that most of the sex workers Zheng describes are rural migrants who have come to the northeastern port city of Dalian in search of increased economic opportunities that will allow them to send remittances to their home villages. Notably, Zheng observes, such women report that the conditions of sex work compare quite favorably to sweatshop or low-wage service work, the only jobs available to them as low-status rural migrants in urban China's burgeoning economy. They often note that sex work gives them a hope for urban social mobility that would otherwise be impossible.

Like Izugbara and Zheng, Treena Orchard also analyzes the disconnects between public policy and everyday practice in her chapter on *devadasis*, women who practice sex work as part of an ancient Hindu practice that has come under increasing scorn by the contemporary Indian state. She describes the similarities between colonial and post-independence efforts to "reform" such women as deeply embedded in moral-medical discourses of hygiene that, in turn, deeply contradict *devadasis'* understanding of their work as religiously motivated. This repositioning of sex work as a social problem in India, in turn, mirrors broader global debates regarding its appropriate role in neoliberal economic systems. Patty Kelly, for instance, documents the establishment of a government-owned brothel in the troubled Mexican state of Chiapas as part of broader efforts to modernize the region by extending state control, particularly via the implementation of agribusiness and other initiatives that generate revenue for elites through the privatization of large-scale agribusiness, while disenfranchising the poor.

Dawn Pankonien and Susan Dewey also draw an explicit connection between state economic policy and sex work, as both note the elaborate intersections between neoliberal reforms and poor people's increased need to devise creative strategies for survival. Pankonien describes the dramatic growth in the number of women who describe themselves as "single mothers" in Huatulco, a federally developed tourist region on Mexico's southern Pacific coast. Like the women in the chapters by Izugbara and Zheng, mothers in Huatulco are often rural migrants who have come to this beach town in search of economic opportunities in a tourist economy. Pankonien characterizes the strategic relationships these women engage in with men as "smart sex," a calculated set of practices in which men are sought out for their ability to temporarily provide for a woman and her children in what are, at best, unstable economic circumstances.

It is difficult to ignore the cross-cultural parallels prompted by the growth of neoliberalism, an economic and moral philosophy in which sociologist Zygmunt Bauman notes, "the responsibilities for resolving the quandaries generated by vexingly volatile and constantly changing circumstances is shifted onto the shoulders of individuals—who are now expected to be 'free choosers' and to bear in full the consequences of their choices" (Bauman 2007:3–4). Bauman essentially argues that neoliberalism's deceptively seductive offer of increased individual choice comes at a heavy price, rendering individuals more and more vulnerable. Neoliberal economic policies have increasingly impacted individual lives throughout the world through the unprecedented untethering of workers and the workplace so that those in positions of power and privilege have less direct contact with or responsibility for those who work at the lowest levels of the same industry. Such new labor practices are a constant reminder to workers that they are expendable, easily replaced, and thus not in a position to negotiate the terms and conditions under which their labor is carried out.

Such vulnerability is even more pronounced for those who already inhabit the margins of social life because of their poverty or other forms of social exclusion. This is particularly true for situations wherein particular types of state-endorsed socioeconomic inequalities create a larger pool of feminized labor that is typically lower paid, less respected, and less able to unionize. For instance, Zosa De Sas Kropiwnicki analyzes apartheid's enduring legacy of inequality on the lives of South African adolescent sex workers in their complex use of racialized discourses of danger in avoiding clients from particular ethnic backgrounds while adhering to "the language of the new democratic 'rainbow' nation of South Africa." Just as the marginalized South African sex workers described by De Sas Kropiwnicki alternatively embrace and reject the broader social frameworks that structure their lives, so, too, do many sex workers actively negotiate economic systems that equate feminized labor with low pay. Thaddeus Gregory Blanchette and Ana Paula da Silva explore this issue at length by noting the importance of situating sex work in the macroeconomic context of feminized labor. Seeking to escape the ghetto of female sub-employment otherwise available to them, the Brazilian sex workers the authors describe consistently mention that the conditions of their labor are not significantly worse than other forms of work open to them.

Yet such statements should not be read as a ringing endorsement of sex work; though it is true that this volume features many examples of how rural to urban migration does create new opportunities for social mobility that may involve sex work, these are often part of what anthropologist Denise Brennan has called "the opportunity myth" (2004:14), whereby individuals become sex workers in the hope of eventual upward mobility but generally end up living in increased poverty after they leave prostitution. Part of the power of ethnography lies in its ability to illuminate the minutiae of individual life circumstances, and in the case of sex work it can be exceptionally revealing. Many of the authors who tackle this issue clearly demonstrate that much of the autonomy that rural-urban migrants ascribe to their independence is, in fact, quite precarious. Pankonien notes that the ability of Mexican women in Huatulco to freely choose and abandon male partners at will stems from the absence of older family members, who remain in the countryside. Zheng similarly observes how women's efforts to subvert the urban-rural hierarchy through their migration to the city are constrained by the Chinese state's severe limits on rural-urban migration, much of which is forbidden and subject to a residency permit system, and the violent environment in which their work takes place.

The advent of the neoliberal era has ushered in a host of complex new relationships between the state and workers, raising, in particular, the problematic question of how states both pursue and reinforce the "global race to the bottom" while maintaining strict border control and limitations on citizenship. This practice is most evident in the contemporary focus on anti–sex-trafficking initiatives in countries that receive large numbers of migrants. Contemporary sex work is in many ways a microcosm of broader neoliberal labor practices, and it is hardly coincidental that sex trafficking has become a matter of international concern at the same time that large numbers of women (and men) are forced to seek work outside their home countries because of economic hardship. Erica Lorraine Williams tackles this issue in examining how trafficking-related discourse is often explicitly racialized in ways that eerily mirror state migration policies. This, she notes, raises a timely question with respect to the Afro-Brazilian women of Bahia, who are depicted as uniquely "at risk" of victimization by the predominantly white European male tourists who engage in relationships with them: "Who is allowed to enjoy the privileges of transnational mobility, and who is not?" Williams argues that, in this case, trafficking discourse is used as a convenient mechanism to deny Afro-Brazilian women their right to freedom of movement.

The vicissitudes of global mobility for the privileged undeniably influence the number of tourists and sex workers in locations that prove particularly popular for various reasons. Gregory Mitchell, for example, notes the disturbing introduction of a 6,001 percent annualized inflation rate in Brazil alongside dramatically increased numbers of both sex tourists and heterosexually identified sex workers who cater to gay male clients. Pankonien also notes this phenomenon in Huatulco, as this state-developed tourism region on Mexico's Pacific coast has attracted a number of rural migrants, many of them women, whose precarious economic situation necessitates multiple sexual partners chosen for instrumental reasons.

These seeming contradictions between sex workers' professions of agency and the severe socioeconomic constraints and stigma that shape their lives is particularly evident in chapters that deal with the politics of activist organizing and donor aid. In her powerful chapter, Heather Montgomery documents the huge amount of international attention granted to pedophilia and child-sex tourism in Thailand, resulting in the passage of Thai laws that in no way benefit minors who sell sex. Such minors, Montgomery reports, see sex work as a more lucrative choice out of a number of equally exploitative options that are more highly paid and used to support their families; in many ways, such Thai laws were developed along Western European/North American discursive lines. Mitchell presents a striking parallel as he describes why *michês*, heterosexually identified men who sell sex to gay North American and Western European tourists, refuse to become involved in Brazil's sex worker movements because they feel their work is temporary, they fear being labeled as "gay," and their machismo prevents them from engaging in activist organizing with one another. Orchard similarly traces the moral-medical discourse with respect to *devadasis*, which has serious health implications, particularly in terms of international, donor-funded, anti–HIV/AIDS campaigns that focus solely on condom use rather than the more substantive issues of sustainable alternatives to sex work. The frequency of such public-policy failures prompts us to ask a significant question: What can the ethnography of sex work offer public policy on sex work?

Ethnography, Sex Work, and Public Policy

Chapters in this volume, largely written by anthropologists, offer a number of concrete suggestions and recommendations to policy makers regarding how public policy on sex work could be improved in a diverse set of cultural and geographic contexts. In the volume's sole non-ethnographic chapter, Goodyear and Weitzer present a case for evidence-based public policy on sex work that is amply supported by ethnographic evidence documented in the rest of the chapters. The authors argue that many contemporary public policies on sex work are ineffective precisely because they are based upon morally loaded assumptions about sex work that do not draw upon actual research on the subject. Numerous chapters in this volume provide examples of the myriad ways in which such policies are often unable to meet their goals because of policymakers' lack of knowledge about the circumstances under which sex work takes place.

Kelly, for instance, documents the failures of moral-medical reform efforts in a state-owned Mexican brothel that strictly regulates its women workers under the premise of moral and medical hygiene but fails to protect them from violence or stigma. The ostensible public health-related goal of state involvement in sex work in this case is the reduction of HIV and other STIs through mandatory testing of sex workers, although their clients are not similarly screened. The obvious result of such a skewed policy, of course, is the state sanctioning of sex workers as vectors of disease despite vast amounts of evidence that sex workers are far more likely than non–sex workers to consistently use condoms during sex (Waddell 1996). By placing sex workers under its watchful eye, Kelly argues, the state asserts control in ways far more beneficial to the state than to those the state is regulating. Kelly's chapter opens with the murder of a sex worker in a state-owned brothel, a particularly jarring reminder that state involvement does not, ultimately, trump social stigma and deeply ingrained disregard for the dignity of sex workers.

Such violence is clearly evident in Susan Dewey's discussion of how exclusionary zoning policies in a mid-size U.S. city that never recovered from deindustrialization in the 1970s combine with the feminization of poverty to create a dangerous work environment for topless dancers. Dewey offers examples of dancers' efforts to obtain autonomy through increased earning power and flexible working hours, yet their constant fears of violence stem from a vast array of institutional and interpersonal obstacles that render them vulnerable to harassment in the isolated regions where they work. Izugbara similarly describes the intricate set of arrangements that sex workers employ to protect themselves and one another from violent assaults by police and clients in Nairobi, where sex work is made illegal via a number of municipal by-laws. He notes the frequency with which sex workers clearly named criminalization as the source of their stigma, unfavorable working conditions, and, most notably, the consistency with which they confronted violence in their everyday lives.

Similarly, Mitchell argues that activists and state officials alike ignore the heavy toll of stigma and its impact on particular communities at high risk of

HIV infection at their own peril, and sometimes with disastrous and counterproductive results. He commends the laudable efforts put forth thus far into raising awareness and changing risky sexual behaviors among heterosexually identified men who have sex with men, noting that such energies successfully recognize "the separation of identity and behavior." Nonetheless, Mitchell also takes such actors to task for failing to understand the complex cultural reasons why such men resist involvement in sex workers' rights movements. In order to be more successful, Mitchell argues, such efforts must make a deeper effort to understand the powerful role stigmatization plays.

Ethnography's greatest potential contribution to public policy lies in its ability to represent the everyday realities of life for individuals who often constitute a population invisible to policy makers. This is particularly notable in the case of laws that do not benefit the intended party, as Montgomery observes in her discussion of Thai anti-pedophilia laws passed under heavy pressure from Western European and North American governments. Although these laws were passed with positive intentions, they erred by failing to consult the very individuals they were meant to protect. She notes that "focusing on the perpetrator meant that the children themselves became marginal to discussions about their own lives."

When contextualized within the broader realities of many sex workers' everyday life experiences cross-culturally, public policy on sex work is often shown to be seriously lacking. The infinitely more pressing issues at stake for many sex workers around the world, as the chapters in this volume amply illustrate, include the lack of sustainable economic alternatives and a pervasive risk of violence. These chapters clearly demonstrate that the continuum of control sex workers experience in their work is a significant factor in the amount of violence they experience, both from state agents and their clients. For instance, Henry Trotter argues that dockside prostitution in South Africa, which involves in-port sailors and independent local sex workers who have significant control over the terms of the exchange, serves as a model style of sex work that, if used to inform public policy, could significantly reduce the otherwise endemic violence against sex workers.

Trotter argues that if all forms of South African sex work followed the model presented by dockside prostitution, sex workers would likely find themselves in a much safer environment in which they incur far fewer risks to their health and safety. He offers recommendations for prostitution's decriminalization and the provision of independent-operator status to sex workers alongside the promotion of ancillary third-party involvement. These recommendations may seem surprising given popular perceptions that dockside prostitution is associated with violence owing to its clientele's transient nature. Because ethnography is based, as noted, in the everyday life experiences of sex workers, it has enormous potential to offer such recommendations. The following chapters encourage us to come to terms with the reality that sex work exists nearly everywhere in the world and warrants serious attention from policy makers.

NOTES

1. Chapters throughout this volume follow geographer David Harvey's definition of neoliberalism as

a theory of political economic practices that proposes that human well-being can best be advanced by liberating individual entrepreneurial freedoms and skills within an institutional framework characterized by strong private property rights, free markets, and free trade. The role of the state is to create and preserve an institutional framework appropriate to such practices. The state has to guarantee, for example, the quality and integrity of money. It must also set up those military, defense, police, and legal structures and functions required to secure private property rights and to guarantee, by force if need be, the proper functioning of markets. Furthermore, if markets do not exist (in areas such as land, water, education, health care, social security, or environmental pollution) then they must be created, by state action as necessary. But beyond these tasks the state should not venture. State interventions in markets (once created) must be kept to a bare minimum because, according to the theory, the state cannot possibly possess enough information to second-guess market signals (prices) and because powerful interest groups will inevitably distort and bias state interventions (particularly in democracies) for their own benefit. (Harvey 2005:2)

2. Particularly nuanced examples of this kind of ethnographic writing can be found in Brennan 2004; Brents, Jackson, and Haubeck 2009; Cabezas 2009; Day 2007; Dewey 2011, 2008; Kelly 2008; Padilla 2007; Zheng 2009a.

3. There have been many divisive and bitter polemics among scholars and activists about the nature of sex work in general and prostitution in particular. Melissa Farley (2004) perhaps most fully captures the contemporary perspective that prostitution is not work but is exploitative gendered violence that embodies women's inequality. Cosi Fabian's statement that "by using a pre-patriarchal model of female sexuality as a noble, even divine power, I have constructed a life that is extraordinarily sweet" (1997:45) would likely be greeted by Farley and other antiprostitution activists with cries of false consciousness, whereas those in agreement see sex work as a valid and even spiritual path. For an excellent discussion of the diversity of contemporary scholarly perspectives on sex work, see Weitzer 2009b.

4. Although dissent and collective organizing are possible under neoliberalism, many scholars have characterized these policies as potentially politically demobilizing (Brooks 2007; Farmer 2003; Farthing 1995; Gill 2009).

5. Studies of more lucrative forms of prostitution are outside the scope of this volume and might result in a different set of policy recommendations, as the privacy of such exchanges results in reduced public scrutiny. Analyses of more "upscale" forms of sex work can be found in Bernstein (2007b), Kokken, Bimbi, and Parsons (2010), Kuo (2002), and Lucas (2005), as well as in Viviana Zelizer's (2007) fascinating sociological analysis of the commodification of intimacy. Social scientists interested in sex work might do well to heed anthropologist Laura Nader's (1972) call to "study up" in this regard.

6. For examples of this perspective on sex work, which is often termed "abolitionist" because it advocates outlawing prostitution on the grounds that it constitutes violence against women, see Barry 1996; Dworkin 2006; Farley 2004; Jeffreys 2008; Raphael 2004.

2

International Trends in the Control of Sexual Services

MICHAEL GOODYEAR AND RONALD WEITZER

States vary in the ways they have attempted to control prostitution, ranging from total prohibition to decriminalization and legal regulation. Some nations prohibit the purchase but not sale of sex (Sweden, Norway, and Iceland) or prohibit the conditions necessary for commercial transaction such as "soliciting," "loitering," or "communication" related to a sexual transaction.

This chapter identifies two major trends in how governments recently have dealt with sex work: (1) intensified *criminalization* designed to eradicate it; and (2) *liberalization* based on principles of harm reduction, labor rights, and civil regulation of commerce. We suggest that such policies are shaped by the interplay of forces at the national and international levels, and we examine the roles played by key actors in shaping policies in three nations: the Netherlands, Sweden, and New Zealand.

Much research on sex work is now available to guide policy makers (Weitzer 2010a), yet this body of evidence is often disregarded in favor of simplistic, ideological methods (Weitzer 2010b). Our three cases differ based on the extent to which their policies are evidence-based, with New Zealand at one end of the continuum and Sweden at the other (Goodyear 2007). Support for this argument is presented below.

The Netherlands

During the last quarter of the twentieth century, state policy in the Netherlands consisted of de facto legalization of prostitution, with some official oversight of premises where sex was sold. Police conducted periodic checks on brothels and window units to ensure that minors and illegal immigrants were not present, but otherwise regulation was limited and third-party involvement, although illegal, was tolerated. Red light districts expanded in the late 1970s, and by the 1990s public opinion favored formal legalization. A 1997 poll, for instance, revealed that 74 percent of the Dutch population regarded prostitution as an acceptable job and 73 percent favored the legalization of brothels (Brants 1998). In the World Values Survey, the Netherlands ranks as the most tolerant of prostitution of any European nation except Switzerland. Only 20 percent of the Dutch population considers prostitution to be "never justified," whereas twice as many people in Sweden subscribe to this view (World Values Survey 2006).

Several abortive attempts have been made to pass decriminalization bills in the late 1980s and 1990s, culminating in a 2000 law repealing the brothel ban. Those who owned and managed brothels, escort agencies, and window-prostitution units were no longer criminalized under the law. The remaining prostitution offenses centered on violations of personal freedom, protection of minors, and trafficking.

Frames and Actors

During the two decades preceding the 2000 law, the women's movement in the Netherlands gradually embraced what Weitzer calls the "empowerment paradigm" (Weitzer 2010a), partly because of concerns about portraying women as victims without agency, which is the hallmark of an opposing perspective, the "oppression paradigm." Liberalization of the law was seen as a means of improving the position of sex workers, and self-determination was held to include the right to have control over one's body, including selling sex (Outshoorn 2004). The dominant official discourse increasingly described prostitution as work inscribed with contractual rights, so long as the worker is a Dutch citizen or from one of the European Union (EU) nations. Symbolically the 2000 law was an important milestone in recognizing prostitution as legitimate work, distinguishing "voluntary" from "forced" prostitution, and separating criminal corollaries such as organized crime, violence, and drugs from the sexual exchange itself.

In recent years the "rights" discourse has been challenged by a parallel discourse grounded in the oppression paradigm and focusing on trafficking, underage sex work, and coercion. Concerns about such abuses provided the incentive for recent legislation, including Bill 32211 which proposes raising the minimum age of participation from eighteen to twenty-one, compulsory registration of sex workers, and criminalization of clients who visit unregistered providers.

The sex workers' organization Rode Draad (Red Thread) opposes the compulsory registration of sex workers and raising the minimum age. Red Thread and independent analysts also point out that most of the criminals involved in prostitution are located in the illegal market, not the legal, regulated sector. Their position is supported by social and health professionals and women's groups (Wijers 2010). Yet, for the most part, these voices have been ignored during the past three years.

Implementation

Implementation had not been a priority in the parliamentary debates preceding the 2000 law, despite the immense task of transforming a marginalized industry into a mainstream business sector with all the rights inherent in legal work. This transformation took place in an administrative void, with little precedence for guidance. The challenges included conflicts between the government and the owners of sex establishments, and tensions between municipal authorities and central government. Administrative law in the Netherlands devolves to municipalities, which assumed responsibility for regulating the newly legal sex trade. Municipalities varied considerably in their motivation, understanding, resources, and prior relationships with the sex industry, and in the degree to which municipal authorities consulted or collaborated with sex workers, concerned residents, and sex entrepreneurs (Wagenaar 2006). Contested issues included taxation, licensing procedures, monitoring and enforcement, public safety, working hours and conditions, health and safety regulations, and the fate of migrant workers.

Recently the federal government has assumed a stronger role in establishing norms that apply to all municipalities. Sex proprietors have been targeted by the authorities. For instance, the Public Administration Probity Screening Act of 2003 has been used to deny licenses to third parties suspected of criminal activities. All that is needed under the Act is simple suspicion that an individual may be involved in money laundering, for example, with the onus on the accused to prove their innocence. This measure is responsible for much of the recent reduction of windows and brothels in Amsterdam, although application of the law has been less rigorous in other cities.

Evaluation

The Ministry of Justice has carried out two formal evaluations of the effects of the 2000 law (Daalder 2004, 2007), documenting some improvements over time but problems in other areas. The number of minors involved is fairly small and has not increased since 2000 (Daalder 2007). Prior to 2000 street prostitution was tolerated in designated areas of the major cities, most of which have now been closed by municipalities. Today street prostitution constitutes a tiny sector of the market overall, and it is almost nonexistent in the vicinity of the red light districts. Organized crime played a larger role in the sex sector in the past than it does today, and organized crime is much more involved in the drug trade (Huisman and Nelen 2007).

Some legal prostitution systems distinguish themselves with costly or cumbersome regulations, and this tends to catalyze a parallel illegal sector seeking to avoid such restrictions. This is the trend in the Netherlands. The number of legal prostitution establishments has decreased over the past decade; the size of the less visible market (independents and illegal underground establishments) is difficult to measure given the lack of a pre-2000 baseline, but it has likely grown as a result of technological innovation (cell phones and the Internet). Many of the legal owners claim they are being "over-regulated" while their illegal counterparts operate with impunity. There is some basis to this charge, especially in Amsterdam, but enforcement actions against illegal operators have taken place as well.

The position of migrant sex workers has attracted much attention. One objective of the 2000 law was to reduce coercion and facilitate voluntary sex work. This is particularly relevant for non-EU and hence illegal migrant workers who are often under some type of third-party (though not necessarily coercive) control and are more vulnerable to exploitation. Some migrants are unaware of their rights or how to seek help or redress if they are being abused or exploited, so the migrant population (both legal and illegal) remains vulnerable and of particular concern to the authorities. There has been an increase in Eastern European workers, reflecting expansion of the EU, and it is possible that the number of illegal immigrants (i.e., non-EU) has increased as well—though this is chronically difficult to estimate.

Analysis

Although critics claim that legalization has done little to normalize sex work, it has extended rights to workers and given brothel owners a new legitimacy as quasi-conventional "entrepreneurs." Some of the changes since 2000 have been motivated by the goals of harm reduction and normalization, but other changes are designed to exert greater control over the sex industry simply in order to contain it. As in all such transitions, the Netherlands has seen both unintended consequences and unrealized goals of legal reform. As indicated above, greater regulation is not always welcomed by owners or sex workers. No evidence supports the claims that liberalization has created *major* problems, but much still needs to be done to address the needs and welfare of Dutch sex workers. Overall, there has been little documented improvement in the well-being of workers, partly because of the usual difficulties in de-stigmatizing sex work (Daalder 2007). Development of better labor standards and mechanisms for redress are required, as well as active discouragement of discrimination against workers. The Red Thread considers the new law to be an improvement but has also called for further reforms—including a hot-line for reporting abuse, encouragement of independents, and small worker-owned and -operated businesses (Altink and Bokelman 2006).

Policies that seek to empower sex workers can run up against local author-ities' desire to maintain control over this sector. Dutch cities differ in the ways and degree to which they have attempted to exert control. In Amster-dam, for instance, the dominant political forces have squeezed a number of brothel and window owners out of business, pushing workers into the illegal sector or into red light areas in other cities and countries, but Amsterdam's aggressive approach has not been followed in most other cities where orga-nized prostitution exists.

In evaluating the evolution of Dutch prostitution policy and practice since 2000, it should be borne in mind that the Netherlands has persisted with this legal regime in the face of intense international condemnation. Influential prohibitionist forces (mostly from outside the country) have tar-geted the Netherlands, in an effort to embarrass the government and catalyze repeal of the 2000 law. The Dutch state seems committed to retaining some form of legal, regulated prostitution, but it has also taken steps to impose new restrictions on sex workers and businesses. As we discuss below, Sweden differs dramatically from the Dutch approach.

Sweden

The sale and purchase of sex remained legal in Sweden until recently, but third-party involvement was illegal. The situation changed dramatically in 1999 under a law that condemned the clients of sex workers and criminalized the purchase of sexual services.

Debates

A 1981 commission concluded that prostitution was *not* a question of gen-der inequality, was declining as an activity, and that criminalization would drive it underground and worsen stigmatization (Statens offentliga utredningar [SOU] 1981). Among those opposing criminalization were the police, judiciary, ombudsman, gay rights groups, and the sex-education association. Most women's groups, however, supported criminalizing prostitutes' clients and defined prostitution as an institution of male domination, incompatible with equality and requiring suppression.

Between 1983 and 1993 some fifty bills dealing with prostitution were presented in the Swedish parliament, partly the result of lobbying by women's groups inside and outside the government. Some MPs articulated the oppression paradigm in parliamentary debates on these bills. For example, in a 1991 debate, Social Democrat Ulla Pettersson stated, "By accepting prostitution society tolerates a humiliating perception of women. The view that women can be bought for money expresses a disdain for women as human beings" (quoted in Dodillet 2004:4). In 1993 another commission advocated criminalizing both buyers and sellers in sexual exchanges, but most political parties rejected blanket criminalization. Subsequent bills called for the criminalization of clients exclusively on the grounds that criminalizing the sellers would only compound the victimization of women.

In 1998 the Kvinnofrid (Peace for Women) Bill was introduced by the ruling Social Democratic Party—an omnibus bill that dealt with crimes against women in general but also included a measure to criminalize those who purchased sex. There was virtual unanimity on most aspects of the bill except for this last point. The Justice Committee doubted that criminalization would reduce prostitution but still recommended the bill (Svanström 2004). The discourse was lacking in empirical referents and rooted instead in claims about gender relations and the threat that prostitution posed to women in general. As the leader of the Swedish Left Party Gudrun Schyman declared, "A law that criminalizes the purchase of sexual services will mark how the society shall look on the unequal distribution of power between men and women" (quoted in Dodillet 2004:6). The law was depicted as an integral part of Sweden's much vaunted egalitarian society, as Social Democrat Inger Segelstrom stated in parliament: "We Social Democratic women in the world's most emancipated parliament cannot allow that men buy women for money" (quoted in Dodillet 2004:3). The bill passed 181 to 92, becoming law on January 1, 1999. Those who purchase sex are now liable to a fine or incarceration for up to six months.

A government fact sheet published six years later showed that the law is firmly rooted in the oppression paradigm: "In Sweden, prostitution is regarded as an aspect of male violence against women and children, it is officially acknowledged as a form of exploitation of women and children . . . which is harmful not only to the individual prostituted woman or child, but also to society at large" (Ministry of Industry 2005).

Frames and Actors

The women's movement lobbied strongly for the bill. Opposition was muted. Sex workers and their organizations were virtually silent, and there was very little public debate over the bill until *after* the legislation passed. Notably the police opposed the bill, as did Liberal and Moderate members of parliament, while Christian Democrats abstained during the vote. An alternative perspective, the empowerment paradigm, appeared late in the debate and only outside of parliament.

Proponents of the bill argued that there was a need to send a message against oppression and trafficking (Gould 2001), insisting that prostitution and trafficking were manifestations of the same male predisposition to "violence against women and children" and that prostitution does serious damage to society (Ekberg 2004). They maintained that it was not about women's sexuality but about *men's* access to women's bodies that interfered with women controlling their own bodies.

During the parliamentary debate, legislators seemed cognizant that they were breaking new ground in shifting the onus onto the clients and thus "protecting" women. The Minister of Gender Equality predicted, "I believe that in 20 years, today's decision will be described as the big leap forward to fight violence against women and to reach *Kvinnofrid* [peace for women]" (Messing 1998).

Implementation

Implementation was not part of the debate, but the government provided 7 million crowns (U.S.$1 million) to the National Police Board for enforcement. Extra police were hired, and vehicles in street prostitution areas were placed under greater surveillance. There was an immediate decrease in the visible street market, followed fairly quickly by displacement to the less visible spectrum, as seen in other countries introducing repressive legislation. The difficulties of enforcement and conviction were immediately noted by the police, as sex workers were reluctant to testify against their clients. Importantly, the legislation provided no support for the prostitutes themselves, and Sweden has paid little consideration to harm-reduction practices. As Susanne Dodillet notes, "Since it came into force, nothing has been done to improve the situation of women in prostitution. The same feminists who lobbied for the law argued against any measures that could make things easier for those in prostitution" (quoted in Sullivan 2009). Despite claims that the law was a success, the government announced a new Action Plan on Prostitution in 2008, the investment of another 200 million crowns, and further educational measures to "help them [the population] rethink their attitudes" toward prostitution (Ministry of Integration and Gender Equality 2008; "Government Gets Tough on Trade" 2008).

Evaluation

Evaluation of the law created a considerable conceptual burden, given the law's broad goals of eradicating prostitution, violence against women, and cultural inequity. There has been a great deal of triumphalism on the part of the law's champions, as typified in this editorial: "No proper evaluation of the law has yet been undertaken, and it appears unnecessary. The law has the support of 80% of the Swedish people" (*Sydsvenskan* 2007). Foreign media coverage reflected this in such headlines as the one that appeared in the German periodical *Der Spiegel* (November 8, 2007) "Prostitution Ban Huge Success in Sweden." The most recent data show that 71 percent of Swedes support the law, but only 20 percent thought the law was working and more than 50 percent wanted the sale of sex also criminalized (Holmstrom and Skilbrei 2009; Kuosmanen 2010). In the 2006 World Values Survey, 40 percent of Swedes felt that prostitution can "never be justified," up from 31 percent in 1996 prior to the legal reform (World Values Survey 1996, 2006). Thus it appears that the law and the debate surrounding it contributed to a less tolerant attitude toward sex work in the population.

The National Board of Health and Welfare (Socialstyrelsen) has produced three evaluations of the law (2000, 2004, 2007), which provide no evidence that it has achieved its objectives. In 2000 it noted that estimating the extent of sex work was almost impossible and that workers and their clients might be relocating to more clandestine locations (Socialstyrelsen 2001). The 2007 report states that street prostitution is on the rise after an initial decline and that customers and sex workers have gravitated to the Internet and mobile phones to set up meetings.

There appear to be unintended consequences of the legislation—namely, that it drives workers underground, increases the risk of violence, harms the most vulnerable, and is difficult to enforce (Clausen 2007; Dodillet 2004;

Scoular 2004). No evidence suggests that the law has reduced violence against women, which appears to have increased instead, as have sexual offenses ("Pedophiles Slip through Net" 2005; Swedish Crime Barometer 2008). A number of other measures indicate that the law is not achieving its objectives despite claims by the authorities. Approximately two thousand men were arrested during the decade since the law's passage (Sullivan 2009), about fifty of whom have been convicted each year. All those convicted have been fined, and none has been jailed as a result of a court ruling that stopped this option from being applied.

The relatively low number of convictions and the mild penalties imposed anger some supporters of the law who have called for a minimum one-year jail term ("Jail Men Who Pay for Sex" 2008). If the law is not a great success instrumentally, official discourse has increasingly stressed the *symbolic* nature of the law—"sending a message" about buying sex. But the symbolic function itself is in question, since a subsequent commission found little evidence of a change in men's attitudes toward women (Leander 2006).

By 2008 the media both within Sweden and in other countries had begun to question the efficacy of the law ("Swedish Prostitution" 2008). A 2010 commission's report on the law's effectiveness concluded that it was a success but recommended stronger sanctions (Skarhed 2010). The report was criticized for being speculative and lacking supporting evidence, and research on the sale of sex through the Internet casts further doubt on the validity of the Skarhed report (Olsson 2010). Notably a number of candidates in the 2010 parliamentary elections announced their opposition to the 1999 law.

Analysis

The Swedish developments resulted not only from a well-organized women's movement and its allies inside the state but also, and more generally, from Sweden's lack of a liberal tradition and its national isolationism. Sweden's cultural tradition has long favored a strong state over individual rights and has been protectionist and paternalist under almost continuous Social Democratic governments. The country prides itself on being unique, and unique "solutions" are expected. Despite its reputation as a progressive nation, Sweden follows a zero-tolerance rather than harm-reduction policy toward drugs, and much of the prohibitionist rhetoric in the prostitution debates resembles that of drug debates (Gould 2001). That Sweden has taken such a vanguard role in the international debate on prostitution policy is surprising, given that sex work is such a small part of Swedish life (in 1999 only about twenty-five hundred prostitutes were working in Sweden out of a population of 9 million). We have suggested that the move toward prohibition can be explained by the nation's dominant social forces and political culture, coupled with the marginalization of Swedish sex workers, who have had no effective voice in articulating their interests prior to or after passage of the 1999 law (Clausen 2007; Dodillet 2009).

Immediately after the law's enactment, Swedish authorities and activists launched an international crusade to promote the unique "Swedish Model"— hosting conferences on trafficking, sexual violence, and prostitution; issuing fact sheets outlining official policy in a variety of languages; and subsequently lobbying other governments, the EU, and the United Nations (Ekberg 2004). Alliances were formed with prohibitionist groups outside Sweden, such as the European Women's Lobby and the Coalition Against Trafficking in Women. This campaign has been relatively successful at exporting Sweden's demand-side solution to some other nations. Norway, Iceland, and South Africa criminalized the purchase of sex in 2009, and Finland (in 2006) and Britain (in 2009) criminalized those who buy sex from trafficked or controlled women. Sweden, in short, is a good example of a remarkably influential policy that is primarily ideological in origin; during parliamentary debate the law was neither grounded in evidence nor informed by harm-reduction principles.

New Zealand

New Zealand inherited British laws that criminalized soliciting, brothel keeping, procuring, and living off the earnings of prostitution. The Massage Parlors Acts (1978–2003) effectively allowed indoor commercial sex under a façade, by requiring massage workers to register with the police.

Debates

The Labor Party came into power in 1984 with an agenda that included the decriminalization of homosexuality. Growing concern over AIDS led to the rethinking of prostitution laws and a decision to fund the New Zealand Prostitutes' Collective (NZPC) in 1987 (Chetwynd 1996; Jordan 1991; Lichtenstein 1999). Over time the NZPC became increasingly aware that legislative reform was necessary to achieve its objectives and began to advocate law reform (Healy and Reed 1994).

In 1997 a number of organizations came together to form a working group that developed a draft bill. This included the NZPC, academics, women's health and legal groups, and some parliamentarians. After losing power in 1990, Labor returned to power in 1999 and, in 2003, introduced the Prostitution Reform Act (PRA), which decriminalized prostitution throughout the country.

Frames and Actors

Health played a major role in this debate. The Health Department used health promotion principles of empowerment through peer-driven initiatives to fund sex workers, recruit them as partners, and provide legitimacy that became increasingly incongruent with the extant prohibitive legislation. The NZPC worked to transform the image of sex worker as disease vector into one of health educator and protector of public health. The NZPC's own research demonstrated that the high-risk actor was not the sex worker but the promiscuous heterosexual male. The Public Health Association, AIDS Foundation, and Law Society were important allies, as were human rights groups. The opposition framed the issue as state-sanctioned immorality, although the government was careful to frame its support as independent of any moral position other than that of improving the lives and welfare of sex workers. The police remained neutral in the debate, and religious and women's groups were divided, as was the public. In a 2003 poll 43 percent supported the bill and 42 percent were opposed, with 15 percent undecided ("Poll Steels Anti-Prostitution Resolve" 2003). On the larger issue of the acceptability of prostitution, however, New Zealanders are more liberal than citizens of many other nations. In a 2004 survey only 25 percent of respondents took the view that prostitution is "never justified" (World Values Survey 2004).

Implementation

The Act largely removed voluntary adult prostitution from the criminal law by decriminalizing soliciting, brothel keeping, and living off the earnings of prostitution. These controls were replaced with civil and administrative regulations at the national and local levels. A distinction was made between voluntary and involuntary prostitution, with coercion remaining an offense. Sex work was prohibited for those with temporary visas, as was immigration with the intent to work or invest in sex work. Contracts between providers and clients were recognized, providers having the right to refuse services and refer disputes to a tribunal. Advertising was banned with the exception of certain print media. Other statutes fill the gaps. The Summary Offenses and Litter Acts continue to penalize offensive behavior and other public nuisances, and the Clean Slate Act (2004) allows sex workers to apply to have previous convictions removed from their records.

Sex work is recognized (but not promoted) as legitimate work by government agencies and, like other businesses, operates under employment and health and safety standards devised in consultation with the NZPC. Employers and employees are obliged to promote and practice safe sex, enforced by the Health Department. Employment disputes can be referred to the Labor Inspectorate. Registration of sex workers was replaced by certification of brothels employing three or more workers, shifting the onus from worker to operator. A certificate can be refused for past criminal offenses unrelated to prostitution. Police activities shifted from arrest to protection, and their training manuals have been amended accordingly.

Local government was empowered to develop by-laws for zoning and advertising, but municipalities cannot prohibit sex work. Model by-laws and procedures were created and distributed and, by 2006, seventeen of seventy-four local governments had drafted or implemented a bylaw, but court challenges have overturned those that violate the spirit of the Act (such as restricting the location of businesses to such a degree that it constitutes virtual prohibition) (Abel, Fitzgerald, and Healy 2010).

Evaluation

The Act established a Prostitution Law Review Committee (PLRC) tasked with conducting research and providing reports on the effects of the law. This proved invaluable in countering opponents' claims (Mossman and Mayhew 2007a, 2007b; Prostitution Law Reform Committee [PLRC] 2003, 2005; Abel, Fitzgerald, and Healy 2010). A comprehensive assessment found that the total number of sex workers remained largely unchanged after decriminalization and that there had been no increase in underage sex work or trafficking (PLRC 2008). Sex workers showed little incentive to leave prostitution and they seemed more empowered as a result of the new law. Problems included some violence on the streets, perceived stigma, problems with working conditions, inconsistent safe sex practices (particularly oral), distrust of authorities and conflicting objectives between central and local governments, the latter having a more restrictive view (Abel, Fitzgerald, and Healy 2010; PLRC 2008). Overall the PLRC felt that the Act had achieved its purpose. The government welcomed the report, and the general response was positive.

Analysis

New Zealand is known for its socially progressive tradition and a tolerant political culture. Although the opponents of the decriminalization bill largely relied on moral objections, the bill's supporters prevailed by focusing on rights, health, and the reduction of harm. The bill passed, however, by the narrowest of margins (one vote), and many citizens felt that the legislature had acted without a clear public mandate, as the population was evenly split on the issue of decriminalization. This might suggest some precariousness in the existing legal order, but subsequent attempts to reverse the law have failed and, despite a change of government, there has been no serious effort to reverse the policy. A key feature of the New Zealand model was the decision to consult and fund the leading sex workers' organization (NZPC), thereby legitimizing and empowering it and perhaps diluting some of the stigma of sex work itself. New Zealand also demonstrates the importance of building periodic evaluation into law reform to provide evidence-based assessments and to address any problems that might be identified. This is institutionalized in the PLRC but is lacking in some other nations where prostitution has been decriminalized. Just as Sweden's system has been emulated by some other nations, New Zealand has been a model for others as well, including Western Australia in 2008, where both the decriminalization bill and the debates surrounding it were similar to New Zealand's (Weitzer 2009a).

Conclusion

In recent years the oppression paradigm has influenced public policies in many countries. It has been used successfully by prohibitionist forces in their efforts to convince governments to pass punitive laws. Lacking in most cases is an evidence-based framework. Instead, the debate has been overshadowed by claims about the immorality of prostitution or the victimization and exploitation of women, or both. In most cases, the voices of sex workers have been ignored. But it would be a mistake to think that policies are uniform throughout the world, even if the oppression discourse is pervasive. There are some exceptional cases where a counter-discourse rooted in harm-reduction and workers' rights has successfully challenged the oppression discourse, for example, in Western Australia (Weitzer 2009a) and in a successful constitutional challenge to Canada's prostitution laws in 2010, a ruling currently being appealed by the government (*Bedford v. Canada* 2010).

This chapter demonstrates how a spectrum of approaches to the regulation of sex work evolved in three nations and how local cultures have shaped these policy outcomes. Whereas the Netherlands is liberal, tolerant, diverse, inclusive, and relatively pragmatic, Sweden is socially conservative, fairly homogeneous, and absolutist in its approach to commercial sex. In addition, prostitution was long tolerated in the Netherlands prior to formal decriminalization in 2000, and it has a much larger and very visible sex industry compared to Sweden's. This cultural and historical background played an important role in shaping the recent legal reforms. In the Netherlands, preventing trafficking and liberalizing the approach to voluntary prostitution were seen as parallel and *complementary* objectives, unlike in Sweden where they were depicted as *antagonistic*. Differing national orientations to social citizenship and social control created the backdrop for changing prostitution policies—contexts that created different *political opportunity structures* for forces seeking to repress sex work in one case and legitimize it in the other. These considerations point to the need to be cautious about the validity of translating contextually dependent "solutions" to other cultures.

New Zealand provides a contrasting model to both the two European approaches, although it is closer to the Dutch system. In New Zealand sex workers themselves occupied center stage as actors who defined the issues and framed the debates within a socially progressive political culture, and were granted legitimacy by the state. Along with their allies in the state and civil society, sex workers have played a much larger role in policy formation than in the other two societies. New Zealand differs from the Netherlands in imposing fewer regulations on sex workers and sex businesses, and its system has been less controversial than in the Netherlands in the post-decriminalization period. This is partly owing to the sheer size of the two sex markets, with the one in the Netherlands much larger and more difficult to manage than the one in New Zealand. Sexual commerce is also much more visible in the Netherlands—with its distinctive, heavily visited red light districts—which makes it easier for opponents to claim that the sex sector is "out of control" and in need of further restriction.

Decriminalization is a necessary but insufficient condition for destigmatization and normalization. Equally important are attention to the wider context of laws and regulations around health and safety, employment standards, and taxation. The control of abuses within an employment sector may be better achieved by empowering individuals, as in New Zealand, than by coercive and punitive approaches that effectively disempower sex workers. Other problems may arise in decriminalized systems as well. There have been problems in nations where powers are devolved to local authorities (creating disparities across the nation), over-regulation that pushes resistant workers and proprietors into the illegal sector, and reliance on police for monitoring and enforcement, especially if they have not undergone special training and lack sensitivity to sex workers. Each of these policies can undermine the intent of legislation whose express purpose is to give sex workers rights and reduce exploitation.

At the same time, and importantly, an examination of the outcomes of those jurisdictions that have liberalized control fails to support the claims of the oppression theorists who predict that conditions will only deteriorate under legalization (Weitzer 2010b). It is by no means preordained, as prohibitionists claim, that conditions will worsen where sex work has been decriminalized and regulated. Much depends on the nature of the regulations.

There are limits to the regulation of vice, not only in implementation and enforcement but also in the likelihood that a segment of the sex industry will operate in the grey zone outside what is legally permitted. What is needed, in all cases, is that law and policy are evidence-based and that there is ongoing evaluation in order to further reduce harm and improve working conditions for sex workers without infringing on the rights of those who are not involved in the sex industry.

3

Into the Galactic Zone

Managing Sexuality in Neoliberal Mexico

PATTY KELLY

> All this garrulous attention which has us in a stew over sexual-
> ity, is it not motivated by one basic concern: to ensure popu-
> lation, to reproduce labor capacity, to perpetuate the form of
> social relations: in short, to constitute a sexuality that is eco-
> nomically useful and politically conservative?
> —Michel Foucault, *Discipline and Punish*

On a warm August day in 2003 Teresa Aleman Che, who worked as
a prostitute, was killed by a client. It is said that he stabbed her in the neck,
though the story is told differently each time. Those who saw him flee say
that Teresa's killer must have been a police officer or a soldier, for he had
the telltale crew cut. The murderer was never caught. People were afraid of
Teresa's blood, fearful of contracting HIV, although there was no evidence
that she was HIV-positive. She died quickly.

The story is not a surprising one. Lurid, almost pornographic, color
photographs of dead women, often sex workers who have been murdered,
haunt the back pages of local newspapers in urban Mexico, their bodies
twisted into unnatural poses only a corpse could maintain. The murders
of female sex workers make the papers not because such events are rare or
considered important and thus newsworthy. Nor do they elicit public out-
rage. Their deaths simply make good copy. There is often no investigation,
no organizing on the part of mothers or feminist groups—only images in
the local papers.

Of interest in this chapter is not how the deaths of Teresa and women
like her are treated by the media, law enforcement, and society. The killings
of women who work as prostitutes, although sometimes sensationalized, are
sadly mundane. What is unusual in this case is where Teresa died. Not hidden away in the back room of an illicit *nightclub*. Not in the street. Not in

a hotel or an *autohotel* (which has covered parking for cars, ensuring total privacy) where sex workers and clients meet.

Teresa was murdered in her room in the *Zona Galáctica*, a legal, super-modern, state-regulated brothel where municipal police search clients before they enter, where sex workers undergo mandatory testing for HIV and other sexually transmitted diseases in the on-site Anti-Venereal Medical Service (SMAV), where sex workers are registered with the municipal government, their highly stigmatized work made legal, though not respectable, by state authorities.[1] The entire complex is surrounded by a high fence, designed in a panoptical fashion, surveillance and discipline being its central architectural features.

Constructed with public funds in 1991, the Galactic Zone is located in Tuxtla Gutiérrez, a city of some five hundred thousand people and the capital of Chiapas, one of Mexico's poorest states best known for impoverishment, ruins, and rebellion. The Galáctica, as it is known by locals, was the dream of Governor Patrocinio González Garrido, a *priista* (or member of the PRI [Partido Revolucionario Institucional], Mexico's long-ruling center-right party) whose political career was characterized by human rights abuses, strict crackdowns on rebellion and dissent, and the implementation of neoliberal economic policies. The creation of the Zona Galáctica may be seen as part of a larger state effort to modernize Chiapas. Just as the state began to cut support for subsistence and small-scale agriculturalists in favor of agribusiness (ravaging rural economies and engendering increased rural to urban migration), it also took a renewed interest in the social and sexual lives of Chiapas's urban working classes. By regulating and controlling prostitutes (long linked to deviance and disorder), the state hoped to discipline and bring into the formal modern market an activity that had previously existed in the margins, beyond state control.

In an era marked by global neoliberalism and its attendant privatization, there has been much discussion about the weakening power of the state (Otero 1996; Teichman 1996). Scholars and popular mythology alike have suggested that economic globalization is engendering a "stateless" world in which federal governments will become all but obsolete.[2] But neoliberalism is less about the withdrawal of the state from public life than about changing arenas of state interest and action. Far from disappearing, under neoliberalism, the state is responsible for creating and maintaining institutions, laws, and a social order that support free markets (Harvey 2004:2). What is seen in the Zona Galáctica is a renewed focus of state energies toward the social and symbolic control of disenfranchised populations, specifically of the socio-sexual and economic lives of Tuxtla's working classes.

Accordingly, this chapter questions the ostensible social and public health benefits that accompany the state-regulation of prostitution in southern Mexico. I argue that as the relationship between commercial sex and the state grows ever more intimate in southern Mexico, reports of the death of the state under global neoliberalism have been, to borrow a phrase, greatly exaggerated.

Sexual Commerce and the State in Modern Mexico: A Brief History of a Changing Relationship

Mexico is hardly unique in its politicization, scrutiny, and contestation of gendered and sexual practices and beliefs during periods of politico-economic transformation. Concern with *mujeres publicas* (public women) was intensified in the years before and after the Mexican Revolution (1911–1917). During the regime of dictator Porfirio Díaz (1876–1911) the state sought to modernize through economic liberalism (the antecedent to contemporary neoliberalism) and advocated the eradication of vice and the inculcation of values such as family, thrift, and hygiene (French 1992:529).[3] Political strategizing, intimidation, and sometimes force were used to maintain power. The "Porfiriato," as the period came to be known, was heavily influenced by rationalism and science. Not unlike neoliberal Mexico, during the Porfiriato industry and foreign investment grew (aided in part by an 1883 agrarian law that opened rural lands to foreign companies). Not unlike today, a move from subsistence to commercial farming compelled many to seek their fortunes in rapidly industrializing cities. But the costs of modernization (then as now) were steep for many Mexicans who were increasingly impoverished by the brutality and socioeconomic transformation that marked the time.

For poor women in urban Mexico, prostitution offered a solution. Constructed as promiscuous deviants beyond redemption, during the Porfiriato women over age fourteen who worked as registered prostitutes were subject to the *Reglamento para el ejercicio de la prostitución en México* (Regulation for the exercise of prostitution in Mexico) which called for medical and legal surveillance. An updated 1898 Reglamento increased the minimum legal age to sixteen (Bliss 2001:32)

Mexico's late-nineteenth-century prostitution policy was intended to protect the citizenry from then debilitating sexually transmitted diseases like gonorrhea and syphilis, as treatments at the time were not widely available. Women suspected of working as clandestine prostitutes (being out alone on the street at night could be enough to raise suspicion) were subject to arrest and compulsory medical inspection and registration. Porfirian values of female honor and purity did not extend to the poor women who worked in urban Mexico's bordellos, hotels, and streets. Though predicated on ideas of modernity and hygiene (social and otherwise), the enforcement of the *Reglamento* and the prostitute's presumed moral failings were also marked by religion; Catholicism's strict sexual morality and patriarchal *doble moral* (moral double standard) all but guaranteed the marginalization of women who sold sex (Bliss 2001:29).

The Porfiriato bred both marginalization and rebellion. The ensuing Mexican Revolution that followed left more than one million Mexicans dead; exiled to Europe, Porfirio Díaz survived the upheaval. The revolutionary state that replaced the Porfiriato took a different approach to prostitution and its practitioners; the "modern" and "revolutionary" Mexican society sought an eventual end to state-regulated prostitution, seen as a distasteful remnant of the Porfirian state. Prostitutes were then viewed as victims of poverty, male lust, and Porfirian false modesty; those who, as historian Katherine Bliss writes, could be rehabilitated through revolutionary social change:

> Legislators, public officials, and private citizens alike invoked the "redemption" of "fallen women" as their *cause célèbre*, promoting legislation to ban procuring, to train women to work in alternative occupations, to persuade clients to restrain their tendency toward sexual promiscuity, and to abolish the Reglamento itself. (Bliss 2001:1)

But the revolutionary version of the *Reglamento para el ejercicio de la prostitución* created by the new government in 1926 was still somewhat rooted in beliefs regarding acceptable male promiscuity and enforced female purity (prostitutes withstanding). While the new revolutionary government continued the medical and legal surveillance of female prostitutes in the name of public health, revolutionary reformers also sought to transform *male* sexual promiscuity, reform public women, and reframe sexuality itself as a scientific rather than moral issue, thereby creating what they regarded as a modern nation (Bliss 2001). But revolutionary social reformers, Bliss (2001) writes, "had long deplored prostitution because of what they perceived to be its negative implications for economic development and national progress" (214–215). Continuing debates concerning state-regulated prostitution, along with the activism of both feminists and eugenicists, eventually led to the abolition of the *Reglamento* in 1940. But the temporary suspension of state-regulated prostitution did not, as Bliss notes, put an end to prostitution.

In contemporary Mexico government-regulated prostitution exists in thirteen of the nation's thirty-one states, including Chiapas. The creation of the Galactic Zone in 1991 coincided with a period of rapid economic change, cultural transformation, simmering political hostilities, and the militarization of civil society (not unlike the Liberal period of a century earlier). Unlike the social reformers of revolutionary Mexico, political elites like Governor González Garrido viewed state-regulated prostitution in neoliberal Chiapas as a path *to* modernity and development. Such policies indicate great ambivalence toward sex workers, who are stigmatized by those who seek to control prostitution (and by society at large) and at the same time are viewed as capable of redemption through, as I heard many times, "reintegration into normal society." Prostitution remains a controversial issue in Tuxtla, even within the municipal government itself. During a meeting I attended with political leaders at City Hall one afternoon, the mayor, a gynecologist and a member of the conservative political party Partido Acción Nacional (PAN, whose members are known as *panistas*), described prostitution as an "economic and a moral problem." The mayor's *panista* colleague, the municipal director of public health (also a gynecologist), strongly disagreed, insisting that sex work is purely a socioeconomic issue, outside the moral realm.

That, during the period of my fieldwork, Tuxtla's mayor and its director of public health were both gynecologists should not go without remark. Being a politician and gynecologist is not unusual in Mexico; in fact, the mayor's father was Tuxtla's first *panista*-gynecologist-mayor in the 1970s. As sociologist Maria Mies (1986) has observed, gynecologists, along with the state, are the "guardians of modern patriarchy" (24–25). When gynecologists run the state, such guardianship is furthered. Doctors and public health specialists have long been involved in political affairs in Mexico—during the revolutionary period, such men (referred to as *higiensistas*), along with criminologists and social workers, were at the forefront of a "social hygiene" movement that sought to control, among other things, female prostitution, sexually transmitted illness, and the "white slave trade" (Bliss 2001:15).

The Birth of the Galactic Zone

In keeping with federal neoliberal reforms in the 1980s and early 1990s, Chiapas's Governor González Garrido (1988–1993) cut state support such as loans and credit for small-scale agriculture while promoting large-scale agricultural exports and the privatization of state industries. Such policies devastated rural areas, generating both rebellion and increased rural-to-urban migration in Chiapas. In 1970, 28 percent of all Chiapanecos lived in urban areas; by 1994, 44 percent were city dwellers (Rojas Wiesner, Luz, and Tuñón Pablos 2001:85). At nearly half a million people, Tuxtla Gutiérrez is one of the state's fastest-growing cities; at the time of my research in 1999 the annual population growth rate was 7.3 percent. I often heard the mayor worry aloud about how to handle the large numbers of new arrivals who came seeking escape from rural poverty.

The politically ambitious Governor González Garrido also dreamed of modernizing sexual commerce in Chiapas.[4] As in Porfirian Mexico a century earlier, neoliberal Mexican cities frequently featured economic modernization projects alongside legislation focused upon sex and social order. As the state withdrew from sectors of the economy such as agriculture, it simultaneously sought greater control over commercial sex in Chiapas through the 1989 Zona Rosa Project, which sought to transform prostitution in the state by creating highly regulated government-run brothels. This effort by Governor González Garrido was probably linked to the militarization of the state and was a way to prepare for dealing with the coming Zapatista uprising,[5] along with other social tensions such as uncontrolled population growth in the city. Among the goals of the project were the relocation of existing unregulated brothels to "appropriate" sites "outside the perimeters of the city," far from homes, schools, government offices, and churches; the registration and medical testing of female sex workers; and the supervision of sex workers and clients by municipal authorities in order to prevent alcohol abuse as well as drug use and distribution within the confines of the brothel (*Servicios Coordinados de Salud Pública en el Estado de Chiapas* 1989).

Governor González Garrido played an unusually large role in the creation of the Zona Galáctica, thereby provoking a great deal of gossip about the governor and his sexual habits. As one official in the State Department of Public Health told me, "That guy was *really* interested in prostitution," underscoring the rather unusual level of involvement the governor took in what is ordinarily a matter of municipal rather than state concern. In addition to his activities in the zone, in 1990 Governor González Garrido also passed a "public health" law banning transvestism, although *travestis*, as transgendered or female-identified male sex workers are known, continued to appear in public in defiance of the law.[6] Between 1991 and 1993 fifteen gay men, mostly *travestis*, were murdered in the streets of Tuxtla with high-caliber weapons. Though police arrested a suspect who was sentenced to eight years in prison for homicide, many believe the case remains unsolved and that the man convicted was a scapegoat. According to Amnesty International, Jorge Gamboa

Borraz, the special prosecutor assigned to the case, resigned in 1994 because of "lack of cooperation" from government officials (Amnesty 1997:15–16).

Because these seemingly systematic murders were committed with high-caliber weapons used only by police and military, many residents believed that Governor González Garrido and the state police force were linked to the killings. Local gossip suggested that Governor González Garrido's interest in regulating prostitution stemmed from his own sexual activities with the *travestis* of Tuxtla. Whether true or not, his interest in controlling prostitution was certainly related to his political goal to make Chiapas modern and suppress dissent, whether among prostitutes or agrarian activists. Despite the rumor and discontent surrounding him, Governor González Garrido was rewarded for his work in Chiapas; he was appointed to the powerful position of Secretary of the Interior in the federal government until public pressure in the wake of the Zapatista uprising led to his eventual political downfall and self-imposed exile.

Borrowing from social theorist Karl Polanyi, who viewed governmental control as essential to market economies, sociologist Gerardo Otero (2004) agrees that "far from minimizing or reducing state intervention in the economy, the self-regulating market requires intervention to create markets and sustain them" (3). The government's decision to withdraw state support from small-scale agricultural producers while at the same time promoting free-trade policies actively creates a situation in which farmers who are unable to compete with cheap imports must enter the labor market on terms favorable to elites. Contemporary prostitution policy similarly creates the infrastructure to control female prostitutes who previously worked independently or informally, while also serving elite interests by creating an orderly urban environment and highly regulated workers and consumers. Regulating and confining prostitution makes prostitutes "legible," allowing the state to see them, administer them, control them (Scott 1998:2).

When it comes to sexual labor, the question of visibility is an important one; official discourse surrounding prostitution focuses not only on public health but also on its spatial regulation. City officials in Tuxtla approach the perceived problems of urban life, such as disorder, social hygiene, and contagious disease, through arrest and confinement. Unregistered prostitutes working outside the legal zone are swept from city streets during raids by municipal police and public health authorities; legal workers remain confined in the Zona Galáctica where they are visible to authorities but not to citizenry. The zone's location at the end of a lonely dirt road five miles from the city center is itself a testament to the status of commercial sex in Mexico:

available yet, ideally, invisible. I attended many government meetings where city officials repeatedly referred to visible street prostitution as "out of context" while discussing the need to place unregulated workers in "appropriate places" like the Galactic Zone.

Thus, in December 1991, Governor González Garrido, along with city officials, inaugurated the Galactic Zone. Such ceremony is commonplace in Mexico, where political officials at all levels, from the president of the republic to the mayor of a small village, preside over the openings of schools, highways, and, in this case, a brothel. Such festivities, which often include the cutting of ribbons, live music, and speeches, are a validation of both government authority and benevolence. They make the power and generosity of the state visible through public spectacle. Smaller government successes, such as the installation of a streetlight or placement of public trash cans, do not go uncelebrated: a new lamppost in a low-income neighborhood in eastern Tuxtla is dwarfed by a large sign advertising the current municipal administration's program for providing lighting. In the Galactic Zone the state's presence is felt everywhere. Trash cans installed years earlier still bear the insignia of the previous *priista* municipal government. On an outside wall between the men's toilets and the Anti-Venereal Medical Service (SMAV) is a large plaque celebrating the state's creation of the Galactic Zone. The entry tickets that clients must purchase at the main gate bear the *panista* administration's slogan, "Tuxtla Needs You. Participate!"

Regulating and Rehabilitating Sex Workers

The official document titled "Regulations for the Control and Vigilance of Prostitution in the Municipality of Tuxtla Gutiérrez, Chiapas," which dates to 1993, lays out the basic rules of the Galáctica (some of which are arbitrarily enforced). City regulations list the multiple prohibitions and myriad requirements for sex workers in the tolerance zone (unregistered sex workers are free of such restrictions). Workers may not practice if they lack the health certificate given by the city, if they are pregnant, or if they suffer from contagious diseases; each worker must be a Mexican citizen over eighteen years of age, "demonstrate that she is able to discern the risks of the activity," be in "full use of mental faculties and not addicted to drugs," and "carry out her activity in the tolerance zone called Zona Galáctica" (Archivo Municipal de Tuxtla Gutiérrez, Expediente Zona Galáctica, n.d.). Clients of sex workers do not appear in the regulations; their sexual consumption is unimpeded by municipal rules.

The zone is open from nine o'clock in the morning until nine in the evening (there are two nightclubs located outside the main gate that open only at night). The zone's operating hours reflect municipal concerns with social order and maintaining the brothel as a place for contained sexual practice. As sociologist Héctor Carrillo (2002) writes in his study of sexual culture in Guadalajara, the night is a transgressive time, one of danger and sexual diversion. Under cover of the night, anything can happen. The zone's regular and "respectable" business hours lend it a symbolic sense of order and safety. Many zone women prefer to work only during the day; keeping "regular" working hours not only enables women to care for their children when they return home from school but also gives workers the sense that they are operating within cultural norms, despite the stigmatized nature of the work.

During the early years of the Galactic Zone's existence, authorities allowed alcohol consumption there, though this conflicted with Governor González Garrido's original plan. Some workers fondly recall these days, particularly the time following the 1994 Zapatista uprising, when zone workers were always busy with soldiers newly stationed at Tuxtla's nearby military base, and the beer flowed freely. Yet *panista* authorities who later gained control of the city (and therefore the brothel) felt that the consumption of alcohol was excessive, often leading to violence and arguments among and between both workers and clients. Particularly problematic was El Pollo Galáctico (The Galactic Chicken), a restaurant within the zone that authorities felt was selling alcohol in excess and violating the *ley seca* (dry laws that prohibit the sale of alcoholic beverages on election day and other national political holidays). Eventually alcohol consumption in the zone was banned entirely by *panista* authorities (although today alcohol is once again available in the Galáctica).

Although the women and men who work as prostitutes in Tuxtla's streets are symbols of social decay (as well as visible reminders of the failures of neoliberalism to provide economic equality), the Galáctica, with its rules, on-site medical testing, and location far from the city center, became a source of pride and a symbol of progress to government officials, a place where suspect individuals could be contained and surveilled.

The government regulation of sex workers in the Galáctica disciplines and individualizes the women, making collective action or revolt challenging. Such disciplinary practices, when combined with the unbridled free market that reigns in the zone, produce a heightened sense of economic competition that further increases isolation and individualization among workers. Workers who undercut others by charging too little are viewed with open hostility. Those who provide "special services" (oral and anal sex) are seen by colleagues who do not perform such acts as immoral and are judged accordingly. The atmosphere is more divisive than collegial.

Municipal police guard the entry, providing constant surveillance in the zone, even after hours. The front gate serves as both exit and entrance, allowing the movement of both workers and clients to be controlled. The high fence surrounding the zone serves as a subtle form of coercion: unable to exit without the notice of a police officer, individuals are less likely to misbehave within the confines of the zone. Two small jail cells inside the brothel contain those who do. "Discipline," writes Michel Foucault (1977:138), "increases the forces of the body (in terms of economic utility) and diminishes these same forces (in political terms of obedience)." The body of the regulated sex worker is then, in part (and only in part), Foucault's "docile body"; like the soldier, the sex worker has been made useful as she sells her services within a modern economy of pleasure.[7]

While medical testing is the main focus of regulation inside the zone, most prostitutes are not considered beyond redemption by municipal authorities. As in revolutionary Mexico City, when the redemption of "fallen women" through vocational training and education became the chosen cause of social reformers, the women of the Galactic Zone are not considered to be lost causes. But some women are considered better choices for "rehabilitation" than others. When it was decided that I would be giving English classes to zone workers, I strolled about the modules with Héctor, a municipal worker stationed in the zone. As we knocked on women's doors to let them know about the classes, Héctor carried with him a list detailing who occupied each room and sometimes led me past a worker's room, claiming she would not be interested because she was too old. Age was considered a major factor in a woman's ability to "rehabilitate." Women who had been working as prostitutes for years and even decades were believed to have fallen too far to ever come back to "normal" society.

Municipal efforts at rehabilitating sex workers in the zone include not only lectures on mental and physical health but also job training workshops in dressmaking and baking. But zone women are not unaware of the realities of the Mexican economy—Viviana took part in cooking courses not because she wished to leave prostitution to work longer hours for lower pay in a bakery. In baking, she found a hobby she enjoyed and could share with her family. State-sponsored vocational training does not provide structural change; rather, it reinforces patterns of gender and class inequality by preparing zone women for jobs that pay less than what they earn as sex workers but that are considered suitable for poor women.

Courses sponsored by the National Institute for Adult Education (INEA) held in the Galáctica are, in some ways, a more appropriate response to the marginality of sex workers. Profe (short for Professor), an aging retiree, teaches the classes; he is a frail man with rheumy eyes and a soft and raspy voice that sounds like bare feet walking across a gravel path. His skin hangs down from his thin face like a hound dog's jowls. When he writes on the blackboard, his hand gently shakes, leaving behind a scrawl that looks more like an echocardiogram than words. Bored staying home, he felt there was a need to educate the women of the zone so that they would not be "marginalized from society." Of his eight full-time and eight occasional students, he says they are not *malcriadas* (poorly raised). His class runs smoothly, he says, because, "I respect them and they respect me."

One-third of zone workers cannot read or write. This figure is about equal to the number of Chiapas residents over the age of fifteen who are also illiterate (30%) but is far greater than the 10 percent of residents of Tuxtla over the age of fifteen who cannot read or write (Centro de Informacíon y Análisis de Chiapas [CIACH] et al. 1997:35–36). Literacy statistics starkly highlight women's tenuous position in Mexican society—illiterate women outnumber illiterate men in Chiapas by two to one (ibid.:36). Some students have learned to read in Profe's class. When Roxana arrived at the zone, she could not read at all. Now she sat in class, struggling but proudly reading aloud: "I . . . live . . . with . . . my husband." Primary- and secondary-school classes do not give women the means to find well-paid employment elsewhere. Though poverty and a lack of education frequently bring women to the zone, educating sex workers does not necessarily cause women to leave prostitution; sex work offers even educated women more money than they can earn using their training because of the nature of the Mexican economy, depressed wages, and their gender. What education *does* do is provide workers with a sense of community and self-worth. Though located within the zone, the makeshift classroom was a space apart, where prostitutes otherwise engaged in an economic and sometimes moral competition against one another became fellow students learning together. The classroom provided a safe space for workers to show their vulnerabilities and experience their strengths.

Medical testing is the primary form of regulation found in the zone. The Sanitary Control Card that workers must purchase before working at the zone not only declares a woman's health status but also strips the woman of the anonymity associated with illegal street prostitution.[8] The card declares the woman a prostitute as a matter of public record. Workers must purchase a new card every three months for 50 pesos (U.S.$5.90). On the back of the card is a calendar in which a zone health inspector marks the date of the medical visit; the worker's photograph, name, room, building number, and landlord appear on the front of the card. Attached to the lower-left-hand corner of the card is an HIV-negative certificate, which also bears the woman's name and photograph. This card, too, must be purchased.

The worker's weekly visit to the municipal Anti-Venereal Medical Service is the centerpiece of medical control. Each morning, with the exception of Sundays and holidays, a group of workers enters the SMAV. Some arrive ready to work, fully dressed and made up; others are in street clothes, long nightshirts, and plastic sandals. Those who wear complicated high-heeled shoes that must be tied usually stroll in with the laces undone, so they may easily slip the shoes off when their turn comes. They wait, holding their control cards, standing or sitting in the white plastic chairs in the hall that leads to the examination room.

The weekly vaginal examination includes a swabbing for illnesses such as vaginosis, yeast, and other types of infections, as well as gonorrhea. During the exam, a worker may be tested for syphilis (every three months), HIV (every four), and receives a Pap smear twice a year. Twice a month a worker receives a free box of one hundred condoms. Workers themselves must pay all laboratory fees. If a worker tests positive for a transmissible illness, she is suspended until cured. If a worker is HIV-positive, she is suspended permanently. A worker who tests positive for illness is said to be *ponchada*, or punctured, a word often used to refer to flat tires. Like a car with a flat tire, a zone worker who is *ponchada* is of little use.

On Prostitution, Public Health, and the State

The stated goal of the regulationist system of prostitution is to protect public health. Regulating prostitution and subjecting female sex workers to mandatory testing scapegoats prostitutes, implying that they are a major vector of disease and that testing will prevent transmission (McClintock 1993). Yet the incidence of sexually transmitted illness in Mexican states and other countries that regulate prostitution is no different than in places that do not (Uribe et al. 1998:184). That regulation does not stop sexually transmitted illness should be an old lesson; in revolutionary Mexico City, where prostitution was regulated, it was found in the late 1930s that men who had contracted gonorrhea reportedly did so from both sex workers and from women who were not prostitutes (Bliss 2001:204) The regulationist system (and the *Reglamento*) was eventually abandoned shortly thereafter.

Furthermore, compulsory HIV testing for sex workers is not an effective way to prevent the spread of the illness, given that workers in the Galactic Zone may serve up to two hundred clients each month and that there is a three- to six-month window of time between initial infection and seroconversion (the formation of antibodies to the virus that would indicate a positive diagnosis). Also, a narrowly focused prevention effort targeting a small sector of society (such as female registered prostitutes) is not likely to have a tremendous impact upon HIV transmission in Mexico or anywhere else (McClintock 1993); prostitutes themselves are not the primary or sole source of HIV in Chiapas. In addition, the incidence of HIV infection in female Mexican prostitutes is relatively low (various studies put the percentage at between 0.5% and 2.2%) (Rivera, Vicente-Ralde, and Lucero 1992; Uribe et al. 1998.). The lack of intravenous drug use among female Mexican sex workers (far more common in Europe and the United States) contributes, in part, to this relatively low rate of HIV infection (ibid.). Also contributing to the low prevalence of infection is that many prostitutes are informed about HIV risk and adopt preventative measures. In fact, sex workers may be more likely to know how to protect themselves than other sexually active populations such as teenage girls engaging in noncommercial sex and housewives who have little negotiating power to insist upon condom use with their husbands (Delacoste and Alexander 1987). Sex workers have a powerful interest in staying disease-free, both personal and professional; as Lorena told me, "It's like a secretary with her typewriter. I've got to keep my machine clean."

In modern Mexico, then, state-regulated prostitution went from "modern" under the Porfiriato to antiquated following the Revolution and, once again in neoliberal Tuxtla, to "modern." Through the case of the Zona Galáctica, we see a neoliberal state that is not withdrawing but that is shifting its energies more deeply toward other arenas of interest. Along with the privatization of state industries, the reduction of social welfare spending, the withdrawal of state support for small farmers, during the neoliberal era there also exists the reassertion of the state's presence in the lives of sex workers, individuals suspected of selling sex, and, to a lesser degree, consumers of commercial sex.

Yet if regulating prostitution does not protect public health, why regulate it? Walking down the cobblestone streets of San Cristóbal's historic district, I pause to read graffiti on the wall of an old building that, in part, answers the question: *Nos quieren domesticar* (They want to tame us).

1. For further discussion of how legalization does not necessarily lessen stigmatization and how the medical management of sex workers in the Galactic Zone is infused with beliefs about the sexual and gender inequality of women in general and sex workers in particular, see Kelly 2008.

2. For a further discussion of debates about the meanings and impact of globalization, see Held et al. 1999.

3. It should be noted here that the Liberal tradition in Mexico is different and in some ways in opposition to a U.S. understanding of the term "liberal." In the Mexican context, Liberalism in general, and economic liberalism in particular, are associated with policies such as free trade, privatization, and social conservatism.

4. González Garrido's interest in matters of sexuality were not strictly limited to prostitution. During his governorship, abortion was decriminalized in Chiapas in December 1990. The new legislation, which allowed for abortion as a means of family planning, had a life of only twenty-two days, when, following pressure from the Catholic Church, it was suspended. Abortion was recriminalized with a few exceptions, such as when the pregnant woman is HIV-positive. Abortion following rape is legal in all Mexican states but is often actively discouraged by government and medical authorities. For more on this topic, see Human Rights Watch, *The Second Assault: Obstructing Access to Legal Abortion after Rape in Mexico,* available at http://hrw.org/reports/2006/mexico0306.

5. In 1994 a group of peasant farmers known as the Zapatista Army of National Liberation (EZLN) staged an uprising against the neoliberal government; though the fighting subsided after a week, the Zapatista struggle continues and may be characterized as a low-intensity conflict marked by community building, occasional skirmishes, and paramilitary violence.

6. Similar acts that target *travestis* continue to be passed in Tuxtla and elsewhere in Mexico. In 2002 government officials in Tecate, Baja California, amended the city's "Police and Good Governance Act," criminalizing and punishing "men who dress as women and move around public places, causing perturbation" (see Gay Mexico News and Reports, "Action Called Against Tecate Council Discrimination," n.d.; available at http://www.globalgayz. com/mexico-news00-03.html, accessed April 6, 2005). In 2004 a headline in the Mexico City daily *La Jornada* posed the question: "Vestidas under house arrest?" The article that followed detailed the efforts of Tuxtla's new mayor, a *panista* and the first female to occupy the office of municipal president, to wipe *travestis* completely from the urban environment. In contrast to her *panista* predecessors with whom I worked who framed the prostitution issue as a problem of public health and order, and who were relatively mild in their social conservatism, the administration of Mayor Vicki Rincón proclaimed that the arrest of any *travesti* in the street at any time was part of a broader municipal program to halt "moral offenses."

7. The idea of the prostitute as a docile body can only be taken so far. I have written elsewhere (Kelly 2008) about resistance among the women of the Galactic Zone, including a 1996 strike in which they held the administrator of the zone hostage.

8. In Tijuana, Baja California, city officials recently revamped local prostitution laws and issued high-tech identification cards (resembling credit cards) to sex workers that bear the woman's photograph and a magnetic strip that, when scanned, instantly reveals a worker's medical status. See McKinley 2005.

4

Sex Work and the State in Contemporary China

TIANTIAN ZHENG

"Urban men take advantage of us both emotionally and physically" opined Min in describing her experience as a rural migrant to Dalian, a northeastern Chinese city. Like ever increasing numbers of other young Chinese women, Min moved to Dalian seeking unskilled work and found labor conditions that posed uniquely gendered risks; in Min's case, these resulted in her being raped by one of her customers when she worked as a waitress. "We cannot be too innocent [*tai chunjie*] or devoted" Min continued, "otherwise, we will be tricked, used, and abandoned. Only women who are not pure can protect themselves." Min's colleague, Guang, echoed her experiences as she described being raped three times by her male employer while working as a live-in maid for a Dalian family. Disgusted with such abusive working conditions and in search of a labor environment that could provide them with the potential for more economic security, Min and Guang eventually entered sex work at one of Dalian's burgeoning karaoke bars, many of which also function as brothels. In this environment, they could at least control and benefit from sexual encounters.

"We men are just performing here because we all know hostesses only recognize money, not us," businessman Hu explained to me over the din of music at one such karaoke bar in Dalian, "However, there are also cases where men fall in love with them and are eventually cheated by them." Just as karaoke bar hostesses Min and Guang describe their survival strategies in a system that clearly denigrates their rural origins, gender, and lack of formal education, men such as Hu that patronize their establishments clearly demonstrate an understanding of the economic motives underlying hostesses' behavior. Such seemingly discordant realities among individuals who spend a considerable amount of time together raise a series of questions about a phenomenon that has become increasingly popular in Dalian and, in turn, a focus of intensified prohibitionist activity on the part of the Chinese state.

This chapter discusses how sex workers have been adversely affected by China's abolitionist policy, which conflates all sex work with forced prostitution and results in anti-trafficking campaigns that do little to improve the living conditions of migrant women workers like Min and Guang. The argument developed in this paper is based on more than twenty months of fieldwork between 1999 and 2002 in Dalian, where my research sample included approximately two hundred bar hostesses in ten karaoke bars. During my research I worked with and became intensely involved in the lives of karaoke bar hostesses and interacted with patrons such as Hu, in order to ascertain how these individuals make sense of relationships between men and women and, indeed, between individual bodies and the state, in the ever accelerating marketization and globalization of Dalian's economy. In this chapter I examine the factors that facilitated the growth of Dalian's karaoke bar industry and the political sentiments that inform China's anti-trafficking campaigns. Such campaigns have a significant impact on hostesses in karaoke bars by depicting them alternately as victims or deviants when, in reality, the vast majority of such women resemble Min and Guang in having chosen what they perceive as the best option for social mobility from a limited menu of life choices.

The Social Meaning of Dalian's Karaoke Bar Industry

The development of karaoke bars in Dalian closely mirrors the post-1978 reforms and rapid economic growth that have made China the world's third-largest economy, and these establishments are themselves inseparable from such socioeconomic shifts. In contemporary Dalian, entrepreneurs and government officials routinely use the services and facilities offered by karaoke bars to build business networks and negotiate contracts. Anthropologists Helen Siu (1993, 1989) and Gan Wang (1999) make explicit connections between the relatively nascent cultural practices found at karaoke bars and Chinese economic reform by arguing that such establishments provide a level of civic organization that is otherwise lacking in post-Mao China. Entrepreneurs and government officials alike routinely partake of the "coordinated sequence" (*yitiaolong fuwu*) typically featured in karaoke bars and consisting of luxurious banquets, singing, and sauna massage. These institutions are not confined to the Dalian elite, however, as blue-collar urban and migrant male workers with limited wages also patronize karaoke bars, albeit low-tier ones that do not feature the same array of services.

"Singing-and-dancing" ballrooms (*gewu ting*) reemerged with the initiation of Chinese economic reforms in the late 1970s after being banned for nearly thirty years. Although officially tolerated, these businesses came under severe supervision both nationally and locally, and sociologist James Farrer (2000) documents how Shanghai, a city famous for its dance halls, saw the first reappearance of Western-style ballrooms in 1979. Farrer (2000) notes that even in the relatively open environment of Shanghai, dance parties were organized by labor unions and youth leagues, and had to be endorsed by the work unit's letter of introduction.[1] The events were closely supervised by monitors whose job it was to keep men and women from dancing "too close together" (Farrer 2000:230).

In 1984 the first dance hall appeared in Dalian, featuring a band of six singers and a capacity of three hundred people.[2] It was not until 1988 that the first karaoke bar, named "Tokyo 898," was opened. Financed by a Japanese businessman and run as a Sino-Japanese joint venture, the bar's karaoke equipment was said to be imported, brand new, from Japan, which was an extravagance almost unheard of at that time in China's economic development. Following the success of "Tokyo 898," new karaoke bars mushroomed throughout the city, and quickly became the most fashionable male recreational and commercial activity. They are closely associated with Western audio and video technology, splendid exterior and interior furnishings, neon lights, high prices, and beautiful hostesses. They suit the desires of the more economically privileged to experience a "modern" form of consumption, display their vocal talents, and display power and wealth. Patronizing luxurious karaoke bars became a way of life, a modern and prestigious symbol, often only afforded by such wealthy clients as foreign travelers and sailors, government officials, and the local nouveaux riche, though, as noted, blue-collar urban men and migrant workers occasionally visit low-tier karaoke bars to imitate this lifestyle.

Through a former classmate, Xie, I was able to experience a karaoke bar scene from a patron's point of view.[3] A high-level official in Dalian, Xie frequented karaoke bars with his three friends Hu, Ren, and Jin, who had helped him to secure his official position and wealth. Hu and Ren were owners of private enterprises, and Jin was the head of a police bureau in the central district of Dalian with more than one thousand karaoke bars, hotels, restaurants, sauna salons, and nightclubs under his jurisdiction. Xie emphasized to me the importance and inherent danger of these connections, as no one can rise to power without the help of one's friends, and no one can maintain that power if one of those friends fails. Each "friend" contributes and receives in what can develop, if successfully cultivated, into a long-term exchange relationship. Each of the friends had resources to offer the others: Xie, his official power; Hu and Ren, their economic power; and Jin, his legal and administrative power. To strengthen their ties, they often gathered in restaurants, karaoke bars, and sauna salons. The bill was always taken care of by the entrepreneurs Hu and Ren. It is this kind of alliance that becomes solidified in clients' consumption of hostesses' services in karaoke bars,[4] although karaoke bars, since their emergence, have been consistently under attack by the Chinese anti-trafficking campaigns.

The Impact of Chinese Anti-Trafficking Campaigns
On Karaoke Bars

Beginning in 1989, with the appearance of karaoke bars, the Chinese government has launched periodic nationwide antiprostitution campaigns to ensure "security and state control."[5] The campaigns are aimed at "cultural purification" and "spiritual civilization." The "erotic company" of hostesses, pornographic TV shows, seductive performances, and prostitution within karaoke bars are condemned as "cultural trash" that "destabilizes state rule and the socialist system." Restrictions stop short of an outright ban, intending, instead, to bring karaoke bars into line with state-defined socialist culture.

China's abolitionist stance deems prostitution (or third-party involvement in it) an illegal form of violence against women. Chinese antiprostitution legislation is predicated upon the belief that no woman would choose prostitution voluntarily and that prostitution strips a woman of her "natural" and legal rights. This legislation includes the First Criminal Law in 1979, the 1987 Regulations, the 1984 Criminal Law, the 1991 Decision on Strictly Forbidding the Selling and Buying of Sex, the 1991 Decision on the Severe Punishment of Criminals Who Abduct and Traffic in or Kidnap Women and Children, the 1992 Law on Protecting the Rights and Interests of Women (the Women's Law), the Revised Criminal Law of 1997, and the 1999 Entertainment Regulations.[6] Because the government holds the belief that women would not choose a profession that violates their own human rights, the purpose of these laws is to prohibit a third party from organizing prostitution, engaging in illicit relations with a prostitute, and trafficking women into prostitution.

The "erotic service" (*seqing peishi*) offered in karaoke bars is deemed counter to China's "socialist spiritual civilization."[7] The exchange of sexual services for money is an "ugly social phenomenon" associated with capitalism and should be wiped out to maintain a healthy socialist cultural environment and "civilized consumption." The main responsibility for administering state policy regarding karaoke bars is divided between the Bureau of Culture (BC) and the Public Security Bureau (PSB). These two agencies, respectively, represent the government's dual strategy of soft and hard administrative measures. The BC is responsible for ensuring that karaoke bars are managed according to socialist standards of civility and morality through a variety of administrative and regulatory measures. For instance, the BC maintains detailed records of bars' business location, name, proprietor, exterior and interior design, audio and video machines, and other information. Strict approval procedures were introduced to reduce the number of karaoke bars. In addition, the BC organized monthly classes on state policy and law that bar owners are required to attend. Those achieving high test scores are awarded a plaque denoting the establishment a "Civilized Karaoke Bar" that can be displayed inside their bars. The BC also mandated that karaoke bars should display "Chinese" and socialist characteristics, including, for example, mainland Mandarin music, "healthy and inspiring" revolutionary songs, Chinese-style wallpaper, Chinese paintings, Chinese-style bar names, and Chinese food and snacks. Lurking beneath these regulations is a palpable sense of crisis induced by the idea that Western influences have begun to erode Chinese culture. As a BC official explained to me:

> The imported Western culture in China is like an aircraft carrier—high quality, durable, and powerful. Chinese culture, however, resembles a small sampan, only able to float a hundred miles. We need to develop a singing-and-dancing business with Chinese characteristics to attack the foreign cultural market in China.

The PSB acts as an "Iron Great Wall" (*gangtie changcheng*), providing the muscle behind state policy. The main vehicle for PSB intervention is the antipornography campaign (*saohuang dafei*), itself a part of a wider comprehensive attack on social deviance known as "crackdowns" (*yanda;* literally, to strike severely). These campaigns run for three-month spurts and are repeated three times a year, strategically centering on important holidays such as National Day and Army Day as well as other events. Crackdowns target a potpourri of social ills, ranging from unlicensed video-game arcades (said to corrupt the minds of the youth) to undocumented rural migrants (said to disrupt urban management).

The PSB employs a complex system of raids to attack karaoke bars, which it describes, notably, as "guerrilla warfare" (*da youji*) in reference to the heroic efforts of the communist revolutionaries against the Japanese invaders and nationalists. There are several types of raids, including regular raids and shock raids, timed raids and random raids, systematic raids and block raids, daytime raids and night raids. PSB units and individuals that perform well, determined by the number of hostesses arrested and the amount of fines levied, receive high honors and cash bonuses from their municipal government.

Local Officials and Bar Owners

The complex interactions between hostesses and their patrons and state agents reflect a gap between the "theory" of policy and the "practice" of enforcement. State policy is distorted, even derailed, by the self-seeking behavior of local officials, particularly because karaoke bars are an important source of extralegal income. As one PSB official candidly remarked, "Karaoke bars and hostesses are our sources of livelihood. We basically cannot live without them." Because these officials have the arbitrary power to arrest and fine the hostesses, the latter are extremely apprehensive when they are chosen by an official, as they know that they must obey the his demands.

Officials extract economic benefits from karaoke bars through bribes and fines, but local officials' exploitation of hostesses is not limited to economic benefits. PSB officials maintain a group of "spy hostesses" (*xiaojie jianxi*) who report on the conditions of the bar and also act as these officials' personal harem. In exchange for their services, hostesses gain immunity from police sanctions. Hostesses, in turn, allow corrupt officials to get rich, contribute to regional economic development, and advance officials' political careers. Further, while local officials manipulate state policy to exploit bar owners and hostesses for their personal gain, bar owners also improvise creative maneuvers to counter local officials.

According to one city official, 1995 marked a change in relations between hostesses and bar owners from the contract system to an exploitative system. Before the police crackdown in 1995, hostesses were hired by the hundreds on contracts with bar bosses. According to the contract, hostesses received fees from the customers for their services. Bar owners also awarded them a percentage of the customers' bills. To explain the change that came about in 1995, we must go back to the early 1980s.

With the rise in popularity of karaoke bars in Dalian, a red light district sprang up in the center of the Zhongshan district. At some time around the end of the 1980s and in the early 1990s, a number of karaoke bars were opened on Stalin Road. By all indications, the scope of business was considerable. Every night hostesses, by the hundreds, scoured the city's seaport for tourists and brought them back to the bars to engage them in sexual activities. During this period both bars and hostesses prospered.

One morning in 1994, a foreigner was seen running out of the area in only his underwear.[8] A group of Chinese men followed him, shouting curses and flourishing clubs. It was said that the foreigner could not afford the tab for the previous night's sexual encounter. Managing to escape with his life, the foreigner subsequently brought charges against the bar's proprietor for exploiting him. The matter quickly escalated into an international conflict between the two affected embassies. The incident even made front-page headlines in the *Hong Kong Gazette* (*Ta Kung Pao*) in an article titled, "Dalian Red Light District on Stalin Road." Fearing that the scandal would taint the image of the socialist regime, the CCP Central Committee immediately ordered that the area be cleaned up. Having to overcome tremendous difficulties in breaking up patron-client ties between local officials and bar owners, the police finally cracked down in 1995.[9] To erase public memory of the incident, the name of the street was changed from Stalin Road to People's Road.

Ever since this extreme police crackdown disrupted the system that had been in place, bar hostesses and owners have been under the strict control of local government. Bar owners no longer view themselves as dependent on the hostesses; instead, they see themselves as the hostesses' saviors because they provide them secure housing and jobs. Since 1995, owners require hostesses to hand over 10 percent of their fees.

In the particular upscale karaoke bar where I conducted my research during the antiprostitution campaign, the bar owner extracted additional profits from the hostesses by charging more for their uniforms than they were actually worth. He also seized this chance to record every hostesses' biological data.[10] He asked the hostesses to give him their duplicate hometown IDs and their Dalian temporary residence cards (TRCs), and urged those who had not yet purchased or renewed their TRC to do so quickly. He claimed that he would compile a book with a record of their pictures, names, and photocopied TRCs, through which hostesses would be transformed into formal employees working as waitresses. He also effectively controlled their mobility and behavior. Prior to the crackdown, hostesses were brought to any karaoke room for selection, but afterward they were grouped in tens and assigned to different sections of the bar, with ten karaoke rooms in each section. Instead of standing together in the entrance hall, they now gathered at their designated section, waiting to be chosen. Every hostess was required to wear the uniform dress bearing a name card, in a color that matched her particular section. Hostesses had to report to the directors (the madams) if they were going outside the bar (*chutai*: to offer sexual services in hotels) with clients. They were ordered to arrive at the bar at precisely 7:30 pm every evening and not to leave until 12 am unless they went out with clients. Hostesses arriving late or leaving early were fined 600 yuan (U.S.$75). If they wanted a leave of absence or a night off, the director had to give his permission, which, as a matter of principle, was never granted. Bar owners also demanded that hostesses be trained and disciplined in how they walked, spoke, and sang. All these new demands, controls, and restrictions on hostesses emerged at this moment of conflict between bar owners and officials. Bar owners ensured the prosperity of their businesses by manipulating hostesses and maneuvering ways around state policy.

Hostesses and Their Aspirations

Local implementation of the state's antiprostitution policy has failed to reach the proposed objective of eliminating prostitution and has only aggravated hostesses' working conditions. Police raids of karaoke bars make hostesses legally and socially vulnerable. Were clients to disclose the women's sexual services to the police, the women would be subject to humiliation, arrest, fines, and incarceration. Because of this potentially horrific outcome, hostesses do not disclose their true identity, which then makes it easier for men to be violent toward them or even commit murder. It was reported that in Shenyang alone more than one hundred hostesses were murdered in 1999 ("Sanpei xiaojie de Falu Baohu Wenti" 2002). In Dalian, hostesses' bodies were found murdered on the street, but the police could not identify them (Sun 2003). When I accompanied my hostess friend Wu to her hometown, I asked her mother if she worried about Wu's safety in Dalian. Her mother's face sank with distress and torment, and she kept silent for a long time before gaining the strength to respond:

> I did not hear from her for three months. She did not call me. I did not have her phone number . . . I really thought she was murdered. You know, it's so common in Dalian. I always heard the news about hostesses' dead bodies found there. I believed Wu was one of them. I was worried sick. I got so sick that I couldn't get up. I thought I was never going to see her again.

In the upscale bar where I conducted research, the main task of the security guards in green pseudo-military uniforms was to keep the hostesses from leaving before midnight, ensure that clients tip the hostesses, and maintain bar security. Occasionally a team of security guards would rush upstairs like soldiers to quell fights in the karaoke rooms. The suppression of disturbances itself always involved violence and blood. Unarmed or armed (with beer bottles, knives, and glasses) fights between drunken clients and between clients and hostesses were daily occurrences. At times hostesses came downstairs crying from their injuries: their legs, arms, and breasts black and blue from clients' hard pinches. Some hostesses chose to endure the abuse, but others quit and consequently received no tips for the time they had put in. Those who clenched their teeth to see it through with big bright smiles would hold back their tears and complaints for later, when they sent off the clients and returned to the crowd of idle hostesses.

The low-class bar called Romance Dream is located in the crime-plagued red light district. The staff includes three multifunctional staff members (madams/doormen/janitors), two bar managers, approximately twenty-seven hostesses, and a barkeep/security guard (*kan changzi de*). As with the high- and medium-level bars, blood ties link the bar proprietor and management into a relatively cohesive group. Each bar on this street has to hire a thug as the barkeep. This person must be a good fighter, otherwise, the bar would be forced to close down because of the harassment of gangsters and thugs roaming the streets. During my research in the bar, I witnessed numerous bloody fights between the barkeeper, a man named Bing, and bar waiters and gangsters, clients, and passers-by. I saw Bing and waiters throw heavy stones and chairs at clients and at the heads of some passers-by until blood streamed down their faces. The bar owner told me that Bing, after having killed and severely injured many men in previous fights, was once sentenced to death. The bar owner spent a great deal of money to finally get Bing out of prison before hiring him as the bar guard. Bing's mere presence in the bar kept many gangsters and thugs away. According to the owner, if Bing were not in the bar, it would definitely be a disaster: all the hostesses would flee in fear, and everything would be plundered by gangsters. She entrusted my safety to Bing and the bar managers.

Gangsters and other bar owners, all local, often came to visit. Upon seeing pretty hostesses, they would drag them upstairs and rape them. When they saw less attractive hostesses, they slapped their faces and beat them up. The hostesses, of course, were extremely apprehensive about some of the toughest gangsters and thugs and would run as fast as they could to escape them. I once fled along with the hostesses. We escaped by climbing onto the overpass built over the bars, losing our shoes and cutting our feet in the process, a very unpleasant experience indeed. Most of the bar hostesses have been raped one or more times by gangsters. Twice the gangsters came in and started to pull me into a karaoke room. Luckily Bing and the bar managers stopped them, saying: "She is not a hostess here. She is my friend." That assurance saved me from imminent danger but the fear lingered.

To protect themselves, almost all the hostesses were connected with one or two street gangsters. When a gangster came in, a hostess who was linked with him or a thug in his group would not have to escape. My friend Wu did not like the bouncer of a neighboring bar, a thug, but he favored her strongly. To gain his protection from other gangsters, she had to develop a relationship with him. She told me,

> In my home town, nobody dares to touch me because I have a wide net-work of friends. It's so different here. Here I don't have anyone. No one cares if I am bullied. He is a thug, and he is local. I have to be good to him. I need someone to turn to when I encounter trouble on this street.

When Wu was harassed by someone in a different gangster group or by drunken clients, she would call the bouncer for help. On several occasions he led a few gangsters into the bar to beat up the drunken client at Wu's request. Wu also started a relationship with a bar owner in the city. She told me that these were the key people she turned to when she needed help. Like Wu, other hostesses were connected with a bar owner, a bouncer, or a skilled street fighter. They frequently joked, "We hostesses are relatives of the underworld."

Despite their uneasy relationship with criminal elements, many rural migrant women quickly find that hostessing provides a lucrative income, independence, and self-esteem. Because of the dearth of jobs in the private sector, rural women have limited employment opportunities in the city. As migrants, they often lack the social connections essential for finding a job in the already over-saturated urban labor market. Their ability to find work is further hindered by a discriminatory government policy that denies migrants equal status with urban residents. Among the jobs that are available to rural women, most are in low-paid, labor-intensive industries. Under these circumstances, hostessing is a highly attractive employment option. Hostessing also holds out the allure of earning high incomes over a brief period of time. Hostesses typically entertain a customer for one to two hours and earn an average tip of 200 to 400 yuan (U.S.$25–$50), at least the equivalent of, but often more than, other rural migrants' monthly wage and almost half the average monthly wage of an urban worker. In addition, working as a hostess provides rural women access to a wide network of influential male figures in the city's business and political sectors. Hostessing requires a minimal upfront investment. Newly arrived hostesses typically borrow money from other hostesses or friends to purchase the clothing and accessories worn while servicing clients. Because of the high profitability of hostessing, the borrower can typically settle her debt with the earnings from one or two sessions with clients. Thus rural women who lack economic resources can nonetheless enter the workforce as hostesses.

Migrating to countries such as Japan and Singapore to conduct sex work is a dream for many hostesses. During my research, three hostesses managed to travel to Japan and Singapore as sex workers, and they were the models for many other hostesses. Each of these three hostesses had to pay out 20,000 yuan (U.S.$2,500) and pass the interview before being permitted to go through the visa process. After having worked in Japan and Singapore for a year, they returned to Dalian and expressed their ambition to return to these countries and continue working as sex workers.

Karaoke bars, as flourishing new cultural spaces in the city, are places where rural migrant women can achieve a certain degree of self-esteem by being accepted and desired by the urban men who choose them as companions for the night. The karaoke bar is also where these women can find secondary socialization by mingling with urban clients, where they feel "urban and cosmopolitan," both culturally and socially. Yet hostesses' experience of rape and abandonment in the city teaches them not to be duped by men's romantic words and to embrace independence through hostessing. They commented, "Dalian men try to cheat both our bodies and our emotions. Without spending a cent, they get what they want from us."

Han worked as a hairdresser in the city. She lived with an urban man for three years in his home. During this time, she suffered from all kinds of physical and verbal abuse from his aunt and mother. For instance, they accused her of stealing their jewelry and associated her "thieving habits" with her "inferior" rural background. Han made every effort to endure all this inhumane treatment. Her urban boyfriend, however, also worried that her rural family would become a bottomless pit, eventually draining all his money, and so he abruptly abandoned her, saying, "Our social status just doesn't match." Devastated, she believed that she would never find happiness unless she became the social and economic equal of the urbanites. She started working as a hostess. Five years later she was very successful: she possessed two household registrations—one urban and one rural; she purchased two houses, one in her hometown for her parents and one in Dalian for her siblings; she supported her two younger sisters and a brother through school; and she paid for the weddings of her four older brothers and sisters. She is now married to the financial director of a prestigious hotel chain.

Another hostess, Hong, broke up with her client boyfriend when he failed to offer her the amount of money she expected. She commented:

> I myself can earn 100,000 yuan [U.S.$12,500] a month from hostessing. To exchange this for his several thousand yuan—so little money—I have to obey everything he says. Who will do that? He thinks I am fresh from the countryside, so I can easily be cheated. With so little money, he wants me to be his second wife and control me as his possession by tying my arms and legs. That's impossible. I want to earn money for myself and spend it happily as I want. There is no way for me to spend his little money at the price of abiding by whatever he has to say.

If rural origin and cultural inferiority is the root of the hierarchical relationship between rural migrant women and urban men, then hostessing offers an opportunity to escape subordination. As paid work, hostessing represents an act of defiance against the urban men who freely exploit the women's bodies and emotions. At the bar, men have to pay a high price to hostesses even to approach them. This transaction transformed the situation that existed when migrant women were available to men as free dinner at the men's whim.

Hostessing allows women to gain an economic profit and therefore independence from men. In the monetary transaction, hostesses attain a certain equality with the urban men by taking advantage of the men's resources. Having financial resources at their disposal brings the women power and confidence. Many hostesses who are married or are kept as second wives sneak out of the house to work. Setting up their own separate account allows them to spend their own money at will and secretly support their natal families. The economic power gained by hostessing earned Han and Hong a great degree of independence and equality in social and gender status within their biological families and their relationships with urban partners.

Conclusion

This chapter points out the discrepancy between policy and practice in Chinese anti-trafficking discourse. The anti-trafficking policy is manipulated and usurped by local officials against the interests of hostesses, leading to a violent working environment. Far from the state rhetoric of forced prostitution and the need for rehabilitation, hostesses are agents who actively choose hostessing as an expedient route to achieving a certain degree of social mobility. I argue that the anti-trafficking discourse of forced prostitution ignores the larger context within which force is used, that is, the global inequities of capital and labor that rob women of viable options and force them into sweatshop labor or lucrative sex work.

NOTES

1. A place of employment in Maoist China was called a "work unit" (*danwei*). The term refers to a place of employment during the socialist economy with state-owned enterprises. Each work unit provided its employees with housing, child care, schools, clinics, shops, services, and other subsidies.

2. Reconstructing the history of karaoke bars in Dalian proved to be exceedingly difficult. A combination of official denial and embarrassment has ensured that no publicly open records were kept on the subject, and the same attitude undoubtedly dissuaded any interested parties from prying. Therefore, to piece together the story, I had to rely entirely on the oral accounts of government officials in different divisions of the municipal Bureau of Culture.

3. For more information on hostesses' social networks, see Zheng 2009a. For more on HIV/AIDS transmission, see Zheng 2009b.

4. For more information on clients' alliances, see Zheng 2009a, 2006.

5. The phrase "security and state control" has been the overarching political language disseminated throughout China. Because of this political language's pervasiveness, interviewees would repeat these words as part of the steadfast belief that China's economy would not accelerate unless Chinese leaders maintained state control and political stability.

6. Antiprostitution legislation became a priority in China following the 1978-initiated market reforms which prompted unprecedented feminized rural-to-urban migration as well as increased numbers of karaoke bars and other entertainment industries.

7. Consonant with the 1978 economic reforms, the Chinese Communist Party (CCP) began a campaign to build a "socialist spiritual civilization" that included specific social and political values and morality to offset emerging negative social aspects such as consumerism, nihilism, and hedonism. Deng Xiaoping first proposed this concept in 1980, and the subsequent political regimes continued the campaign. The "socialist spiritual civilization" was intended to create a superior set of moral codes (including discipline and hard work) and political consciousness without caving in to the influences of Western bourgeois lifestyles.

8. That the person involved was not Chinese is significant, as the disclosure of the red light district to the outside world embodied national shame and political disgrace. China wanted to present an ethically moral and economically developed image to the outside world, not the tarnished image of rampant prostitution.

9. This information was gained from my interviews with political officials in the municipal government.

10. Rural migrants, to remain legal in cities, are required to pay a certain fee each month to purchase a temporary resident card. These resident permits are related to the household registration system initiated in 1958 that outlawed rural migration through the management of resource distribution, thereby establishing a two-tier urban-rural caste system in the society.

5

Smart Sex in the Neoliberal Present

Rethinking Single Parenthood in a
Mexican Tourist Destination

DAWN PANKONIEN

Oraida and Fernando arrived in Huatulco from Oaxaca City four years ago with four children. They brought just enough money to pay one month's rent and invest in what is still today their Huatulco business venture—a semi-formal stand from which they sell sandwiches along with Coca-Cola products and goods from the giant Mexican bakery Bimbo. Fernando's parents watch the children while Oraida and Fernando work. Despite Fernando's research and ever evolving marketing strategies, his business, like most in Huatulco, barely survives—even with Oraida delivering sandwiches to doorsteps, free of charge, on her rent-to-own motorcycle.

When Fernando is alone at the business, he fills the empty hours, sometimes days, thinking. One day in January 2009 I sat before him at the counter of his stand, and, aware that I was studying the lives of single parents in the region, he asked: "Do you know why matrimony has changed in Mexico?" Fernando, one of my most eloquent interlocutors, then pivoted to open the coke cooler. "This," he exclaimed, holding up a twenty-ounce bottle of Diet Coke, "this is what changed matrimony in Mexico. Do you understand me?"

I did not understand.

"Fine, I'll tell you." Fernando sighed, with exaggerated impatience which I believe he thinks builds credibility. "Think of it this way," he went on. "The people drink Coca-Cola and they love Coca-Cola. Everyone loves Coca-Cola. And Coca-Cola has a great taste, but it also has calories. You just know—that's one part. But then one day Coca-Cola comes out with this." He holds up the bottle to remind me. "*Coca-Cola Light.* And what? I tell you, now you have all of the good taste of Coca-Cola and none of the calories. This is what happened to marriage in Mexico. The people have learned to want all of the taste with none of the calories. But marriage isn't like that. There's good and bad. Now people want it without the bad."

This conversation took place in Huatulco, Oaxaca, a twenty-five-year-old federal tourism development project located in the south of Mexico on the Pacific Coast. Journalists describe Huatulco as pristine and idyllic, and tourism promoters overuse descriptive terms such as "natural" and "virgin." Anthropologists, on the other hand, write of the region's seclusion, economic instability, out-migration, and manufactured authenticity, though, in their footnotes, they recognize that tourism has sometimes produced benefits (Barkin 2000, 2002; Gullette 2004, 2007; Long 1990; Pankonien 2008). Residents are more attentive to the cost of living. Whole milk, tortillas, and other staple foods cost 15 to 20 percent more in Huatulco than in Mexico City and as much as 35 percent more than in surrounding areas of southern Oaxaca. "Huatulco is expensive," I am told again and again.

The percentage of births among women who are single, separated, divorced, or widowed is 50 percent higher in Huatulco than in Mexico City (Instituto Nacional de Estadística y Geografía [INEGI; Institute of Statistics and Geography] 2000), and local discourse suggests rates that are even more extreme: "Half of the women here are single mothers," say most Huatulco residents willing to venture a guess. By claiming that this is the result of Diet Coke, Fernando is locating the cause in a global, political, economic, and now cultural shift toward instantaneity and cyclical consumption fostered by the neoliberal ideology guiding capitalism today.

In this chapter I examine the interrelation of neoliberal tourism development, urbanization, and the formation of single-parent families. I represent cross-class, indigenous, and non-indigenous single parents as economic actors and am concerned with the ways that political, economic, and cultural shifts might render single-parent families increasingly viable, attractive, and perhaps even necessary. I suggest that single parents, unconstrained by the institution of marriage, are free to wield sex and sexuality as tools. And I argue that this is key to surviving the economic instability wrought by high unemployment rates and seasonal employment in neoliberal tourism development zones. Sex, in this context, is smart, economically motivated, and easily called sex work without at all resembling what we have come to call "sex work." This micro-level manipulation of sex, of course, makes sense only inside a macro-level analysis of history and political economy.

In my attempt to understand the evolution of family forms in their economic contexts, I look at the works of Victorianists Lewis Henry Morgan (1877) and Friedrich Engels (1884). My goal is to create an argument for today's single-parent families according to a simple formula: monogamy replaced the pairing family which replaced group marriage. Charles Darwin's evolutionary schema provided a framework for understanding shifting social institutions, inspiring Morgan, Marx, Engels, and countless other contemporary scholars. Engels argued that the pairing family already represented an end of the natural selection process: "In the pairing family, the group was already reduced to its last unit, its two atom molecule—to one man and one woman." Engels told us it was the unnaturalness of capitalism that necessitated monogamy. I am convinced that it is just as neat, just as simple, to posit that the unnaturalness of capitalism now relatively privileges poor, single-parent families, often in ways we do not notice. I suspect, in the cases of women in particular, that this is because single parenthood allows women to maintain the rights to their sexuality or even to sell their sexuality of their own will.

Welcome to Huatulco

Huatulco, Oaxaca, Mexico is a federal tourism development project that has grossly underperformed compared to the projections accompanying its design and implementation. Proposed by the creators of Cancun, Loredo, Los Cabos, and Ixtapa, Huatulco's master plan details the construction of hotels, restaurants, and an eighteen-hole golf course, all situated along thirty kilometers of coastal terrain which, in the mid-1980s, held fewer than four hundred people. Federal statistics from that time suggest a region that was 0 percent urban with inhabitants divided into small communities situated on the beaches of varied bays (INEGI 1985). Development was to bring ten thousand hotel rooms by the year 2000; at the end of 2009 there were twenty-five hundred hotel rooms in the Huatulco development zone (INEGI 2000; Ana Laura Valderez, Huatulco director of SECTUR: personal correspondence 2009). In other words, Huatulco was 75 percent short of a planning goal that was, in 2009, nearly one decade old.

Despite many failings, Huatulco is a region of great hope, partly because those who have lost hope have sold out or moved elsewhere and partly because the federal government still heavily invests in Huatulco. Roads are straight and repaired annually, and tap water is chlorinated so that too many showers over too many months leave one's hair falling out, but tourists don't get sick from the ice cubes. Hedges are manicured; palm trees are aligned; and low-waged gardeners keep the region green many months into the dry season. The countless projects that have been abandoned before completion—now half-built structures dotting the Huatulco landscape—suggest to the unknowing onlooker investment rather than desertion. And even when one knows what Huatulco was supposed to be by now, the region still evinces rapid, radical redevelopment and urbanization: the municipality that was 0 percent urban, is now, according to INEGI, more than 80 percent urban, growing by at least 8 percent annually into the mid-2000s (INEGI 2000; Ramon Sinovas, Huatulco director of Fondo Nacional de Fomento al Turismo [FONATUR], personal correspondence, 2005).

The many single parents in Huatulco have gone unnoticed in anthropological studies of the region. And though scholars, who have worked elsewhere in Mexico specifically with single mothers, have documented the ways in which women stress chastity and religious faith in attempts to salvage honor (Hirsch 2003; Murphy 1998), my observations in Huatulco do not conform. I find, instead, a community of women and men who are unapologetic regarding their single parenthood.

The lives and choices of the single parents with whom I worked make politico-economic sense. To say this requires that I define single mothers and single fathers, and, in Mexico, where free unions are not only an accepted form of marital union but in some places are increasingly preferred, this is not easily done. In my project a woman who identified herself as a *madre soltera* (single mother) at any point in her life qualified as a single mother. Those I might call the "purists" in the region spent two and a half years telling me that my project was deeply flawed, as "everyone knows" that a single mother can only be a mother who has never married. All those women who are separated, divorced, or widowed are not actually *madres solteras,* I was told. And although the federal statistics agency INEGI would agree, I chose not to and stayed with my own definition. (Mexicanist scholars have remedied this by using *madre sola* in place of *madre soltera*.) Regarding my definition of single fathers, I exclude men identifying as single fathers who had never been in contact with their children.

This left me with forty of eighty-eight formal informants who identified as single parents at the time of their interviews. Only fifteen of those would have been labeled "real" single mothers by the "purists." Five were single fathers. All the others looked more or less like real single mothers, although that varied greatly over time, for single motherhood is as impermanent an identity as many others. Just as the residents of Huatulco move in and out of jobs, in and out of work, in and out of the region, so, too, do they move in and out of relationships.

Single parents, in fact, are somewhat more likely to be first-generation migrants to Huatulco than residents as a whole. In the sample of seventy-six residents I constructed to represent Huatulco's diverse population, 82 percent were first-generation migrants to the region. Meanwhile, 90 percent of the single parents in my study were first-generation migrants, and more than half arrived to the region years before other family members. This is meaningful. Following sociologist Larissa Lomnitz's 1974 study of reciprocity networks in Mexico,[1] scholars examined the ways in which kin and fictive kin relationships mitigate poverty. Such strategies become particularly important among immigrant populations, as suggested by the works of anthropologists Cristina Oehmichen Bazán (2005), Li Zhang (2001), and others. Yet my work, along with many other recent studies, indicates that it is becoming much harder to sustain such reciprocity networks. Neoliberal policy immiserates all, eroding support systems today based both on kin and fictive kin (Gonzalez de la Rocha 1994, 2000, 2002; Willis 1993, 1994).

Sex as Strategy

In Huatulco, where residents are necessarily incorporated into the market economy, where consumption costs are high, wages are low, and employment is seasonal, single parents must become even more creative in their attempts to sustain themselves and their children. As neoliberal policy reform continues to roll back social programming, this means that single parents are providing their own safety nets. Sex-based relationships, whether temporary or permanent, become ever more vital.

Single fathers who are quick to assume girlfriends suggest such economically based sexual strategizing. The unpaid household labor of a girlfriend functions just as does that of the bourgeois wife in Engels's work. The status of single father might even work as bait: three of the single fathers in my work, all of the professional class, described women's attraction to them as single fathers. Women, they told me, see them as caring, invested in their children, and good fathers, and thus as good long-term relationship partners.

For women, the employment of sex as an economic strategy looks far different. I used to tell Alma with a laugh that she was my study's outlier, and at first glance she looks little like the other women in my study. She is the single mother of three boys to whom she gave names such as "Divine Confidence" and "Gandhi." In Huatulco, she survives by reading tarot cards, teaching yoga, giving massages, tailoring clothing, and taking people into her home so they might learn healthy living. Alma rarely has excess pesos and never has secure employment, but like many of the single parents in the region she patches jobs together and sometimes pays her rent a bit late. Upon closer examination, she is not so much of an outlier.

In 2008 Alma's landlord grew stricter on rent payments at the same time the economy tightened. As Alma's clients became boyfriends and boyfriends became clients, onlookers became confused. "Alma's a prostitute," they murmured, quietly at first. But Alma wrote up a resume, in which she announced that she gives sexuality conferences, that she will teach women to reach orgasm and men to "be alive between their hips." Alma had a friend who promised to teach her how to advertise on the Internet.

The single mothers of my study said repeatedly in their interviews that one difficult aspect of being a single mother is that people think you are *facil* (easy). The mothers described extravagant strategies to test potential boyfriends for sincerity. Some wait a year or more before introducing a man to their children. Yet almost all the women showed, through the course of their narrative accounts of life in Huatulco, that they could switch from mother to martyr to girlfriend and even to the sexualized single mother troped as easy—as in the example of Alma above.

Nayeli claimed that, at the gas station where she worked, the trick is not to ask if a customer wants his or her windshield washed. You just do it, and they will give you five pesos and sometimes more. It helps to wear sexy clothes. Lupita, who works at the gym owned by her cousin, told me that the men like her to tell them how to use the machines, to show them how to work out different muscles. She would grin and tell me how they like to flirt and that this makes the time pass much faster. As female laborers of Huatulco have grown prominent in receptionist positions at hotels and restaurants, at gas stations and gyms, they have grown increasingly adept at enacting various identities. Single mothers, with children as scarlet letters, are particularly free to sell sex and sexuality to today's global consumers in the local, tourism-dependent economy of Huatulco.

In September 2009 Lupita and her fifteen-year-old were competing to see who would find a boyfriend first. Lupita explained that her relationship with her daughter is much different than the way her parents treated her. Local restaurant owner Paola said that was true for her as well, that her parents' strictness drove her to seek freedom, the kind that comes with rebellion and results in teenage pregnancy. Both women agreed that Huatulco is a good place to raise children—small enough that your friends will tell you if your children are in the streets but not as small as other places. Small towns, big gossip, they warned. Many used this phrase to describe the towns from which they migrated. In Huatulco there is more privacy and less gossip, they maintained. On a bad day, however, the women with whom I spoke would forget this and contradict themselves, telling me there is too much gossip in Huatulqu-ito, "little Huatulco."

What the single mothers in my study did not say, but which I nonethe-less suspect, is that much of the privacy in Huatulco stems from the absence of extended family members. Almost all who live in Huatulco now do so neolocally. Rural migrants have left communities where siblings build houses on land owned by their parents or on communal land. They have left com-munities where three- and four-generation families remain in daily contact. Similarly, longtime inhabitants of the Huatulco development zone were relo-cated from the beachfront, where they farmed, fished, or ran small conve-nience stores, to a designated residential sector. They were given plots of land measuring ten by twelve meters and the materials to build concrete homes. But families soon outgrew these plots, or they sold out. Others learned that establishing small businesses or renting rooms to outsiders was more profitable than housing adult children. Households, whether headed by migrants or by Huatulco's original inhabitants, are now far less likely to be multigenerational.

Although single parents in Huatulco are more likely to be first-generation migrants than other residents, they are also more likely than the population of residents as a whole to set up independent households. Eighty-eight per-cent of the single parents with whom I worked live in rooms, apartments, or houses which they rent or own and fund in their own names. As *jefes* and *jefas* (heads) of households, they increasingly depend on themselves. Might this turning inward suggest more than the corrosion of kin and fictive-kin relationships that results from neoliberal policy? Might this also imply attempts to escape social stigmatization made possible by women's increas-ing incorporation into low-waged service sectors everywhere? Is this turning inward an indication that women want to make decisions independent even of those to whom they are closest?

Virtual relationships leave single parents turning inward and outward at the same time. Jenyfer, Lili, Carlos, Memo, Alma, and many other single par-ents with whom I worked shared the conviction that, even with one's own space, Huatulco grows too small. Nearly one-quarter of the single parents in my study dated online. Alma was the most enthusiastic in her promotion of Internet relationships, and she maintained the most profiles on the most social networking sites. On my last day in the region I stopped by with my camera because she needed digital photos for a second Tagged profile: "I'm going to wear a hat and sunglasses, and I will dress like this isn't the beach. No one knows my given name, I'll use that. I'm going to friend the actor, the one who quit talking to me. I know he likes sexy women. These will be sexy pictures. He will try to talk to me, and I will ignore him."

Alma had been sure, one week earlier, that this actor, with his photos of yachts and mansions, would invest in her dream to build a little café filled with food for the body and spirit. The German scientist Alma dated online the year before had arrived in Huatulco six months into their relationship and decided that he didn't like the fuchsia bedroom walls at Alma's; communication was much more difficult without the online translator. Alma had also envisioned this man as a potential investor in her dream.

Jenyfer who has had the same Internet boyfriend for four years tells me there are no men in Huatulco—her boyfriend lives somewhere in the Yucatan Peninsula. Alma says, "Why would I limit myself to Huatulco when I have access to the whole world on my computer?" Jenyfer talks with her boyfriend daily, although she has not yet seen him in person. Her friends call her crazy. "Actually, this is perfect," she answers, "because it doesn't take time away from my children, and I don't have to worry if he gets along with my children. This functions for now." With more than twenty Internet cafés in the town's center and a cost of U.S.$0.66 per hour online, such Internet-based relationships do in fact function in Huatulco.

I also find that single mothers, with ever greater frequency, are choosing to assume multiple lovers. Polyandry, once one is free, or perhaps freer, of the institutions and social relationships that limit the performance of polyandry, becomes smarter than monogamy. Such choices are historicized with local meanings: "We are from the beach, from the hot zone, we are a hot people. This is why our daughters develop early," explained Doña Chayo, days into my stay in the region, but I would hear this many more times before I left. Oaxaca is renowned for its many indigenous residents. Here, as in many tropical regions where the exotic, dark-skinned other is perceived as hypersexed, the hot temperature is conflated with hot bodies, sexual bodies, and is used to explain the sexual activities of adolescent and adult women.

Additionally Huatulco is three hours up the coast from the Isthmus of Tehuantepec, a region long famous for its pre-Hispanic three-gender system, matriarchal families, and *macha* women (Chiñas 1991; Stephen 1991). I once asked a girlfriend, as we watched a drunken man stumble past our table in the coffee shop at midday, why I kept seeing drunken men in Huatulco but had not yet seen any drunken women. Magda smiled knowingly:

I'll tell you. Think of our friend Dani. She's from here, from the isthmus. You see how she's very strong, very *brusca* [abrupt]. This is how the women here are. The men, they get here, and they have come from places like Mexico City or Acapulco. They have come from places where they are used to being the men, and they arrive here, and here they learn that they are not the men. Because here the women are the men. And that's why they [the men] drink.

Local discourse depicts Oaxacan women as *machista* and coastal women as highly sexual. Thus the local social expectations are that women have sex, repeatedly, even casually. This notion is increasingly exploited, and the histories that create it are continually reworked to give new meaning to the growing number of single parents.

Politicos on the Family

The politicians who occupy my field site readily confirm the presence of many single mothers in Huatulco, and their campaign strategies to pitch to single-mother voters further indicate political recognition. I asked, "*Si haya una interés*—is there an interest—in single parenthood in the region? "Yes, yes, we are very interested in the family," federal development director Ramón Sinovas answered: "Work brings people here, but marriage keeps them here." Municipal vice president and one of the largest business owners in the region, Don Wilo Garcia, responded, "The nuclear family is the base of all; when nuclear families learn to live together this then becomes a community and these communities, ultimately, form a society." Politicians are concerned with economic stability, and in their efforts to map the path to such stability, they imagine social typologies with the nuclear family unit as a foundation.

Huatulco's politicians have read sociologists' reports on out-of-wedlock childbirth. They understand that single parenthood correlates positively with poverty and suspect that single parents are unstable residents in a region already overflowing with cyclical migrants. These politicians, nearly all from large urban centers in central and northern Mexico such as Guadalajara, Monterrey, and Mexico City, then blame a dysfunctional educational system and high percentages of indigenous residents for the many unwed mothers. But many other factors are at least as culpable when one shakes free of the idea that "Oaxacans are *IOPs* (*Indios Oaxacos Pendejos*[2])" which lends itself to racist, classist interpretations of all that might be deemed problematic in Huatulco. The next most common explanation for single motherhood in the region, for example, is "the taxi drivers—it's because of the taxi drivers." Thus I learned that Huatulco's taxi drivers have reputations for infidelity. But although this explanation seemed to escape the racism of other explanations, and indeed this one hinged on indigenous taxi drivers' abilities to usurp class boundaries (and thus lure women) through access to cars and tips, this did not explain the lives of any of the single mothers with whom I worked.

What did account for these single mothers were factors spawned by politicians' own development policy and implementation. Neolocal living, the absence of parents, grandparents, siblings, and in-laws who might judge, neighbors from different regions with new traditions and understandings, smaller households, shared apartment buildings, the impermanence of work and residence (replacing coworkers and neighbors with strangers)—all characteristics tied to migration and urbanization—now shape the quality and character of the social relationships that single parents maintain in Huatulco. Women's access to paid labor positions enable them to raise children in the absence of a partner. The sexualization and then commodification of the exotic other, fostered by the architects and promoters of tourism, create positions that skew earnings scales for the better if one can deliver sexualized otherness. Labor casualization allows one to work multiple jobs; at the same time the devalorization of labor makes working multiple jobs a requirement for many who hope to sustain a family.

Just Plain Smart

Judith Stacey argues that "marriage became increasingly fragile as it became less economically obligatory" (1997:461). Women's ability to raise children independent of husbands has led many to do so. Anthropologist Mary Weismantel found in Zumbagua, Ecuador, that many of the market women with whom she worked "became mothers for reasons that had little to do with male desires . . . They became mothers because they wanted children, and remained unmarried because they did not want—or need—a spouse" (2001:234). Sociologists Kathryn Edin and Maria Kefalas (2005) also found impoverished women in the urban United States choosing motherhood before marriage, deciding they were fit to parent, yet certain that they had not yet met their life partners; they chose to have children in the meantime. Feminist scholar Geraldine Heng and scholar-journalist Janadas Devan wrote of women who suggested, ironically, in response to the prime minister of Singapore's call for elite women to have children out of patriotic duty, that "if increased numbers of superior children were exclusively the issue, then women ought to be encouraged, nay, urged to have children outside of the institution of marriage" (1997:111). Their informants, too, described the many women who wished to have children without marrying.

In the case of Huatulco in 2009, I argue, single parenthood increases in popularity not because marriage is no longer economically obligatory but because it is, frequently, no longer economically sustainable. In many ways, choosing single parenthood from within a tourism economy as precarious as that of Huatulco limits an individual's risk of poverty. If one begins as a single parent, there is not, at any point, a partner who might lead one down the slippery slope to dependence and then disappear. Unmarried, one also maintains the freedom to trade one partner for another as all individuals move in and out of employment throughout the year—single parenthood thus allows one to hedge one's bets in a low-wage, high-unemployment service economy.

Juanita has been a single mother twice—once with her thirteen year old and once with her ten year old. At the time of our interview, she was married to the father of her youngest children, ages three and one. "Don't ever marry a man without knowing two things about him first," she warned, during our conversation at her house located in a town outside Huatulco. "You need to know how his mother washes his clothes and how she prepares his food. This is what he is used to. Then you decide if you want to marry him." She told me this lack of information at the outset of her relationship was now causing her many problems:

J: He lives with me, but we have many problems.
DP: What does he do? (I am asking about work.)
J: Nothing. That's the problem. He's *flojo* [lazy].
DP: But does he work?
J: No. He doesn't do anything.
DP: Does he take care of the kids—is he like a house-father?
J: Sure, something like that. But my mother comes over to take care of them so he doesn't have to. . .
J: I married the father of my last child. It was what he wanted. But civil marriage is bad luck. And divorce is very expensive.

Even while the development discourse in Huatulco and other tourist destinations continues to relate to nuclear family structures and social stability, the politico-economic shift, and the policies that drive such a shift, increasingly necessitate both family structures and family members that can accommodate instability. Anthropologist Mercedes González de la Rocha (1994, 2002) has argued repeatedly that women's control of resources—in the absence of a male head—has led to more equitable distribution of resources among household members, and therefore "is a crucial factor for well-being achievement and protection" at the household level during economic downturns (2002:15). Geographer and gender studies scholar Sylvia Chant (1985, 1991) has argued, similarly, that the nuclear family structure "often mitigates against economic progress" (1985:27). Male heads are likely to prohibit females from working, limiting women's autonomy and earning potential. Men often contribute less of their total incomes to household costs than do women. While findings such as these are rarely contested, they have done little to undermine the social and political correctness of the nuclear family.

One-third of the single mothers and fathers I interviewed outsourced the care of their children to parents in lower-cost rural regions. Two others, single mothers, both college-educated with professional positions, chose to bring their mothers to Huatulco so that these mothers could share their homes and assume child-care responsibilities there. Yet another, Viki, brought eight siblings, one by one, to care for her child as he grew from an infant to a teenager. As the siblings adapted to urban Huatulco, they would get a job in the formal sector, and the next brother or sister would arrive to care for the child.

All non-*originarios* in my study, female and male, cited a need for money, the need to work, as their motivation for migrating to Huatulco. And though single fathers were more likely to become single fathers once in Huatulco, more than half of the single mothers I interviewed arrived following the births of their children. They are not, it seems, the ignorant, unsuspecting, new arrivals to the city and thus unprotected, accidentally impregnated, and then abandoned single mothers that middle- and upper-class residents in the region describe. Nor are they the asexual and pious single mothers that scholars describe as attempting to correct for the discourses of immorality that surround single mothers.

Huatulco's single parents reinterpret matrimony and polyamory. They manipulate transnational and transregional relationships that they construct both in shared geographic spaces and via the Internet. The anonymity of an urban tourist destination filled with migrants, the abundance of commodified sex and sexuality, and the sexualization of indigeneity (catalyzed by the tourism development project) provide both context and tools for experimentation. Fishermen bake, daughters drive taxis, work gets harder to gender, and everyone has access to pesos, however limited. Here single parents are smart, sexual, and are challenging norms in order to transform the institutions that suggest they are other than this; in so doing they are transforming the institutions that have organized urban social interaction in the past. Meanwhile, they are constrained by new structural conditions arising from current neoliberal development practices.

Rethinking the Family, Rethinking Economic Policy

The existence of so many single mothers now residing in Huatulco and comparable regions already suggests our need to radically rethink today's family. Rethinking the family, in turn, requires us to rethink family policy, which includes economic policy that inadvertently shapes the family. That policy is currently neoliberal.

Worldwide, neoliberal reforms have protected private property rights and free markets while steadfastly eliminating social programming. Mexico, because of its proximity to the United States or perhaps because of its untimely bankruptcy, has served as a neoliberal playground of sorts; repeatedly it has been one of the world's earliest nations to adopt neoliberal reforms. The most prominent example is the ratification, in 1994, of President Salinas's North American Free Trade Agreement (NAFTA) to the vociferous praise of his U.S. and Canadian neighbors. Two years later more than two million Mexicans had lost jobs, more than twenty-eight thousand Mexican businesses had declared bankruptcy, banks were failing, consumer debts were skyrocketing, and the minimum wage had dropped below its level at the time of Mexico's bankruptcy.

Transnational and federal attempts to bolster state economies reflect a generalized shift from industrial to service production. In 2000 the World Bank began promoting tourism as a primary development tool for the global south. State officials in Mexico, as in many countries, now hail tourism as "a costless generator of employment and well-being." Consumption, as Marx warned, is cyclical and approaching instantaneity. Nearly everything has been commodified. Labor is feminized, casualized, pressuring laborers, male and female, to compete for ever lower wages in capitalism's race to the bottom. Failure by systems of governance to provide for citizens is hidden in a discourse that locates blame with the individual. One is poor because one did not pull on his or her bootstraps hard enough.

All this means that individuals need new strategies for survival. Single parents, as I have argued above, are providing their own safety nets. Child care is being outsourced to the country. Single parents are taking up multiple jobs, piecing them together, and paying rents late. Sexual relationships— whether temporary or permanent, multiple, cyclical, local, or virtual—and the (sex) work of sustaining such relationships, are becoming ever more vital.

There is much to conclude, but I leave you with the following: humans now operate inside a political economy that privileges individuality, not interdependence. As a result, smart sex, it seems—the kind that produces wanted children, economic stability, social power, and more—has less and less to do with marriage. Marriage, one could even argue, to the extent it engenders monogamy or a sense that one should be monogamous, might preclude one from obtaining such things. Single parenthood, it turns out, is not pathological but is politically and economically motivated.

NOTES

1. This also follows Carol Stack's 1974 study of "swapping" and interdependence among black residents in U.S. cities.

2. This may be translated as "Dumb-ass Oaxacan Indians."

6

On the Boundaries of
the Global Margins

*Violence, Labor, and Surveillance
in a Rust Belt Topless Bar*

SUSAN DEWEY

"So if I can't call the police, who'll help me?" sobbed Chantelle backstage, her question muffled by the dull throbbing of music pounding outside the door. "This guy who thinks we're destined to be together is sitting outside my house every night, maybe with a gun. He could follow me home tonight and kill me and my baby; he could do whatever he wants." Eyeliner streaming down her face, Chantelle buried her head in her hands and wept as her colleagues, topless dancers at an upstate New York bar I call Vixens, continued to minimize her obvious distress by insisting that there was nothing she could do except wait for the man to lose interest in her. As the newest dancer at Vixens, Chantelle had already acquired a stalker in the form of a frequent visitor to the bar. This man was in his mid-forties and persistently requested her phone number, ignoring her insistence that management forbade dancers from seeing clients outside of working hours. Two months pregnant and without a socioeconomic network of support, nineteen-year-old Chantelle was terrified at the prospect of losing her only source of income and by the very real physical threat the man posed.

One of the Vixens dancers, who called herself Cinnamon, shrugged rather resignedly in the face of Chantelle's highly emotional description and sighed, "Welcome to the business, honey. For every fifty normal guys, you get one complete freak." This disturbing vignette raises a number of pressing questions. How could it be that someone like Chantelle was so completely exposed to the constant threat of intimidation and violence? How could her colleagues be so remarkably nonchalant when the danger was so obviously real? Most notably, what structural, institutional, and individual forms of regulation and surveillance combined to implicate Chantelle and her coworkers in a system that not only consistently placed them under threat but also held them responsible for the consequences of their marginalization? This chapter attempts to answer these questions through an analysis of the complex means by which pervasive neoliberal labor practices, exclusionary zoning policies, and an environment of constant surveillance create a situation with a high potential for the kind of violence that so terrorized Chantelle.

Fear was a constant theme in the lives of Vixens dancers, many of whom had experiences with violence that marked their bodies, shaped their decision-making processes, and kept them in a constant state of anxiety. Such previous experiences often meant that Vixens dancers were keenly aware that the relative degree of autonomy their work provided them, particularly in terms of flexible hours, income, and at least some degree of adulation from male clients, came with powerful strings attached. As with Chantelle, these sometimes entailed life-threatening risks resulting from the elaborate set of exclusionary processes that frame sex workers' lives.

Neoliberal Labor Practices and the Feminization of Poverty

Feminized labor, broadly characterized by the low-paid, part-time, low-status, and often temporary jobs performed primarily by women, is often highly regulated despite the relative lack of benefits and income it provides to its workers. Sex workers, whose profession is perhaps the most feminized of all forms of work, inhabit a social category that positions them in need of (often nonconsensual) state control and assistance as both victims and criminals. Such state interventions have become increasingly common in recent decades as a result of broader social and policy shifts regarding the appropriate role of the state in legislating individual sexual behavior (Wagner 1997). Particularly significant for sex workers like Chantelle and her colleagues is the frequency with which such state interest in regulation has been accompanied by the rise of the neoliberal labor practices that frame their experiences in the workplace.

Geographer David Harvey (2005) defines neoliberalism as an increasingly global politico-economic philosophy which "proposes that human well-being can best be advanced by liberating individual entrepreneurial freedoms and skills within an institutional framework characterized by strong private property rights, free markets and free trade" (2). Despite its rhetoric of freedom and rights, these economic changes often feature an unprecedented prevalence of untethering the workplace from its workers so that those workers in positions of power and privilege have increasingly less direct contact with or responsibility for those who work at the lowest levels of the same industry. This disconnection results in diminished accountability for the powerful and an increased burden for the least-advantaged members of the socioeconomic hierarchy. Notably, this hierarchical separation between individuals in the same workplace is frequently accompanied by a lack of unionization and the rise of part-time positions that require a degree of investment in work akin to that of a full-time employee without offering comparable benefits. A number of changing economic realities accompany these labor practices, and constantly remind workers of their expendability and lack of bargaining power (Newman 2008, 2000; Wilson 1997).

Undoubtedly these destabilizing economic processes have an equally debilitating effect upon individual women's lives, particularly in a region where the legacy of deindustrialization has been so powerfully enduring. Vixens is located in an upstate New York town I call Sparksburgh, which is part of the geographic region often called the "Rust Belt," a disparaging but exceptionally picturesque phrase that captures the landscape of decay so characteristic of a region that has seen almost all its industries close in past decades as well as an exodus of its young people in search of work. This enduring term entered popular discourse in the 1970s as shorthand for the socioeconomic decline in the U.S. Northeast and Great Lakes regions, once vibrant industrial centers that lost their primary economic force when manufacturers relocated farther south in search of cheaper labor and production costs. In Sparksburgh and many other towns and cities like it, one round of destabilization followed another and prompted a generalized shift to the less secure and less well-paid service industry jobs that emerged in the wake of deindustrialization.

Vixens dancers, like many other poor and blue-collar U.S. workers, demonstrated a cultural understanding of wage employment as an inherently negative (and even abusive) part of life's many monotonous and inescapable realities. Dancers called the low-wage labor market available to them outside the sex industry "the straight world," an environment they characterized as exploitative, exclusionary, and without hope for social mobility or financial stability. Far from being a completely separate sphere, however, "the straight world" both set the conditions of their work and informed the way dancers think about their lives. All but one of the women at Vixens had previously worked outside the sex industry, and many had left intermittently for low-wage, service-sector work elsewhere before returning with the recognition that they preferred the topless bar with its possibility of periodic windfalls from customers. This follows similar patterns documented by sex workers in Nevada's legal brothels, wherein sociologists Barbara Brents, Crystal Jackson, and Kathryn Hausbeck clearly note the strong connections between the growth of feminized low-wage service jobs and the number of U.S. women willing to engage in legal prostitution as they "seek alternative ways to make ends meet" (Brents, Jackson, and Hausbeck 2009, 155).

Such overt connections between the feminization of poverty and the institutionalization of neoliberal labor practices are almost eerily obvious in establishments like Vixens. Topless and nude dancing venues present the perfect neoliberal model, featuring nonexistent labor costs, cash income (much of it untaxed), no unions, and a constant supply of workers preconditioned to follow the rules without complaint. In practice, of course, the reality is much more complex, and few dancers would argue that theirs is an ideal form of work for these very reasons. Income is unreliable, social stigma pervasive, clients sometimes dangerous or threatening, and dancing offers absolutely no illusions of long-term support. Fundamentally, this system functions to the benefit of those in positions of ownership and to the detriment of their workers: a familiar (and by now quite clichéd) characterization of the anti-capitalist argument.

The advent of post-deindustrialization neoliberal labor practices coincided in particularly telling ways in the growth of establishments like Vixens throughout the Rust Belt in the mid-1980s (Dewey 2011). This expansion occurred just as strip club owners sought to make their businesses competitive with the expansion of in-home video technology by offering increasingly sexually explicit acts onstage and more physical contact between dancers and clients (Shteir 2005, 317–325). Yet these increased expectations for dancers were not accompanied by an improvement in their earnings or working conditions and, in fact, resulted in their being expected to undergo more risks to their health and safety for less money.

New York State labor law further reinforces dancers' subject position by considering dancers as "independent contractors" who are not formally employed by the bars where they perform. The New York State Department of Labor (2009) defines independent contractors as workers who "are free from supervision, direction and control in the performance of their duties. They are in business for themselves, offering their services to the general public." In practice, this legislation means that the owners of such establishments are not required to pay them a salary or provide health insurance or any form of benefits. Some bars even charge women a "stage fee" ranging from fifty to one hundred dollars to perform as part of a curious labor practice in which the workers pay to use the means of production.

Dancers fall into the "independent contractor" category of state labor law, because they are considered to meet the following specific criteria of this definition: they pay their own expenses, assume risk for profit or loss in providing services to clients, and are (ostensibly) free to refuse work offers (New York State Department of Labor 2009). The first is certainly true, as dancers must incur significant, non-reimbursable expenses in costumes, cosmetics, high-heeled shoes that are attractive and yet allow the wearer to dance for hours, and other paraphernalia. Dancers also have the right to refuse to dance privately for clients, although in practice women are unlikely to assume the risk of not earning any money by refusing work offers.

This rather laissez-faire approach on the part of legislators reveals the ambiguous position of women workers at Vixens and other establishments like it, as in many ways we see assumptions about their lack of entitlement to state protection in their classification as "independent contractors." Such discourse closely replicates divisions between "good" and "bad" women that frame everyday gendered experience in positioning women who fall into the latter category as deserving of any bad treatment meted out to them. This slippery dichotomy, in which the boundaries between respectable and lascivious behavior are not at all clear in practice, results in myriad forms of dancer regulation at both the state and individual levels.

Zoning and Surveillance

The close association that topless dancing has with the exchange of sexual favors for money underlies many of the policies and laws that define what behaviors can take place inside establishments like Vixens. Such regulations shape dancers' work environment in complex ways, from the use of security cameras to its location on the Sparksburgh outskirts because of zoning laws that forbid it from being too close to a residential area. Dancers' subject positions are reinforced by a number of state and local laws concerning prostitution and obscenity, but many of these are tellingly ambiguous in ways that reflect moral and social ambivalence toward sex work in general. Article 230 of the New York State Penal Code, for example, classifies prostitution as a misdemeanor defined as the exchange of "sexual conduct with another person in return for a fee" without elaborating on what such behavior actually entails. Article 235 on obscenity is similarly opaque, holding that:

Any material or performance is "obscene" if (a) the average person, applying contemporary community standards, would find that considered as a whole, its predominant appeal is to the prurient interest in sex and (b) it depicts or describes in a patently offensive manner, actual or simulated sexual intercourse . . . (c) considered as a whole, it lacks serious literary, artistic, political, and scientific value. Predominant appeal shall be judged with reference to ordinary adults. (New York State Penal Code 1965)

But what exactly is "sexual conduct" and who makes up this population of "ordinary adults"? This obliqueness is particularly problematic for Vixens dancers given that the New York State General Business Law defines an "adult establishment" as a commercial establishment where a substantial portion is given to "sexually-oriented activities that do not cross the line into prostitution or obscenity" (New York State Office of General Counsel 2003).

Laws and regulations on obscenity are unclear at best, as they call upon courts to use what they term the "contemporary community standard" (New York State Penal Code 1965) of appropriate sexual practices when evaluating whether a behavior, document, or film is obscene. In his research on the lack of clarity involved in this standard, sociologist Joseph Scott observes that obscenity is the only crime punishable by U.S. law in which the defendant does not know whether he or she actually committed the offense prior to the jury's decision (Scott 1991, 29). Scott's administration of more than seven thousand telephone interviews on the subject clearly revealed that individuals are generally unable to assess what a contemporary community standard is in regard to sexuality (ibid., 44).

Yet this confusion about the boundaries of acceptable sexual behavior rarely tempers the high degree of public and policy concern about the existence of adult establishments like Vixens. Anthropologist Jacqueline Lewis (2000, 203), for instance, has described the effective removal of women's agency in the construction of lap dancing as a "social problem" that constituted an explicit threat to public morality. Lewis argues that the court-mandated ban on lap dancing in Canada positioned sex workers as vulnerable and "in need of protection" (ibid., 215), thereby reinforcing broader sexist stereotypes of women as defenseless creatures who were helpless in the absence of male safeguards. A great deal of both moral and legal ambiguity thus surrounds such businesses, whose appeal lies at least in part in their fringe location.

In her classic text on cultural notions of taboo, purity, and pollution, anthropologist Mary Douglas famously argues that in the Western European cultural template, dirt is "matter out of place" (Douglas 2000 [1966], 36). Douglas believes that one of the primary functions of culture is to create order out of disorder, requiring social systems to rely on a number of strategies to regulate behaviors, ambiguous actions, and beliefs that fall in the substantial grey area between these extreme opposites. These include branding those who engage in such activities as dangerous and to be avoided or assigning them to a particular category so that they become immediately classifiable. The powerful questions and moral debates raised by topless dancing indicate the uneasiness that surrounds the boundaries between the theoretical concepts of licit and illicit sexual exchange.

Nor are these lines obvious in practice, and dancers themselves complain that they are often unable to resist customers who, during a private dance, want to touch their breasts and hips for extra money, which Vixens management does not consider to constitute "sexual conduct" as defined by the state prostitution law. A manager always sits in the main office to monitor activities in the curtained room reserved for private dances on a television screen via security cameras mounted there, because violations of these rules could result in forced closure of their business if a plainclothes police officer witnessed them or, less likely, a male patron complained to the police. For dancers, the lines between "sexual conduct" and dancing very close to a seated man while semi-nude are difficult to discern, and are considerably complicated by clients who offer more money for sexually explicit services that involve increased physical contact.

This ambivalence about female sexuality is also evident in sociologist Amy Adler's analysis of two Supreme Court decisions on whether nude dancing should be protected by the First Amendment. Adler posits that these cases were marked by "an unacknowledged apprehension of female sexuality as entertaining, trivial, threatening and sick" (2007, 309). More specifically, Adler finds the Supreme Court decision that nude dancing fell on the "out perimeters of the First Amendment" in itself reveals that a "stripper's speech occupies a liminal space. Condemned to the border between protected expression and unprotected conduct, her body symbolizes the very margins of constitutional 'speech'" (ibid., 311). Such marginality at the legislative level also carries the implicit message that sex workers are somehow unworthy of state protection or, at the very least, unworthy of serious attention.

Even more unclear are the ordinances imposed upon such businesses by zoning laws, which in Sparksburgh do not permit sexually oriented businesses to open within five hundred feet of any area classified as "residential" by the city's Zoning Office. Sparksburgh is divided into thirty zoning districts, each with its own classification into categories of residential, office, local, business, commercial, or industrial, and topless-dancing bars are permitted to operate in all but the first category of these. As the New York State Office of General Counsel has noted, however, municipal zoning regulations raise serious constitutional issues when the regulation regards free expression protected by the federal and state constitutions. Zoning regulations on adult entertainment are thus required to demonstrate prior to implementation that such businesses have harmful secondary effects, such as "urban blight, decreased retail shopping activity and reduced property values" (New York State Office of General Council 2003).

Municipalities in New York State typically choose between two zoning techniques when dealing with adult-oriented businesses: the first concentrates such establishments in a single area, and the second disperses them by using distance requirements. Sparksburgh has chosen the latter, which in theory avoids what has been termed a "skid-row effect" but in practice means that topless-dancing bars are located either on the industrial outskirts of the city or in dangerous or dilapidated downtown areas abandoned by homeowners and thus outside the residential classification.

Outright and de facto bans enacted via zoning regulations are nearly as old as topless bars themselves and have been vociferously encouraged by neighborhood activists, government officials, and small-business owners. New York State first passed a law in 1977 banning topless dancing in bars licensed by the New York State Liquor Authority, but in the absence of a definitive state court ruling following a challenge by a group of upstate New York bar owners, the law was never enforced. The New York State Supreme Court declared the ban unconstitutional on June 10, 1980, when it ruled that the law "amounted to censorship of a constitutionally protected means of expression that the state had failed to justify" (Greenhouse 1981, A–2).

New York State then appealed to the U.S. Supreme Court, which ruled in 1981 that individual states did in fact have the right to ban topless dancing in bars under the Twenty-first Amendment to the Constitution, which repealed Prohibition and declared the right of states to control the sale and consumption of alcohol within their borders. A compromise decision that recognized topless dancing as a form of free expression protected under the First Amendment then forbade nudity in bars regulated by the New York State Liquor Authority unless dancers remain out of customers' reach (Goldman 1981, C–4). Once dancers cover their breasts, they may touch clients.

The New York State Liquor Authority mandates that women must stay at least six feet away from clients and wear panties or lower-body coverings because, as spokesperson Richard Chernela noted, "once you remove your pants, you create an inherent disorder" (Harting 1990, 3). As a result, inspections by the local and New York State Liquor Authority resulted in the arrest of dancers who allowed clients to place dollar bills in their thong underwear while dancing topless in many New York State strip clubs. The dancers' clients, quite notably, were not charged with any criminal offense (Duffy 1995, C1). Social ambivalence toward both topless dancing and its regulation are evident in newspaper coverage of such arrests, with numerous upstate New York letter writers and commentators contributing tongue-in-cheek statements for publications such as "I'm sure the city is much safer tonight because of this [police action]" (O'Hara 1995, B3).

The choice of language employed in such popular discourse indicates the depth of contradictory sentiments toward sex workers and, more generally, women. Chernela's association between the nude lower body, specifically in reference to women, and "inherent disorder," conjures Mary Douglas's (1966) discussion of how cultures function to order the world through classification. City topless-dancing establishments responded angrily to this increased regulation on their operations, particularly in the form of a 1993 Sparksburgh Common Council ordinance banning new strip clubs from opening within one thousand feet of a school, church, park, or residence. In a similar case in Syracuse, New York, an alcohol-free nude-dancing establishment successfully asserted in court that the city had conspired to keep his club closed by delaying his planned opening date as well as permit and license applications until after the ordinance was passed (Wright 1993, B2). Indeed, most arrangements to deal with such establishments are de facto, with consideration beginning solely when community members complain about them.

Regional provisions in upstate New York that sought to force erotic-dancing establishments to move to industrial areas or close began initiation by Syracuse Common Council member Rick Guy in 1995 following a U.S. Supreme Court ruling that former New York City Mayor Rudolph Giuliani's closure of Times Square adult businesses was constitutional. Yet many upstate New York officials were skeptical about the utility of this plan, including Syracuse Common Council President (and later two-term mayor) Matt Driscoll, who noted, "The city is crumbling down around us, our finances are a disaster, the roads have potholes and this is how the administration is going to spend its resources?" (Pierce and McAndrew 1999, A1, A14).

Yet some community members and small-business owners remained adamant that adult establishments warranted relocation to a specially designated portion of the city because of the lowered property values and increased crime that they believed accompanied such businesses. One convenience store owner in a central New York town complained, at a public hearing on the subject, that, "the kind of people that go to these places [to] feed their lusts on naked women and drink for hours" posed a threat to his wife and children at night (Wiley 1996, B4). Community officials who believed that it would simply shift the problem to neighboring communities or further concentrate it in a single location dismissed the relocation proposal (Pierce 2000, B3).

Vixens is located in an industrial section of Sparksburgh immune to such zoning legislation because it is extremely far from any residential area. Yet "industrial area" is something of a tenuous misnomer in a region character-ized by the consistency of its factory closures as corporations continue their search for cheaper labor in the Global South. My drive home from Vixens each night was fraught with anxiety after listening to the stories dancers had told me about infatuated clients who followed them home on the empty highway dur-ing the predawn hours. I found myself constantly checking my rearview mir-ror, relieved when the reflection revealed only the shadowy outlines of aban-doned furniture factories in the former industrial zone of the city.

Zoning is just one aspect of the multiple means by which pervasive social inequalities influence individual women and the elaborate ways social and institutional regulations and structures intersect with their everyday lives. Multiple forms of structural, institutional, and individual forms of regulation function to shape these processes of marginalization, including moral com-petition among dancers. As such, dancers find themselves in a paradoxical situation in which they place themselves, and one another, under surveil-lance in ways that consistently reinforce their own oppression.

Dancers' Regulation of Themselves and Others

Dancers are fully cognizant of their membership in a highly stigmatized group, and they work with constant awareness of the need to preserve what they perceive as the critical boundaries between emotional and physical intimacy. Women frequently complain about clients who wrongly presume they are prostitutes, and often insist on distinguishing themselves from other types of sex workers who have greater degrees of physical contact with cli-ents. Vixens dancers were disturbingly consistent in their stigmatization of prostitutes and nude dancers as part of what they view as a completely separate subculture of drug addicts and vectors of disease. This stereotyp-ing notably mirrors assumptions often made about topless dancers by those outside the profession.

One slow Tuesday night, Vixens dancer Star and I were sitting at the bar when she turned to me with a serious expression on her face and said, "You know, I really am a good person. I'm not a whore. You believe me, right?" Such negative associations with selling sex rather than its simulation onstage were part of a pattern of dancers' broader insistence that they were different and infinitely superior because of the boundaries they set with clients. This was one of the otherwise limited forms of self-esteem and pride they were able to salvage in a society that often views them as little more than immoral objects in need of regulation. Dancers had an enormous amount of pride and self-esteem invested in what they were not, rather than what they were, and this frequently led to arguments between women at Vixens regarding appropriate behavior with clients.

Such moral hierarchies are omnipresent in all areas of the sex industry, wherein sociologist Wendy Chapkis observes that women are not equally victimized by this stigma, because "those whose work most closely resembles non-commercial sexuality generally occupy a place of higher status . . . [and] a similar status distinction may exist between those who turn quick tricks involving less in the way of emotional labor" (Chapkis 1997, 104). Anthropologist Patty Kelly similarly observes that this sort of competition for "good" status is "linked to conceptions of morality, deviance, sexual norms and even the sense of fair play among competing co-workers" (Kelly 2008, 157). Similarly, when sociologists Holly Bell, Lacey Sloan, and Chris Strickling (1998, 360) asked topless dancers about whether they felt they faced social stigma in their work, many interviewees noted that "dancing isn't really a dirty job— prostitution is a dirty job."

Thus what may initially appear as competing discourses of state surveillance and state marginalization are not at all discordant and, in fact, work in tandem with one another. Topless dancing occupies a unique position among different forms of sex work in the United States because it is both legally sanctioned and morally condemned. Perhaps it is not surprising, then, that the many forms of state regulation that dancers experience are also accompanied by clear forms of marginalization that render women responsible for their own safety. For instance, Vixens did not have bouncers or any other form of security, and, on most nights, it fell to the dancers to defend their boundaries when clients became particularly aggressive. The manager on duty would generally intervene when a dancer's physical safety was at risk or a law was clearly being violated, but such intervention rarely took place.

The reality that Vixens dancers could only rely on themselves was painfully underscored for Chantelle one night when she unknowingly violated the law against exposing her breasts in close proximity to a client and was nearly terminated by Paul, the manager on duty that night. Chantelle had not been at fault for the exposure. Paul even acknowledged later that the problem lay with the New York State Alcoholic Beverage Control Law, which forbids businesses with a liquor license from featuring nude performers. The only topless dancers exempt from this law are those who expose their breasts below the areola while performing on a platform stage elevated at least eighteen inches above floor level and at least six feet from the nearest patron. In practice, this law means that New York State dancers may bare their breasts while dancing onstage but must cover their breasts with a cloth or another item in order to accept tips from clients. Tips comprise Vixens dancers' entire income, and dancers often complained that new clients, especially those who had not visited a topless bar before and were thus unaware of this rule, would withdraw their money as soon as a dancer covered her breasts.

Chantelle's transgression took place on a busy Friday night when Vixens was particularly crowded. A group of some two dozen young men who had arrived half-drunk from a bachelor party stood near the stage shouting loudly at Chantelle, who had removed the top half of her negligee to reveal her naked breasts. She left the bottom half on, convinced that her third month of pregnancy was beginning to show.

One of the young men beckoned Chantelle, waving a dollar bill in the air. She walked toward him, carefully pulling the straps of her negligee over her shoulders to cover her chest so as not to violate the law. This was difficult to do on her six-inch heels, and she struggled to move forward toward the waving dollar bill as quickly as she could. Chantelle leaned forward toward the man's hand, when he rapidly shook his head and retracted the bill from her reach, much to his friends' amusement. He then refused to pay until he could see Chantelle's breasts up close, and so she bent forward and allowed him to caress her.

Within the hour Chantelle was in Paul's office, in tears. "What am I supposed to do," she cried angrily, "when you don't explain the rules to the guys who come in, how am I supposed to, when I am the one standing there naked?" Paul softened his tone and explained that she needed to be firm. "Just don't do it, then," he replied rather weakly. Chantelle began to sob, effectively ending Paul's gentle rebuke but by no means clarifying how dancers with little power and great economic need are supposed to enforce rules that most male clients are unaware even exist.

Everyday Forms of Structural Violence

"All women are whores," Cinnamon often said, pausing dramatically, until another dancer backstage would inevitably ask what she meant. "We have to be" she usually replied, "and it doesn't matter how rich you are or how good a job you got. That's the way the world is." It took some time before I understood what she meant. At first I thought she was simply employing the moral typologies that allow dancers to distinguish themselves from prostitutes as part of a broader system of self-empowerment that helps to diffuse some of the stigma surrounding their profession. What Cinnamon actually meant was that, in her opinion, sexism's oppressive weight suffuses even forms of privilege that remained far beyond her reach, including economic stability.

Women at Vixens clearly understand that sex work is just one aspect of an infinitely larger process by which all women learn (and even teach others) that their labor is less valuable. As Cinnamon concisely pointed out, this phenomenon transcends class and occupational status and can be used to describe the life situation of many women. Women throughout the world are socialized to provide the vast majority of unpaid labor, including child care, food preparation, and other caregiving work. Such responsibilities are often incompatible with higher-paid and more secure jobs, so that women are much more likely than men to find themselves doing unpaid work in the home rather than earning a salary through formal employment.

The operations of power take myriad forms in the lives of poor women. These everyday forms of structural violence are compounded for sex workers, whose lives evince the stark inequalities inherent in these practices ever more sharply because of the heavy weight of institutionally imposed social stigma. The lives of these women, although situated at the social and legal margins of life in the United States, consistently speak to the exclusionary forces that impact all women, albeit in different ways. Thus, despite Vixens dancers' best efforts to obtain some autonomy for themselves through increased earning power and flexible working hours, a vast array of institutional and interpersonal obstacles consistently place them in a permanent state of fear.

7

The Virtues of Dockside Dalliance

Why Maritime Sugar Girls Are Safer Than Urban Streetwalkers in South Africa's Prostitution Industry

HENRY TROTTER

South African prostitutes operate in a context characterized by extreme levels of sexual violence. The country has one of the highest rape rates in the world, with one in four South African men admitting to coercing females into sex (Smith 2009) and too many others using rape as a means of enforcing social control (Moffett 2006). According to the literature on township and rural sexuality, transactional (commodified) sexual relationships, aggressive masculine identity formation, and unprotected promiscuity lead many women to believe that sexual coercion is normal (Abrahams, Jewkes, and Laubsher 1999; Delius and Glaser 2002; Hunter 2002; Leclerc-Madlala 2003; Wood and Jewkes 1996, 1998). Although many women resist this aggression, gender violence is maintained by a patriarchal social order, women's financial dependence on men, and a social and legal regime dismissive of women's complaints of abuse.

Prostitutes are especially vulnerable in this context. They are criminalized by law enforcement and stigmatized by their communities. They face assault and rape from clients, harassment from police, and abuse from pimps. Some prostitutes are more vulnerable than others, however. Structural differences between the various sex sectors determine the likelihood of violence within them. For instance, streetwalkers face greater risk from the police than do agency escorts. "Beer prostitutes," as women who consent to sexual relations with men in exchange for beer or other gifts are known, face greater risk from clients than do urban brothel women. And hotel sex workers face greater risk from extortionate third parties than do dockside prostitutes.

This article focuses on the neglected dockside prostitution sector, and shows how that sector's structural features enhance women's ability to avoid violence. By comparing the street, truck stop, brothel, and agency sectors, I argue that sex workers' vulnerability to violence depends on five structural factors: the client's social and legal status, the site of the negotiation, the location of the sexual act, the level of discretion in the solicitation process, and third-party involvement. After discussing how each of these variables affects violence, I provide policy recommendations for industry interventions that could improve prostitutes' safety.

Context, Method, and Profile

Three nightclubs in Cape Town and one in Durban cater to foreign sailors. Located in downtown areas, they resemble other local nightclubs with one exception: they are patronized exclusively by female prostitutes and international seamen. The women interact with the sailors for four to eight hours each evening, dancing, drinking, smoking, shooting pool, singing karaoke, and chatting. After a few hours together, the women initiate negotiations for sexual trysts outside the club. If a couple agrees on terms, they take a taxi to her flat, a hotel, or a friend's house to consummate the contract. In the morning he departs to his ship and she to her abode.

Between 2006 and 2008 I spent 150 evenings interviewing sex workers and sailors at nightclubs in both cities. I usually spent five hours there per night, talking with the women and observing their behavior. In this way I pieced together the outlines of the women's life histories, established how they approached their relations with the sailors, and considered the impact this work had on them. I gathered information through ethnographic participant observation, casual conversations, and intensive interviews. I used an open-ended approach to elicit information, allowing informants to explore issues over the course of multiple encounters.[1] I also met with the women during the day, conversing in English, Zulu, or Afrikaans. I interviewed a total of ninety female sex workers and dozens of club owners, managers, bouncers, barmaids, cab drivers, and sailors.

In Durban most of the eighty women hailed from rural towns outside the city. Others had migrated from other African states. Sixty African women worked alongside sixteen whites and four coloureds (of mixed race) and Indians (Trotter 2007). Most were between eighteen and twenty-nine years of age, and the rest were between thirty and forty. Most spoke Zulu, although all the women had some facility in English, the language of solicitation.

In Cape Town sixty women solicited from three seamen's clubs. Except for five white women, all were local coloureds similar in age to the Durban women. Most spoke Afrikaans, but all spoke English as well. Most also spoke one Asian language—Chinese, Japanese, Korean, Taiwanese, or Indonesian—which they had learned through interacting with the trawlermen, using it as their language of solicitation.

Factors Affecting Violence in Sex Work

This section discusses the five key structural variables that affect the likelihood of violence against prostitutes, focusing upon how each relates to particular sectors of the South African sexual economy.

The Client's Social and Legal Status

The needs and constraints of male clients structure the operations of most prostitution sectors. The dockside scene, for example, is based on the transience and foreignness of international sailors (Trotter 2009), the truck-stop sector around the periodic need for relaxation among long-distance truckers (Marcus, Oellermann, and Levin 1995; Ramjee and Gouws 2002), the upcountry tavern niche around the dangerous labor and low wages of mine workers (Campbell 2000; Luiz and Roets 2001; Meekers 2000; Wojcicki 2002), and the Internet escort market around the wealth, cyberspace connectivity, and discretionary needs of traveling businessmen.[2] Thus the temporal, financial, social, and behavioral properties of an occupationally similar clientele determines the character of each prostitution niche. But whether the clients are local or foreign is crucial. Their differing social and legal status affects how comfortable they feel asserting power over women.

As a rule, the more social stature and legal protection a man enjoys in relation to a sex worker, the greater his freedom to act violently. In almost all sectors, the client's status is far superior to the prostitute's because of patriarchal social norms. Until the end of 2007 in South Africa, the Sexual Offences Act of 1957 had only criminalized the solicitation, sale, or procurement (pimping) of sex, punishable with fines or imprisonment. The (male) purchase of sex, however, remained legal, granting men a much higher status than prostitutes in their relations. Since 2007 the purchase of sex has also been criminalized, rendering the couple technically equal in the eyes of the law. But this has not yet translated to equitable law enforcement. Male clients face little threat for their actions, not only because prostitutes are hesitant to report client abuse (exposing them to legal hassles of their own) but because police do not regard the purchase of sex as a priority.

In the outdoor trades, streetwalkers and truck-stop women are vulnerable because local clients—and especially police officers—know what they can get away with. They realize the constraints facing prostitutes and understand how social double standards protect them in their engagement with sex workers.

The status of brothel and agency women is complicated, as they claim to provide legitimate services. They call themselves masseuses or escorts and say that if sex occurred, it was between consenting adults and not for a fee. This significantly protects the women's social and legal status. Unlike streetwalkers who solicit openly, these women maintain a certain degree of social and legal credibility. Although their clients tend to be local regulars or international tourists who retain a status advantage over them, the clients cannot be certain of impunity if they act violently.

In contrast, the clients of dockside sex workers are strangers to the country and its laws. Although they may enjoy a high level of male privilege at home, they feel much less comfortable asserting masculine prerogatives where they do not know the rules nor have much social standing. Sailors are allowed liberty time in a port as long as they respect the law and do not pose a health or security risk. Sailors who embarrass their employers through dubious behavior abroad face incarceration, deportation, or a ban on working at sea again. This, coupled with their vulnerable social and legal standing, dissuades them from acting violently with local prostitutes.

Thus men who feel legally and socially secure enough to abuse prostitutes (such as police officers) are more likely to do so than clients who are uncertain of impunity (such as foreign sailors).

Location of the Negotiation

The location of negotiation for sexual services determines whether the prostitute can assess a potential client's character and refuse his advances if she desires. In all sectors the locations rarely allow sex workers to reliably evaluate a client's character, but sectoral differences influence whether they can refuse sex.

Streetwalkers who negotiate with clients through car windows have little time to judge the men's character. They rely on immediate clues and intuitive indicators: his vibes, cleanliness, car condition, tone of voice, negotiation style, and so on (Fick 2005). The same is true for truck-stop women who negotiate from parking lots, the side of the road, or passenger seats. In these exposed contexts, a sex worker has only a moment to make complex judgments about her potential safety with a stranger. As long as she remains outside the vehicle, she can usually refuse sex. But she relinquishes much of her power once she enters the vehicle, a space largely controlled by the client.

For brothel workers, the location of negotiation coincides with the location of sex in a place that is managed by a third party. Neither she nor the client controls the space, so both must trust the owner to put their interests first. In some cases, owners watch out for their employees by mandating condom use, providing security personnel, and allowing women the right of refusal.[3] Such rules can be quite helpful given how little time women have to assess clients in the front room—but they can also disrupt business. If a worker refuses clients too often, the owner may start to lose business. This puts pressure on sex workers to accept virtually anybody who walks through the door (Fick 2005).

In contrast, a dockside "sugar girl" spends hours with a man—in a public space—before initiating negotiations. She assesses him during their initial greeting as they converse together, as he chats with his mates, and as they drink, dance, and flirt. Over time, she observes him in multiple registers, assessing his character while maintaining the right to refuse sex. This long assessment period usually allows her to make sensible decisions about the man, increasing her likelihood of safe treatment.

Location of the Sexual Act

Sex workers typically negotiate contracts in one space and fulfill it in another. This distinction usually allows them to reject potential clients if they cannot agree on terms. But, in reality, negotiations continue until the moment of sex and after. Once in bed, a client may refuse to wear a condom, demand extra services, or pay a lower fee than agreed to. According to Campbell (2000), nine hostel prostitutes report that, after sex, some clients threaten them with knives to get their money back. The location of sex has a major impact on whether clients feel comfortable using violence to achieve noncontractual goals.[4] Generally the more control a prostitute has over this space, the less likely that a client will use force against her, and vice versa.

Streetwalkers and truck-stop women typically enact the sexual contract within a client's residence or vehicle. They are strangers in these spaces and so are at heightened risk. The sex worker, especially in a client's residence, lacks information on reliable escape routes and may be isolated by its location. Meanwhile, the terrain is completely legible for the client. His comfort level with asserting demands will be higher in his own space.

Brothel women do not control the space where sex occurs but enjoy some rights within it, because they work under an employer who usually has some interest in their welfare. Prostitutes can feel quite unsettled if their employer does not demonstrate such interest, since failure to do so may indicate that the owner will protect clients' interests first (Fick 2005). Typically, however, the client is surrounded by people who support the sex worker.

Escorts who publicize their services through newspaper ads can meet a client at his house, a neutral hotel, or their own abodes. Escorts often also hire drivers to drop them off and pick them up at their rendezvous points, which makes the client understand that people know where the woman is and care about her welfare. This undercuts much of the advantage the client may have on his home turf.

At the dockside, it is the woman who is the local and the one who chooses where sex occurs. If the client ships out the next morning, she will likely choose a hotel; if he is in town for a few days and available for multiple engagements, she may prefer her home. In either case, she has superior knowledge of the environment and can call on a potential network of contacts. When the woman chooses the space of intimacy, she commands greater control than the man, which decreases the likelihood that he will be violent.

Level of Discretion in the Solicitation Process

Clients and sex workers both value discretion, because prostitution still invites moral opprobrium and social embarrassment for both parties. Hence clients usually reward discreet solicitation with higher fees (Leggett 2001). Such discretion also allows prostitutes to safeguard their reputations, avoiding stigmatization and police harassment. A woman's social and legal status—derived from her public reputation—establish her level of power relative to a client. Sex workers who protect their reputations through discretion generally maintain more personal power than those who do not.

Women who solicit openly are therefore more likely to experience violence than those who solicit discreetly. Open solicitors receive almost no social or legal protection, because they have taken on a publicly criminal identity. A client can abuse a streetwalker with virtual impunity, because she cannot mobilize social or legal support for her complaints.

Escorts, however, often lead double lives and are not publicly known as prostitutes. Their discretion allows them greater flexibility in constructing their identities. Newspaper or Internet advertisements do not expose them

to communal surveillance. Their anonymity protects them from stigmatization and allows them to mobilize legal resources if they get into trouble with
men.

Dockside solicitation is also discreet, because it takes place indoors and
resembles flirtatious activities that occur in normal clubs: dancing, drinking,
singing, talking, and touching. Although the sailors know that the women
are sex workers, whose flirtations are really just solicitous gambits, they lack
the means to leverage this information against them. Sailors have no social
impact beyond the clubs and so pose no threat to the women's reputations.

Role of Third-Party Involvement

Although many South African sex workers are independent agents, their
transactions often involve third parties who exacerbate, or reduce, the likelihood of violence against them. In the streetwalker and brothel trades, pimps,
gangsters, and brothel owners have a direct financial interest in a prostitute
having as many clients as possible. These characters can apply subtle or overt
pressure on a prostitute so that she accepts new clients despite her reserva-
tions. They usually claim to provide a service that justifies her payment to
them. Pimps might provide protection, gangsters drugs, and brothel owners
a place to work (Fick 2005). They all get a cut of her fees and may use physical
force to assure her compliance. But not all are abusive or controlling: some
remain nearby for protection and write down a client's license-plate number
before accompanying the woman home (Pauw and Brenner 2003). Although
this is preferable to an abusive relationship, the pimp still relies directly on
the prostitute's earnings for his livelihood (Leggett 2001). This may lead the
third party to exert pressure, or even inflict violence, on a woman to make
her to go with a client she does not trust.

Dockside prostitutes also deal with many third parties, but these figures
have a vested interest in keeping them safe. The nightclub management, cab
drivers, and hotel owners all derive indirect commerce from prostitutes, and
form part of an informal surveillance network over them and their clients.
In Durban, for instance, the nightclub owner notes which sailors the women
pair up with. When sailors enter the club, they sign a registry listing their
name, nationality, ship, and employer. If a woman has a problem with a client, she can call the club owner, who will talk with the port authority or ship-
ping agent concerning her complaint. Hence sailors are confronted at every
turn by the prostitutes' allies, allowing the women to make sexual decisions
without much threat of violence.

Moreover, because these third parties derive only indirect business from the prostitutes' labor, they provide decent service so that the women will continue bringing them business. The clubs' success depends upon the presence of sex workers who encourage the sailors to spend lavishly in such establishments, and thus owners must keep the women happy so that they continue to solicit from their clubs. The same is true for taxi drivers and hotel owners, who rely on the women to bring in customers. These parties have no incentive, therefore, to pressure the women into choosing bad clients. Instead they provide sex workers with casual surveillance that allows them to move around safely.

Recommendations for Reducing Violence in the Sex Industry

Dockside prostitutes are safer than most other sex workers because of the structural logic of their sector that caters to the needs and constraints of foreign maritime transients. Based on this knowledge, I propose five policy recommendations for making prostitution safer in South Africa, though these are also relevant elsewhere. In this section I discuss how legal, social, linguistic, commercial, and procedural policy interventions can decrease the likelihood of violence, especially in the more dangerous sectors.

Legal Intervention: Criminalize the Purchase but Decriminalize the Sale

The typical clients of the dockside sector do not enjoy a high social or legal status. Although South African society supports patriarchal gender norms and criminalizes sex work, seafarers do not have an appreciably higher status than the prostitutes because of their transience and foreignness. In other sectors, though both parties are legally criminalized, patriarchal double standards ensure that local clients retain a higher status. This inequality increases women's vulnerability to violence, as they lack the credibility to seek redress from judicial institutions. Indeed, in the outdoor trade, clients can abuse prostitutes with virtual impunity. Religious morality and social stigma often end up excusing the non-enforcement of prostitutes' rights.

To remedy this inequality, a positive legal double standard should be established that operates similarly to racial affirmative action. The premise behind affirmative action in South Africa is that the legacy of racism continues to structure social and economic opportunity and that only a legal double standard can help previously disadvantaged groups succeed despite that legacy. The law is used as an instrument to overcome a prevailing social norm—white privilege—that would otherwise remain unassailable through a strictly nonracial legal code.

Given that patriarchal norms continue to structure unequal gender relations, applying *positive discrimination* to the sex industry could also decrease violence against female prostitutes. This would be achieved by leaving the purchase of sexual services criminalized while decriminalizing their solicitation and sale, as has been done in Sweden (Ekberg 2004).

Such a legal double standard would erode the veritable impunity that clients enjoy by redistributing power away from them toward the sex workers. Essentially this would resemble the situation foreign sailors face in South African ports as transient, low-status visitors. Clients would respond by demanding greater discretion from sex workers, encouraging them to seek those who work indoors rather than outdoors. Such a reversal of power would also create a new bargain between the couple: she would honor the man's desire for discretion if he behaves and follows her rules; if he abuses her, however, she can seek legal redress.

This is not an "ideal" solution, in that it does not further legal equality. Nor is it enough. But it is a practical proposal in a patriarchal context characterized by high levels of gender violence. The prevalence of domestic abuse, rape, and violence against the general population of South African females shows that legal equality would not be enough to protect vulnerable prostitutes. Indeed, they require greater legal protection than clients so that, in reality, they might be able to operate as equals.

Social Intervention: Periodically Name and Shame Male Clients

Sailors safeguard their reputations so that they remain employable. They are vulnerable to the negative attention a prostitute can bring if she complains about them to the ship's captain, the police, the port authority, or the ship's agent. Thus they have a financial incentive to behave properly overseas. Clients of prostitutes in other sectors, however, face no such threat to their reputations.

By periodically naming and shaming clients, law enforcement would give teeth to the criminalization of client purchases. Such a practice would warn clients of the risks that they, not just the sex workers, take by engaging sexual services. Not many of these examples would be needed to put sex buyers on alert. The Western Cape provincial government already does this with drunk drivers (offenders are named and shamed in the major local newspapers), an effort that has made the roads safer (van der Fort 2010). The effects of publicly shaming transgressors could be quite severe for clients' reputations, but it would dissuade them from using violence against prostitutes as this would call attention to their illegal activities.

If the likelihood of violence is based on clients' ability to escape public exposure for their actions, then their reputations represent a crucial point of leverage in achieving safety for prostitutes.

Linguistic Intervention: Equate the Moral Position of Buyer and Seller

Social discourse about prostitution relies on a vocabulary that reinforces gender inequality. Currently only sellers are stigmatized, called "prostitutes," a term that sets their identities within conceptual boundaries that are morally, socially, politically, and legally debilitating. (The term "sex worker" is a welcome corrective but has not been adopted by sex workers themselves. Moreover, "sex worker" is as over-determining as the term "prostitute," since many of the women are quite transient to the business.) Buyers of sexual services bear no comparable stigma, referred to by bloodless, amoral terms such as "client" and "john." So whereas the people on the demand side remain free of taint, those on the supply side are marked for life. This reinforces the gendered power imbalance between the two parties. Through a linguistic shift, this imbalance could be tipped somewhat in favor of the suppliers. Just as language identifies sellers (prostitutes) with their business (prostitution) it should identify buyers with their actions by labeling them "prostitutors," a term evincing their agency, complicity, and responsibility for the trade.

Dictionaries define a prostitutor simply as a prostitute, offering yet another redundant name for the seller. But because the term "prostitutor" is almost never used to actually talk about female sex workers, it could be adapted to refer to the other party in the transaction. Thus a prostitute is the seller and a prostitutor is the buyer.

This would add a moral dimension to male behavior, making prostitutors bear moral and social risks comparable to those of prostitutes. Currently South African communities rarely penalize men for sexual purchases. A campaign for substituting the label "prostitutor" for the vacuous term "client," however, would raise awareness about how these gendered identities are unequally constructed. It would also threaten the assumed moral and social impunity that prostitutors enjoy in their sexual dealings. Alone this strategy would achieve little, but in conjunction with other measures it could gradually change the public's understanding of how each gender contributes to the sex business.

Commercial Intervention: Promote Ancillary Third-Party Involvement

In the dockside trade ancillary third parties help protect prostitutes because of their reciprocal commercial relationship with them. Club owners, taxi drivers, and hotel owners, as noted previously, form a casual surveillance network for the women.

In other sectors the women either work alone or are burdened by brothel owners, gangsters, and pimps, who have a direct financial interest in their business. Although it is criminal to profit from prostitution, brothel owners, gangsters, and pimps face little legal threat. Police usually turn a blind eye to vice profiteering. Although some of the services that these parties provide are helpful, they also can entail drug peddling or virtual sex slavery. A preferable option would be if they provided such services for a standard fee so that the women could take or leave such services without coercion.

Admittedly it is difficult to add new parties to niches that are structured around the existing needs of clients. After all, street-cruising clients and truckers do not need the services of cab drivers, hotels, or nightclubs. But if such clients are criminalized and occasionally named and shamed, they might seek discretion and alibis for their sexual purchases. As mentioned earlier, when solicitation is incorporated into regular recreational environments such as nightclubs or bars, the women tend to benefit from third-party surveillance. The more that prostitution-related activities are incorporated into larger fields of legitimate commerce, the safer the industry will be for sex workers.

Procedural Intervention: Enhance Complexity, Value-Added Services, and Discretion

In the dockside trade, sexual engagements follow after hours of drinking, dancing, and conversation at a nightclub. Such legitimate activities shroud the connection between solicitation, sex, and money, masking the work of prostitution and protecting sex workers from legal harassment.

Indeed, when sex is one of many components of solicitation or interaction, prostitutes are rarely targets of the law. When brothels advertise themselves as massage parlors or sex workers market their services as escorts, they add a veneer of legitimacy that provides the women with cover stories and offers greater discretion to prostitutes and their clients. This is not foolproof, but it helps.

Hence South African police officers tend to target prostitutes lacking plausible cover stories, such as streetwalkers (Fick 2005; Leggett 2001).

Legally these women have no defense against the charge of loitering with solicitous intent. If they merely moved their business indoors to a tavern or a nightclub, they could avoid much legal scrutiny and achieve greater stature in negotiating with clients. As it stands, the streetwalker, truck stop, and mine hostel trades cater far too much to the convenience of clients, as they ultimately enjoy massive structural advantages over the prostitutes. This is not what the prostitutes intend but is simply the result of the structural logic of these niches.

Thus, rather than forcing clients to seek socially complex engagements or forcing women to move their business indoors, incentives would have to be crafted to encourage these changes indirectly. Criminalizing clients and shaming selected purchasers would encourage many clients to take their purchases indoors, seek discreet providers of sexual services, involve third-party agents, relinquish their assumed power and comfort, and engage in more complex service arrangements that elevate sex workers' status and enhance their cover stories. Decriminalizing sex work would also allow the women to stop worrying about establishing cover stories to protect themselves. Of course, such measures would not necessarily eliminate the exposed trades, but they would at least alter the bargain between prostitutes and their clients.

Conclusion

South African prostitutes may be restricted by patriarchal gender norms, stigmatized by their communities, and criminalized by the law, but their exposure to violence is heavily dependent upon the features of the sex sector in which they work. At one extreme, streetwalkers are highly vulnerable to client, police, and third-party abuse owing to the structural characteristics of the street trade. Specifically, their clients enjoy a higher social status than they do; the location of negotiation militates against reliable assessments of clients' character; clients control the location of sex; the women solicit openly without discretion; and they are surrounded by third parties that have a direct financial interest in their work.

At the other extreme, dockside prostitutes face little danger of sexual violence because of the structural logic of their sector. For example, their clients have a low social and legal status; the location of negotiation allows for deep assessments of clients' character; the women control the location of sex; their solicitation activities are relatively discreet, because they occur indoors and simulate normal nightclub behavior; and their relationships with third parties are characterized by mutual benefit.

These different experiences have nothing to do with the prostitutes' personal qualities: their race, ethnicity, educational level, and class background have little bearing on whether they experience violence within a given sector. These characteristics certainly affect which sector they might choose to work in, but, once there, sex workers confront irresistible structural forces that determine their likelihood of encountering violence. From a policy perspective, then, the most effective interventions in the sex industry may not revolve around modifying sex workers' behavior, for instance, through workshops or counseling; instead, they may involve altering the structural conditions of the sectors in which the prostitutes work so as to provide disincentives for male abuse.

In this chapter I have tried to counter the image of the typical "comfortable" client with that of the "uncomfortable" one to show how clients' comfort level (i.e., their feeling of sexual entitlement) relates to the probability that they will abuse sex workers. In South Africa's dockside sex trade, clients feel socially and legally insecure and do not control the spaces of intimacy. As a result, they rarely threaten or execute violence against prostitutes, but they are still able to achieve their contractual goals with the women. This insight should encourage the consideration of strategic interventions that help equalize power in the prostitute-prostitutor relationship. Focusing on the structural features of the various sex sectors would allow for the formulation of policies with greater precision and the provision of external support for the women who navigate risk within this industry.

NOTES

A portion of this article was previously published as "Navigating Risk: Lessons from the Dockside Sex Trade for Reducing Violence in South Africa's Prostitution Industry," *Sexuality Research & Social Policy: Journal of NSRC* 4, no. 4 (December 2007): 106–119. I would like to thank the dockside prostitutes, nightclub owners, barmaids, bouncers, and cab drivers of Cape Town and Durban who contributed their time and information to this study. I also acknowledge the support of the Fulbright-Hays Dissertation Field Research Grant, the Social Science Research Council International Dissertation Research Fellowship, and the Yale University Fox International Fellowship.

1. For further details on the dockside context, the participant profile, and my research methods, see Trotter 2011.

2. "Elaine," an elite "escort" or courtesan, maintained a website where she advertised her companionship availability and prices. She charged about ten to fifteen times the rate that streetwalkers charge for comparable durations with clients (Elaine, personal communication, Cape Town, May 5, 2006).

3. Such was the case for one woman who left brothel work in favor of the dockside clubs in Cape Town. Although she was not unhappy with brothel conditions, she moved to the dockside because she thought she could make more money (Moena, personal communication, Cape Town, March 6, 2007).

4. Mine hostels are residential compounds that house mine workers near the mines. Sex workers often congregate in open fields near the hostels, offering their services to the miners passing by.

8

"Their own way of having power"

Female Adolescent Prostitutes' Strategies of Resistance in Cape Town, South Africa

ZOSA DE SAS KROPIWNICKI

Strategic Agents

Adolescents engage in prostitution across the cultural record, and yet their decisions and actions negate what is widely seen as appropriate or desirable behavior for children who in contemporary Western society are viewed as vulnerable, innocent, and dependent "becomings"(Lee 2001, 5). In order to conceptualize this anomaly, adolescent prostitutes are either described as "powerless victims" or "irrational delinquents" acting in conflict with social norms. There is little conceptual clarity or theoretical analysis of the choices these adolescents make and the manner in which they intentionally use their sexuality to fulfill their preferences and meet their needs. This chapter argues that prostitution is a strategy employed by female adolescents in Cape Town, South Africa, in order to resist the structures that bind their decision-making capacity and their actions.

As strategic agents, adolescent prostitutes devise various tactics and use a range of resources to exercise power in the face of exploitation and slavery. Power in these contexts is not owned by any particular actor, institution, or system but is diffused into social relationships and exists only in "action" (Foucault 1982, 794). Action in each power relationship implies a "strategy of struggle" and has the potential for resistance (ibid). Even the "victim" is capable of action and therefore exercises power in a "power relationship" in which "a whole field of responses, reactions, results, and possible inventions may open up"(ibid, 789).

Foucault emphasizes that one needs to consider the "aim of the struggle to overcome the effect of power" (Foucault 1982, 780). Bandura's (2001) model of intentionality elucidates this form of agency. People's intentions are often based on plans of action and forethought. Agents weigh the options they perceive to be available as observed in their environments or as rooted in their value systems or rationalizations. The foundation of human agency is "self-efficacy," the belief that one is capable of exercising some measure of control and power over one's own functioning and environment (Maddux 1995; Schwarzer 1992). This notion of agency can be used in conjunction with Giddens's (1986) theory of "bounded agency" to understand the manner in which agents draw on various norms and resources embedded in the social structure. These resources or weapons are central to agents' strategies of resistance. For example, in his research on peasant rebellions in colonial Africa, Scott (1985) describes the "ordinary" weapons utilized by the "*relatively* powerless" including "foot grading, dissimulation, false compliance, pilfering, feigned innocence, slander, arson, sabotage, and so forth" (29).

Giddens (1986) argues that humans may themselves become resources that others use. This echoes Bandura's (2000) argument that agency can be exercised directly, by proxy, or collectively through or with others who are perceived as more powerful. These resources are therefore derived from relationships and defined in relation to the power exercised by others. In these "power relationships" many children make use of a number of tactics including manipulation and moral reasoning (Harre 1986). Kitzinger (1984) argues that even in the face of sexual abuse,

> children employ the strategies of the most oppressed, dispossessed and victimised: joking and gossip, passive resistance and underground rebellion . . . although such tactics are rarely recognized by adults, children seek to evade abuse with all the resources they have of cunning, manipulativeness, energy, anger and fear.

These tactics amount to strategies in which children act alone or through or with others. Despite their attempts at forethought, many of these strategies are double-edged in that they may ensure the girls' immediate survival but increase longer-term risks of violence and exploitation.

This chapter describes structural constraints on the agency of twenty-four adolescent prostitutes and forty street children who occasionally engaged in prostitution in Cape Town in 2005. It reveals that in the face of poverty and abuse my respondents are active agents who make decisions to ensure their own survival and that of their families and friends. Many perceive prostitution to be a viable and desirable option, given the scarcity of alternative economic choices and mechanisms of social support in impoverished and violent contexts characterized by discriminatory norms and institutions. Such norms lend support to the notion that the differences associated with ethnicity, socioeconomic status, gender, and age are natural and legitimate determinants of the power, control, and freedom that individuals can exercise, and that violence is a reasonable and acceptable way of exercising power and resolving disputes over these differences. My respondents did not passively accept these norms but instead actively interpreted, contested, and revised them depending on the demands of a particular situation. Prostitution was one means by which they were able to resist these structures.

"It is like a wheel; you can't forget": Socioeconomic and Ethnic Constraints

In South Africa ethnic and socioeconomic structures cannot be disengaged. Given the age of my respondents, their awareness of Apartheid structures did not emerge from direct contact with state institutions but was mediated by their caregivers' experiences in the workplace and other social spaces. Their parents either discussed these encounters with them or exhibited frustration and aggression in front of them. Alternatively, children joined their caregivers and other adults in public spaces where they observed and experienced ethnic discrimination. Through these experiences they formed the belief that ethnicity is a marker of socioeconomic status, as well as a determinant of power and freedom. This belief was entrenched rather than challenged by my respondents' experiences in post-Apartheid South Africa. The lack of ethnic integration coupled with extreme deprivation in black and coloured communities have had a significant impact on their options, aspirations, and values so that they perceive prostitution as their only option.

Apartheid's segregationist policies denied the realization of their parents' human rights, circumscribed their movement, limited their employment options, and restricted their social spaces. Their parents "could have got further in life if it wasn't for Apartheid"; they had to carry a "pass" when traveling between white, black, and coloured-designated areas; and "everywhere you went there were signs 'For Whites Only.'" Apartheid affected the composition of my respondents' households during their early childhoods. For example, Jenny attributed her father's absence to Apartheid. She explained, "All I know is that he is a black man and was killed." Frustration and anger—a product of Apartheid—also affected the quality of interpersonal relationships, especially the incidence of intimate partner violence within their homes. As Susanna stated, "My parents used to argue a lot because my mother worked for white people and my father used to have a tough time working for white people on the railway where he worked."

Apartheid's migrant labor system and color bar policies meant that my respondents' parents worked for white employers, which informed their commonly held perception that ethnic differences amount to social inequalities, and that socioeconomic hierarchies exist in which wealth and power are distributed on the basis of ethnicity. Susanna's only experiences interacting with white children occurred when her mother was employed as a domestic worker for a white family. She stated, "We used to play with a white woman's child because we had to look after the child. We could not kiss the child because we were black—that was because of Apartheid."

The democratic transition has not had a marked effect upon socioeconomic inequalities and the differential poverty experienced by particular ethnic groups. Black and coloured people continue to be the most disadvantaged in terms of employment, income, skills, and education. For example, one girl said, "We just want to forget our past, but it is like a wheel, we can't forget." This was affirmed by Melissa, who argued,

> Nothing has changed. The blacks are more advanced but people still do not have jobs. Blacks can go wherever they want to go. I heard and learnt about Apartheid but didn't feel it. But nothing has changed. The president still does not care about us.

These hardships have significantly affected my respondents' options, desired outcomes, and long-term aspirations.

My respondents' perceived options were informed largely by the fact that their parents, siblings, and peers were uneducated and either unemployed or working as unskilled laborers. Despite their aspirations to be teachers, nurses, and lawyers, their lived reality suggests that the immediate financial returns gained from working as a prostitute were valued more out of necessity than the potential long-term benefits of being educated. Emphasis was frequently placed on the absence of alternatives: "Sometimes you think you can't live with yourself, not with what you are doing I mean. If I don't have a choice, what can I do?" By challenging the structures that have failed to provide them with alternatives and solutions to poverty-related stressors, they resist the cultural constructions of themselves as "child dependents." In this context, many engaged in prostitution to assist their families:

The children leave to go look for a job to help and send money to families. They lie to their family and say they doing nightshift. But when your family finds out, you run away because you embarrassed. It is too hard to work on a farm picking oranges for only R250 [U.S.$36.41] a week.

Many tried to reciprocate the care they received from their parents. One factor behind Jenny's decision to start working as a prostitute was that "my mom was suffering for us. Sometimes we go to school and do not have anything to eat. Mom borrowed money. It was hard for her to give it back." Hence their desire to fulfill their obligations at home, to show respect to their mothers, and to seek autonomy emerged as key factors supporting their decision to engage in prostitution. Prostitution was one means through which they could "help out" in contexts characterized by high levels of socioeconomic deprivation.

In their accounts it was evident that many girls wanted more than economic security; they wanted to be wealthy. As one girl stated, "It would be nice to be rich because of the lifestyle. I would like to be rich one day." Others highlighted the "comfortable life" of rich people that included fast food, stereos, clothing, and jewelry. Melissa attributed her desire for material goods to the deprivation she experienced as a child: "I know it's wrong, but I never had those things when I was growing up so now I just want more all the time." Hence my respondents did not criticize socioeconomic hierarchies per se or the value attached to commodities; instead, they sought to improve their position within these hierarchies by accessing goods, even if it involved prostitution.

Although white people were associated with wealth, my respondents stated that "we are all the same" and "we are all human." Nevertheless, when they were not questioned explicitly on this issue, racial prejudices cropped up in their descriptions of their clientele. For instance, Melissa explained how she deliberately chooses white clients because "black clients treat you like a prostitute but white people do not look at me like a prostitute. They could be friends with me." In the accounts of all my respondents, ethnicity emerged as the main criterion for evaluating a client's proclivity for violence. This is evident in the following statements: "I am not racist but I stay away from black guys"; "Black guys . . . do not treat me like I want to be treated"; and "[Black guys] don't play the game right. They are a danger to prostitutes. Once they get you in the corner you must pray." Ethnicity was also associated with socioeconomic status when selecting clients. White clients were preferred, because they "show more money" whereas black guys are "too cheap." The most favored client was a white foreigner from European countries such as Holland, Germany, England, and Sweden with whom the girls tried to establish longer-term relationships. Clearly adolescent prostitutes appeal selectively to certain norms. They challenged discriminatory practices that were constructed during Apartheid by adopting the language of the new democratic "rainbow" nation of South Africa; in their daily practices, however, they use these norms and discourses to structure their behavior and decisions.

The sex work industry is itself divided by racialized barriers. In hostess clubs, escort agencies, and many nightclubs, the majority of prostitutes are white, although a few are coloured. In contrast, in the Cape Town metropol clubs catering to fishermen and in township *shebeens* (illicit bars), prostitutes are mainly black and coloured. The ethnicity of sex workers on the streets varies according to what are still largely segregated communities in Cape Town. The legacy of Apartheid's geospatial politics and socioeconomic inequalities remains in residential spaces divided by ethnicity, to the extent that, in 2001, only eight suburbs in the metropolitan area contained at least 20 percent of African coloured and white population groups (Smith 2005, 14). Their ethnicity and economic standing affects their working conditions, which in turn impacts their ability to make decisions in this context. Their ethnicity, in particular, has an effect on the clients they come into contact with and can choose from.

Children "Fight for Life": Generational Constraints

My respondents believed that age is a marker of one's capabilities, which denote power and freedom. They associated childhood with learning and dependency, adolescence with physiological changes, burgeoning freedom, and increased autonomy, and adulthood with enhanced capabilities as well as complete freedom and control, aptly summarized in the statement: "Adults can do what they want to do when they want to do it." Despite the freedoms adults enjoy, my respondents generally felt that certain constraints should be placed on adults' behavior, particularly relating to the rights and protection of children.

Discussions with street children ("strollers") revealed a disjunction between normative and actual experiences of childhood. Despite constructions of childhood which suggest that children should not work and should be cared for by adults, many of the respondents had to "fight for life" by working and living on the streets. Thus the association of childhood with a carefree, blissful, playful period does not reflect the manner in which child-hood is experienced. Still, although norms surrounding childhood con-strained the girls' agency, these norms were also manipulated by the very same girls. It was held that children, regardless of age, could exercise power over, with, and through others. Infants, for example, may be physically weak, but their mothers exercise power on their behalf: "If you hit a baby, mos, its mother will kill you." Similarly, in the context of abuse, it is held that young children, despite their age and size, can exercise more power than teenagers can, because adults are more likely to listen to younger children while it is assumed that teenagers either can protect themselves or are culpable. Thus, although teenagers are therefore attributed more agency, the support they receive is often reduced.

The adolescents I studied constantly struggled against generational hier-archies. For instance, Sarah threatened to run away from the street shelter where she stayed because the director refused to allow her to date an older man: "If I was her [the director] I would let a child go if she wants to go, because she is a big girl who knows what's right and wrong. I am a big girl. I don't look thirteen, I tell people I am eighteen." Sarah explained that she lies about her age to make herself seem older so that people will acknowledge that she is capable of making her own decisions.

Youth is regarded as a resource in the context of prostitution because "young girls make money easier than old girls." Because younger girls are in greater demand, they can be more selective about their clientele. Youth is therefore a source of power in this context. As one adult prostitute com-plained, "I am getting too old; guys are always looking for young girls." This preference for youth was not often seen as a matter of age per se but reflected the value placed on appearing young. Youth, it appears, tends to be associated with beauty. Rinalda said, for example, "It was easier when I was younger. I had a beautiful build and boobs. I had what men want. Now I am lucky to get one or two a day." She added that young girls "take the business away. Guys go for youngsters. If I had the ability to do so, I would send them home. It is not right."

Younger girls are also regarded as more attractive because of their sexual inexperience. Rinalda stated that "the guys get a kick that they are younger and tighter and have no experience." In other words, men find the experi-ence of having intercourse with younger girls more stimulating and physi-cally enjoyable (Wojcicki and Malala 2001). Reference was also made to the novelty of a newcomer. As one older prostitute pointed out, "There are lots of young girls. When I see them I think business is going to be bad. I don't tell them to go home. The guys know all the old girls, so they want to try young ones out. They don't want to eat meat everyday; they want to try some fish." Such statements demonstrate the women's belief that men seek to engage in a variety of sexual activities with multiple partners of varying ages in order to fulfill their sexual needs.

Hence, for various reasons, girls who are young or appear young are more popular in this context, which often leads to competition between adults and adolescents. As one adolescent explained, "Jealousy is the biggest problem. There's lots of girls who are jealous of me. If you make more money it's a problem. I don't know what I've got that they don't have." That youth was a source of friction, a resource over which many actors competed, was evident from numerous accounts. As Emily stated, "They actually don't speak to one another. The one is jealous of the other. Say now you are a small girl, then everybody's *dik bek* [angry] for you because they take it so you stealing their clients."

Thus, to enhance their popularity with clients, both adults and adolescents readily lie about their age. Many adult prostitutes also attempt to appear younger. As one woman stated, "Guys like me because I look younger. It is not good to lie but sometimes you have to do it." Thus adult prostitutes would often exploit their client's preferences for younger girls by altering their own age and appearance. Adolescents, too, would try to look younger, for example, by losing weight.

This strategy was highly situational. Occasionally my respondents would represent themselves as being older. Adult prostitutes testified that adolescent prostitutes sometimes exaggerated their age in their presence. Elly stated that "although some girls are very young, I'll ask them their age and they'll make themselves seem older." This was echoed by another adolescent. "When we see them we ask them how old they are and they make themselves seem older than they are, but we know they are younger." Some adolescents apparently alter their age to fend off interference from others who may try to restrict their freedom on the streets.

Age was redefined in other contexts as well. Emily reported, for example, that when she was arrested by the police she lied about her real identity and address so that she could not be traced. She also told them she was older than her fifteen years, because she did not want to be taken to the children's shelter, preferring instead to pay the R50 (U.S.$7.10) fine that adult prostitutes were forced to pay. Age was thus readily manipulated not only to increase popularity with clients but also to achieve other outcomes related to autonomy, power, safety, and security. Age was a resource that could be employed or manipulated depending on the situation.

"Being Strong": Gendered Constraints

Violence, which was described in gendered terms, was a common feature of my respondents' local communities. Boys and girls, it was believed, have different capabilities, which is reflected in the power and freedom they wield in the realms of violence and sexuality. My respondents claimed that boys are physically stronger than girls and therefore more capable of exercising violence or protecting themselves from it. Although "boys have their own ways of having power and girls got their own ways of having power," women, it was suggested, have less power than men "because women cannot protect themselves. Men can just punch them." Sexual violence is not a concern for boys, because "girls can get quickly raped but boys can't get quickly raped." This perception, which was repeatedly supported by actual examples of violence, was accompanied by strong feelings of insecurity and fear.

Many girls witnessed intimate partner violence in their homes of origin and were very often subject to rape and physical maltreatment from male peers and other men in their homes, schools, places of recreation, and neighborhood streets. Christeline, for example, stated, "I've seen my mother get beaten lots of times. My father beat her blue eyes many times. Then we could do nothing about it." This violence was related to uneven social, economic, and political change, which was played out in intimate struggles. Violence was also associated with a clash of values and social roles in the domestic domain, particularly regarding the allocation of financial resources: "My father used to hit my mother if he wanted money," one respondent told me. The resort to violence reflects the stress experienced by some unemployed men whose wives are the sole breadwinners in the house. In some cases, the mothers of my respondents cohabited with a man to benefit from additional income and thereby ensure the economic survival of their household. "Because your mother has no money to look after the children," another respondent explained, "she takes in a man," and such men, I was told, were often abusive. Intimate partner violence flared in the presence of alcohol, which in South Africa, as elsewhere, is often related to extreme economic stress. Some respondents protested against such of violence; one girl stated, "I started to hate my father. . . . I told my father it's not fair, my mother does not deserve it."

Violence also characterized my respondents' interpersonal relationships. This abuse was related to a range of factors including age and gender. For example, Jenny lost her virginity to an older man and described the experience as forced and painful: "My partner was twenty-two years and I was twelve years when we had sex. I was very sore. I was bleeding. I didn't know why, maybe because he had a big thing. I didn't want to do it again." Girls who are younger than their partners or less experienced sexually may be unable to assert themselves or resist violence or pressure to have sex. Emily's first sexual experience was also associated with sexual violence and substance abuse. She stated, "I gave him the mandrax and dagga but I did not smoke with him. I just struck the match because I was too scared. When he was done smoking he held me down on the bed and pinned me down. The next day I had to go to school with a sore body."

The girls argued vehemently that incest is wrong and "disgusting." A father who has sex with his child was described as a "dog" because "it's his own child" and "he brought her into the world." They emphasized that a "father should respect the child's body." From their accounts, however, such respect had clearly broken down, since a significant number of the girls had been sexually abused by their fathers and by other male members of their immediate or extended families. Most of my respondents who were sexually abused had no one to counsel them. They told me, for example, that "I just kept everything to myself" or "we had to find our own solution to our problem" or "you just had to cope with it."

Some emphasized that it was difficult to approach their parents to talk about sexual abuse. As Susanna argued, "The men just do [it] and then they say it's the child's fault." Lerato stated that when she told her mother that she was being sexually abused by her mother's live-in boyfriend, she was blamed for the abuse. As Grace put it: "One could not talk about it because it would be said that you are keeping yourself big [acting too mature], that is why you waited till you older then you would talk about these things." Grace's comment suggests that, in some communities, children's concerns are ignored because they are believed to be too young to recognize abuse and are either fabricating it to get attention or are responsible for encouraging or initiating it. The girls complained that little action was taken against perpetrators, because their mothers were too inebriated, dependent, or scared of their male partners. Relatives did not provide the kind of support that they might have and instead often contributed to the violence and deteriorating conditions in the household.

Practitioners such as schoolteachers or social workers also failed to provide support to these girls. One girl stated, for instance, "I told the social worker that my mother was not taking care of us but my mother said I lied. The social worker doesn't care and leaves you with your family when she knows they are not looking after you. So I ran away from Kyelitcha to Cape Town."

This underscores the fact that when a child's word is measured against a parent's, the latter is often given more weight. Combined with the physical act of sexual abuse, this is likely to have a detrimental effect on children's self-esteem and their options. With few people to turn to for assistance, many children may decide to take matters into their own hands. For most of the girls in my study, running away was one of the few options at their disposal. As one girl told me, "Some children have problems at home, they can't solve the problems at home, they run away from home, and come onto the streets." After weighing all options, self-preservation could only be achieved by escaping.

Escaping to the streets, however, failed to provide the desired reprieve from violence. Even when "you are like strong, you don't know if you like safe because you can just be raped or so. You can't just walk anywhere. You don't know what is going to happen." Hence the threat of violence must be considered in their decision to run away. To overcome their low sense of self-efficacy, many girls decide to exercise their agency collectively with their peers. It was suggested that children who have more friends are stronger, because "if you lots, you are more strong; if there are only two of you, you more scared." As a result, many girls living on the streets would join groups of "strollers" for protection and material security. The group would allocate specific duties to each girl such as begging or parking cars, but for many the duty was prostitution.

Alternatively the girls joined gangs for physical protection. In other words, "you have people to sort things out for you." The unintended consequence of this attachment, however, was the greater risk of violence from gang members, as well as pressure to engage in prostitution. Boys in gangs generally have physical and financial power over the girls. As one girl stated, "To be in a gang you have to have a boyfriend in that gang. If you have a boyfriend, that boyfriend makes you have sex nonstop." Girls in the gangs are required to follow the boys' instructions, which include involvement in prostitution; the income from these encounters goes to the gang and their criminal activities. Girls are also used as decoys or "bait" so that they can lure clients, who are then attacked. In many cases they are instructed to do so by the gang's leader. As one respondent explained, "Maybe I am the leader of the gang ne, ok I need money, ne, I can just change my mind and tell you, ok, you gonna go stand on the road for me for money." Sara also referred to her friend's engagement in prostitution:

> Christy likes living on the street because she is a number 28 [the name of a gang]. They stop cars and rob men. The boss is a grownup and tells them

what to do . . . He orders them to do things. They all wear black clothes. Sometimes he tells girls to stand in the street and lift their dress and do stuff to buy drugs.

Many of my respondents' attach themselves to men, whom they describe as boyfriends, for physical security. As Christy put it:

You run away from the shelter because you are used to the street where no one tells you what to do, where to sleep, what to drink . . . when your boyfriend goes to jail you don't know how to survive without a boyfriend. So you get another boyfriend. The girls fight over guys . . . If you don't have a boyfriend, other boys will take a chance with you.

Attachment to one man means protection from many others. But the girls' economic dependency on men also increases their vulnerability for abuse and exploitation. As one girl reported, "they [boys] sleep with you or beat you because they bought you food. You have to do what they want. You never know if he loves you." Another girl said that she doesn't like to ask her boyfriend for money "because I will become a slave." Given the importance of having a boyfriend, many girls submit to coercion and are pressured to engage in prostitution. As another girl stated, "The boyfriend is going to tell the girl to stand on the road for him for money."

Many girls therefore prefer working alone in order to exercise greater control and power over their lives. Even then, violence is a common feature of their working relationships. A number of the adolescent and adult prostitutes working in metropolitan Cape Town had been "dropped," or stranded, penniless and often naked in outlying areas in Tableview, Bothasig, Salt River, and even on top of Table Mountain. This was frequently the case after they had been assaulted and raped. A client of one of my respondents tried to push her out of his moving vehicle on a freeway, and another respondent was gang-raped. Even those who choose not to travel with the client are still at risk of violence. Many of the prostitutes working in the Van Schoorsdrift neighborhood were taken into the nearby park and assaulted. Because the area is off the main road and concealed by trees, the girls are less likely to be targeted by the police but more likely to be attacked by clients.

My respondents did not passively accept or acquiesce to this gender-based violence. Many stated that they would develop positive relationships with other female prostitutes to exercise their agency collectively; in this way they could take note of vehicle registration details, safeguard their money, and keep an eye out for one another's physical safety. My respondents also used violence against aggressive clients as a survival strategy. Jenny maintained that first she would attempt to reason with the client: "I tell clients I am a prostitute, but I am also a woman." If this failed, she would then resort to force, even though she was not physically strong: "I have power only from my mouth to say stop. If they beat me then I will do it. But I will also fight. If I am in the car I will hit him." Another adolescent made a similar point, "If a client hits me I kick him back. Even if he is big I am not scared." Many girls would throw stones at the windshields of abusive clients' cars, aware that such clients would be unlikely to risk being implicated in illegal activities by approaching the police.

Some girls resisted these tactics by exercising violence over other girls. Reference was made, for instance, to an all-female gang called the "Dollar Signs." One member explained that she joined the gang with her friends when she was eleven years old but complained that "you choose to be in the gang, when you are in the gang you can't make your own decision, you have to go the way they going." She was ordered by the twenty-one-year-old female gang leader (the *inchiswa*) to murder another girl who wanted to leave the gang: "Like the *inchiswa* says you must go kill that one. You must go rob that one. You just have to go do it and if you don't want to do it, she is going to tell the group to beat the person that doesn't want to do it."

Some would ask their boyfriends to exercise violence against other girls with whom they were in competition. The relationship between adult and adolescent prostitutes was generally characterized by violence, given the competitive nature of the industry and the attention that young prostitutes drew. As one adolescent prostitute complained, "Sometimes they [adult prostitutes] are nice to you when a guy chooses them, but they get mad when a guy chooses you." Some women complained that girls would "send their boyfriends to interfere with the older girls." In Van Schoorsdrift, adults and adolescents alike constantly recounted Linda's story: she had been murdered by another younger prostitute's boyfriend for poaching her clients.

At times the girls benefit from exploitative arrangements by acting as "middle men" and introducing other girls to so-called pimps in exchange for a fee. Sara explained that in such relationships the third party "tells you that they [the group] sell their bodies on the streets for money and now you got to do the same thing they do." Alternatively they introduce other newcomers to clients and demonstrate how to engage in sexual activities for a fee. Jenny, for example, went with a friend to Van Schoorsdrift "and saw how fast the girls make money. I went with her a second time and the third time I did it by myself." Adolescent girls even employ coercion to force their peers to engage in prostitution. As Sara stated,

> I enjoyed Friday night on the street but not Saturday night. A man tried to take me with him; he had a knife. Christy said that I must go with him because Christy will get money. I said no and spent the night at the police station. On Sunday I came back to Ons Plek [a Cape Town shelter]. I am cross with Christy, but I am also scared of her.

Clearly certain norms support the use of violence against women in general, and adolescent girls in particular, both in their homes of origin and on the streets. My respondents did not simply accept this victimization but actively tried to resist it by seeking the protection of other actors or by using violence and coercion against other men, women, and children.

Conclusion

This chapter has argued that adolescents who engage in prostitution are "bounded" by strategic agents. On the one hand, their decisions and activities are informed by social structures that have been shaped by discriminatory and oppressive discourses, norms, institutions, and the inequitable distribution of resources in relation to ethnicity, socioeconomic status, gender, and age. This social structure has an impact upon adolescents' relationships with others, which in turn influences their identity, self-efficacy, decision-making ability, and actions.

These adolescents do not simply acquiesce to given notions but actively interpret and challenge these norms and institutions by heatedly resisting what they perceive to be an unjust distribution of power in relationships. In these power struggles they develop various strategies using the resources they perceive to be available. These may include their peers, boyfriends, clients, and other sex workers with whom and through whom they exercise their agency. Alternatively they may make use of their gender, age, and other personal characteristics. This chapter has shown how adolescents use these resources to protect themselves from violence and abuse, survive in the face of poverty, fulfill their duty-bearing roles, and earn respect in their homes, in shelters, and on the streets. In asserting their power over others, some adolescent prostitutes perpetrate violence against other children. The binaries "powerful and powerless" and "perpetrator and victim" do not hold true when conceptualizing the lived reality of adolescent prostitutes, who possess multiple identities, assume diverse roles, and act with intentionality to exercise power and control over their lives and others. Even in the context of prostitution, they have "their own way of having power."

9

"Hata watufanyeje, kazi itaendelea"

Everyday Negotiations of State Regulation
among Female Sex Workers in Nairobi, Kenya

CHIMARAOKE IZUGBARA

Just late last night they nearly got me . . . Two of them were
approaching me and I knew they were police. Luckily, there was
this man passing and I walked fast and joined him . . . I said to
him "Boss, please, behind me are policemen, they will arrest me
for walking alone, please pretend we are together." He looked
at me and said "Ok, I will help you." The policemen ran forward and said, "Hey woman you are not with that man, we were
watching you. Follow us; we are taking you to the station." The
man told them that I was with him and that we are going home
together. So, they moved away . . . As we walked, the man said,
"Ok girl, I have helped you . . . let's go to my car . . . it is parked
over there, and you give me some love. I said ok, "if you have
money and a condom." He said "I don't have a condom . . . I
just saved you from the police. You know what they would have
done to you, right?" I told him "Well . . . no condoms, no sex."
He said "Ok, in that case, just give me *kudara* [oral sex]. I will
give you 600 bob [Kenyan shillings, U.S.$7.13]." I told myself . . .
"This is not a bad deal."

—Rose, a Nairobi sex worker

Currently scholarship positing social actors as agentive beings capable of creatively mediating or transforming their own relationships with the
structural forces at work in their lives has led to calls for critical research on
how sex workers, particularly in contexts where prostitution is criminalized,
negotiate the activities of state regulatory agents (Okal 2009). While agency
has offered scholars a conceptual tool for charting sex workers' maneuver-
ability, inventiveness, and reflective choices in relation to the constraints they
face at work (Emirbayer and Mische 1998), it has also inspired two impor-

tant questions: Does sex workers' engagement with the structures governing or regulating their lives actually cancel out the effect of disempowering
social regulations? And, moreover, do sex workers' everyday practices for
managing policing truly promote their well-being? (Izugbara 2007). Without
downplaying the dangers and violations to which criminalization exposes
sex workers globally, this chapter focuses on the strategies used by female sex
workers in Nairobi, Kenya, to avert arrest by law enforcement agents and the
implications of these strategies for their well-being and vulnerability. Nairobi
offers an intensely exciting location for studying sex workers' engagement
with formal policing. Prostitution flourishes in Nairobi despite the 2007 Nairobi General Nuisance By-Laws (formerly The By-Laws of the City of Nairobi of 1960), which directly criminalize it.

I raise two major points in this chapter. First, I argue that the efforts of
law enforcement agents to regulate prostitution in Nairobi unite the city's
sex workers into a community of victims and inventors. Nairobi's antiprostitution laws expose sex workers to a painful list of daily victimization and
indignities. But sex workers in Nairobi are also not passive social agents
struggling against unsympathetic laws, implemented primarily by corrupt
and inefficient state agencies; they have developed strategies for defying
arrest and regulation by law enforcement personnel. My second conten-
tion is that these strategies are paradoxical in nature: while they permit
sex workers to flout formal control, they also reaffirm sex workers' marginality, making them more susceptible to victimization and negative health
outcomes.

The arguments presented here are based on my three and half years of
ethnographic work among sex workers in urban Nairobi, Kenya. During
this time I lived and worked in Nairobi as an ethnographer with a leading
international research organization. Data collection involved an assortment
of qualitative techniques, including ethnographic observation and in-depth
interviews. Informants were mainly sex workers operating in the bars and
on the streets of Nairobi, although information was also sought from groups
and individuals concerned with their lives, including police officers, Nairobi City Council officials, leaders of sex workers' organizations, taxi drivers, male clients of sex workers, human rights activists, lawyers, and night
watchmen. I also regularly visited and spent time in bars and other places
frequented by sex workers observing their behavior, drinking and chatting
with them as well as clients, and eavesdropping on conversations. On many
nights I walked throughout Nairobi's red light districts and conversed with
the street-based sex workers there. Data from formal interviews were audio-

taped and complemented with handwritten notes based on observations and informal discussions. All the materials are presented anonymously to protect the participants' identities.

Prostitution in Urban Kenya: Sociohistorical and Legal Contexts

Certain unique socioeconomic conditions imposed by colonialism led to the rise of prostitution in contemporary urban Kenya. White (1990, 1986) contends that prostitution flourished in colonial Kenya and was central to the political economy of the colonial system. Prostitutes provided sexual services in addition to individual domestic or other tasks that reinforced male power. They supported colonialism by providing sexual and other services that enabled urban-based male laborers to return to their jobs at least slightly replenished. This benefited the colonial system, which, by 1930, had developed policies that forced men moving into the cities to leave their wives and children in their rural homes. Nairobi's Municipal Native Officers wrote, in 1938, that the city saved money on "proper native housing because the needs of eight men may be served by the provision of two rooms for the men and one for the prostitute" (Davis 1939, cited in White 1986).

By the 1800s *watembezi* prostitution (from the Swahili verb *kutembea*, "to walk") had taken root in Kenyan cities. *Watembezi* women were street-based and followed clients home to provide them sexual services in exchange for a fee negotiated in advance. Most *watembezi* women were unmarried, unemployed, and newly arrived migrants in need of an immediate source of income to obtain shelter and sustenance. *Watembezi* prostitutes usually shared rooms and primarily operated along busy thoroughfares and affluent neighborhoods, where they were recruited by men needing their services (White 1986).

Malaya[1] prostitution emerged first in the 1920s, in Pumwani,[2] east of Nairobi. *Malaya* women sold erotic and other forms of domestic labor from their own places of residence. The *malaya* prostitute waited in front of her room for her customers to come. Pumwani's municipal by-laws prohibited outdoor loitering and prostitution. *Malaya* relationships mimicked marriage, thereby conforming to civil law (Bujra 1975; White 1986). Since *malaya* workers usually did not go out to solicit clients or sell sexual services exclusively, they also could not easily be charged with a criminal offense. *Wazi wazi* prostitution, which emerged at the same time and existed alongside *malaya* prostitution, largely involved non-Kenyan women and is historically associated with Haya women from the Bukoba District in (then) Tanganyika, also called Waziba in Nairobi. *Wazi wazi* prostitutes were reputedly aggressive, audacious, and brazen. They had the habit of yelling out their erotic credentials publicly and soliciting clients by moving from the door of one returning worker to another (McClintock 1991). *Wazi wazi* prostitutes rarely sold nonsexual services (White 1992).

Kenya's declaration of political independence in 1963 significantly altered the social organization of prostitution in Nairobi, particularly through mass education and the relaxation of migration and mobility laws. Rural-to-urban migration dramatically increased in post-independence Kenya largely because of the Kenyan political elite's failure to redistribute agricultural land abandoned by fleeing British settlers, prompting an influx of landless young men and women into urban areas. Other social currents that allowed for the expansion of the prostitution sector and made sex work attractive to many women in Kenya include the rise in tourism, urbanization, and industrialization, the liberalization of fishing and other extractive rights, the increase in escort agencies, the intensification of cash cropping, the growth in cross-border trading activities, economic crises, and, more recently, political conflicts in neighboring countries such as Rwanda, Somalia, Sudan, Ethiopia, and Uganda. The devastating impact of the poorly managed famines, crop failures, and droughts that periodically hit agricultural and pastoral communities in the country has also increased the number of women who engage in sex work as a survival strategy.

The uncertainties associated with urban residence in post-independence Kenya continue to force many married men to leave their families behind when they come to the cities. Critical shortages in urban housing and employment opportunities have meant that many migrants entering the city live in the slums. The extreme anonymity and multiethnic character of these settlements have been particularly influential in fostering weak controls on sexual behavior in the city. Further, many migrants have little or no formal education and have difficulty finding jobs in the city that provide a sustainable income. Historic gender inequities regarding access to education in Kenya have also meant that the majority of rural women migrants are less educated than their male counterparts and thus less employable. Perhaps as a result of these socioeconomic factors, a 1999 national survey showed that an estimated 6.9 percent of Kenyan women had sold sex for money, gifts, or favors the previous year (Elmore-Meegan, Conroy, and Agala 2004).

Growing consumerism and the high cost of living also sustain sex work as a lucrative alternative to the poor-paying jobs in the Kenyan formal and informal sectors. The HIV pandemic has also played a major role in the growth of sex work in Kenya, creating a significant number of orphans and widows for whom prostitution has offered a means for caring for themselves and their dependents. Indeed, remittances earned from sex work are used to support whole family units, set up businesses, and fund education. Urban prostitutes vary considerably in their earnings and clientele; while an average of twelve to twenty clients per week has been reported, there are also instances where sex workers have up to six clients daily (Okal 2009). HIV is widespread among Kenyan sex workers, with about 40–88 percent of Kenyan male and female sex workers reportedly infected in comparison with 6–8 percent of the general population (Elmore-Meegan, Conroy, and Agala 2004).

Prostitution is stigmatized in Kenya, and sex workers in the country are common targets of violent physical abuses including rape and murder by clients, community members, and law enforcement agencies. Mistreatment and abuse of sex workers in Kenya are also rarely punished. For instance, when Castro Mwangi killed twenty-five-year-old Vivian, one of two sex workers he had taken home for group sex, because she refused to have unprotected anal sex, he was acquitted. Despite overwhelming evidence to the contrary, the court ruled that Mwangi had killed Vivian in self-defense ("Castro Mwangi" 2004). Also, when nineteen-year-old Frank Sundstrom, an American tourist and naval officer, killed Monica Njeri, a Mombasa-based prostitute and thirty-two-year-old mother of two, for not granting him the kind of sex he wanted, he went scot-free. In fact, Sundstrom admitted to the crime but was never prosecuted. His only sentence was a bond of 500 Kenyan shillings (U.S.$46) and a pledge of good conduct (Migot-Adhola 1982; Omondi 2003).

Sex work in Kenya is currently regulated by a combination of colonial criminal laws, recent legislation (such as the Sexual Offences Act), and municipal councils' statutes (FIDA 2008). Kenya's national legal code, which is based upon Acts of Parliament, neither defines prostitution nor directly criminalizes it nor forbids it. However, several municipal laws, which are rules and regulations for administering local councils, unswervingly criminalize sex work and proscribe it. The focus of Kenya's Penal Code is on third parties gaining financially from sex work or supporting it. For example, willingly and knowingly offering a premise for sex work is a crime. Kenya's Penal Code describes two sex work–related offenses: living on the earnings of prostitution and soliciting or importuning for immoral purposes.

The 2006 Kenyan Sexual Offences Act also focuses on the "exploitation of prostitution." Actions compelling anyone, including a child or person with mental disabilities, into sexual intercourse for gainful purposes or supporting sex work in any way, such as offering premises for sexual acts to take place, are prohibited. Many of Kenya's local and municipal authorities prohibit sex work directly through their by-laws. Examples include the General Nuisance By-Laws of 2007, formerly the By-Laws of the City of Nairobi of 1960 and the By-Laws of Kenya's Municipal Councils of Mombasa, Kisumu, and Kakamega. The Nairobi General Nuisance By-Laws (2007) provides that "any person who in any street loiters or importunes for purposes of prostitution is guilty of an offense," and the Mombasa Municipal Council By-Laws (2003) state that "any person who shall in any street or public place (m) Loiter or importune for the purpose of prostitution (n); Procure or attempt to procure a female or male for the purpose of prostitution or homosexuality . . . shall be guilty of an offense." Part VIII of the Kisumu Municipal Council By-Laws deals with public health concerns and describes "nuisances" as offenses in the following two categories:

A person shall not (m) molest, solicit or importune any person for the purposes of prostitution or loiter on any street or public place for such purposes; or (n) willfully and indecently expose his person in view of any street or public place.

The Kisumu By-Laws introduce the offense of "molesting for purposes of prostitution" and "soliciting for prostitution." Other sections of the code, specifically By-Law (n) concerning "indecent exposure," empower the police to arrest "loitering" women, as well as women who dress in particular ways. Overall, most of Kenya's municipal by-laws regarding prostitution are characterized by ambiguities and give law enforcement personnel extensive powers.

Sex Workers and Nairobi's Antiprostitution Law

Many of the sex workers I studied did not know that Kenya's national law does not proscribe prostitution. Research by the Federation of Women Lawyers (FIDA 2008) in Kenya showed similar results. The majority of sex workers in the FIDA study thought that Kenya's national law prohibits sex work and based their conviction on the frequent arrests and harassment that they experience at the hands of law enforcement officers. My own interlocutors believed that Kenyan national law empowers the police and municipal authorities to regulate sex work in Nairobi. Even when I showed them documented evidence that sex work is not illegal in Kenya per se, my respondents doubted it, wondering how and why sex work would be legal in Kenya but not in Nairobi, the country's capital city.

The antiprostitution stance of Nairobi's municipal by-laws affects sex workers in a number of important and critical ways. First, it criminalizes all prostitutes and increases the risks they face in their work. As criminals, Nairobi's sex workers are frequent targets of arrest, molestation, and harassment by state agents. In the hands of Nairobi's poorly trained and corrupt law enforcement agents, the antiprostitution law translates into a very real, very long, and very painful list of daily mistreatments, victimization, and indignities for sex workers (Jolin 1994). Sex workers in Nairobi are mentored on, and learn the implications of, the illegality of sex work very early in their careers. Often, more experienced prostitutes offered extensive guidance to those joining for the first time. This frequently took the form of buddy systems or casual stories and counsel shared among the women, which Brents and Hausbeck (2005) observed among prostitutes in Nevada's legal brothels. Sanders (2004) also noted that storytelling unites experienced sex workers with beginners, creating solidarity and a mutual sense of community. Work-related stories among prostitutes particularly disseminated information on risk and provided support. They revealed common consequences of prostitution and helped women pass on tips for dealing with risky situations, creating a spirit of camaraderie. Louisa, one of my informants, reported that friends who had introduced her to sex work three years earlier unequivocally told her about the importance of remaining vigilant toward law enforcement officials. Louisa herself has shared her own work-related experiences with hundreds of practiced and beginning sex workers. "We tell each other our experiences and also learn from each other. That's the way to survive in this job," she said.

Judging by the available narratives, the illegality of prostitution in Nairobi made sex workers a particularly susceptible and powerless group, and state-supported efforts to regulate prostitution strongly and at once united the city's sex workers into a conscious community of self-identified victims. Indeed, sex workers' narratives about the criminalization of their work suggested that their common risk of victimization united and propelled them to assist and support one another. Client violence and abuse, especially murder, rape, robbery, denial of payment, forced unprotected sex, payment in counterfeit currency, and coerced anal sex, were also described as common and pervasive. Sex workers also reported cases of clients with HIV or other sexually transmitted infections (STIs) tricking and forcing them into unprotected sex and of mentally ill or maladjusted clients attacking them. "Which other work has these many problems? We are definitely different," declared twenty-five-year-old Leah.

My informants recognized criminalization as the bridgehead of most of the issues they faced in their work. It was blamed for the impudence with which the public mistreated sex workers, for the exploitation and abuse of sex workers by clients and law enforcement officers, and for sex workers' inability to seek and obtain redress for work-related injustices. "People know they can get away with anything they do to you because they know you can't even go to the police," offered twenty-three-year-old Comfort, who primarily worked in bars. Given this scenario, sex workers lived cautiously and watched one another's backs. A sex worker arrested by law enforcement officers reportedly has limited options: she either does what they want or has herself to blame. As sex worker Irene said, "We know what we are doing is illegal. So we are very careful. When they catch us we have no rights to claim. We just have to watch out and act like sisters to each other. The one you help today will help you tomorrow."

Encountering, and Defying, Law Enforcement Agents

My interlocutors' stories of their work were dominated by narratives of encounters with law enforcement agents. Two law enforcement agencies were recognized as constituting a major threat to sex workers in the City of Nairobi: the Kenyan police and the antiprostitution force of the Nairobi City Council, which sex workers refer to, respectively, as *Magava* and *Kanjo*. Although encounters with both agencies were reportedly pervasive and increasing, sex workers told me that they preferred encountering *Magava*, whose officers were easier to bribe into releasing arrested sex workers, whereas *Kanjo* would take bribes and still detain the sex workers. Sex workers admitted that they were aware every day that they might encounter these agents. Nairobi sex workers might encounter law enforcement officers anywhere and at any time—in bars and on the streets, at night and during the day.

Dorcas, who worked in an exclusive bar/sex compound in one of Nairobi's high-class residential neighborhoods, experienced her first arrest by law enforcement officials in broad daylight in the compound where she worked. Dorcas was arrested along with seven others by *Kanjo* in an afternoon raid. She revealed that the sex compound had been targeted because of a quarrel over money which the compound's proprietress had with her boyfriend, a high-ranking City Council official who had been providing her with protection.

Criminalization regularly exposed Nairobi's sex workers to acts of harassment and mistreatment by law enforcement officials. Pubs such as Simmers, Florida 1 and 2, Pavement, Lidos, and Six-Eighty, and streets and lanes such as Koinage, Muindi Buingi, Lithuli, Argwing Kodhek, Wabera, and Utali are notorious for prostitution in Nairobi, and are regularly patrolled by law enforcement. Women in these areas found walking alone or in the company of other women risk arrest. To entrap sex workers, officers sometimes pretend to be clients and then arrest them. Wanjiru, while canvassing for clients, was arrested on Arwing Kodhek Road by City Council officials driving around in a private van. When the driver of the van stopped near her, Wanjiru thought he was a client and went to talk to him, but another man jumped out of the van and arrested her.

Sometimes officers went into pubs to "chat up" sex workers and pretend they wanted to take them home. Then, once outside the bar, they arrest them. Officers also regularly raided streets and bars to arrest sex workers. Jane was arrested during one such raid in a popular bar in the South C neighborhood of Nairobi. She had been drinking in the bar in the company of other sex workers when four armed policemen swooped down on them. The arresting officers claimed that they recognized them as sex workers who collaborated with a notorious robbery gang in the neighborhood.

In the hands of corrupt law enforcement, antiprostitution laws translate into painful victimization and indignities for sex workers (Jolin 1994). My respondents displayed immense apprehension regarding Nairobi's antiprostitution law. As twenty-five-year-old Melissa noted: "It is not that they will arrest you or take you to court; it is that you can't tell what they will do to you once *Kanjo or Magava* catch you." Sex workers' narratives revealed their preference to be arraigned in court once they were arrested, but this rarely happened. Once a sex worker is arraigned, informants said, her physical safety is guaranteed, as the police rarely mistreat an arraigned person. But, until then, "anything can happen to you," Melissa reported. In the court sex workers could secure their freedom by paying fines or hiring a lawyer to argue their case. In some cases the courts set them free for lack of evidence. Court procedures could be time-consuming, however, and their outcomes uncertain. Hiring a lawyer was also very expensive and yet failing to do so often left sex workers at a judge's mercy.

Nairobi's law enforcement agents regularly abuse the law to mistreat sex workers. They rarely arraign sex workers, preferring to extort them. Very few of my respondents who reported having been arrested by the police were arraigned in court, and those who had been often were unable or unwilling to meet the arresting officers' demands. Kadijah was arraigned in court because she could not pay the 2,000 shillings (about U.S.$40) demanded by the City Council officials who arrested her. The four sex workers who had been arrested with her paid bribes and were released. The officers even offered to drive Kadijah to her house to get the bribe money, despite her insistence that she had none. When she refused to have sex with each official in the back of the patrol van, they drove her to the police station and locked her in a cell with two other women, who then beat her up and tore her dress. She was arraigned in court two days later but was released by a female judge for lack of evidence. A different outcome awaited Mary, who was arrested by a patrol team led by a policewoman who was rumored to have lost her husband to a Nairobi-based Rwandan sex worker. Known in the Eastland neighborhood of Nairobi for her toughness against sex workers, the police-woman ignored Mary's pleas and refused her bribe. Mary spent two nights in detention before her arraignment in court, where she was fined 1,500 shillings (about U.S.$20).

The commonly reported extrajudicial activities of enforcement agencies against sex workers were rape, the extortion of bribes, verbal and physical abuse, illegal detention (sometimes in officers' homes), obtaining sex from sex workers by deception, and refusing to pay sex workers after sex. Arrests generally put sex workers at the mercy of the officers. Bribe amounts usually depended on the discretion of the arresting officers. Instances have been reported where sex workers paid as little as K 150 (U.S.$7) and as much as K 3,000 (U.S.$70) to be released. One informant had been arrested up to fifteen times in the past nine months, and another twelve times in the past year. All bribed their way out. One respondent reported spending nearly U.S.$200 in bribes in the past year. Generally sex workers considered it more convenient to negotiate with and pay officers a bribe than to be arrested and taken to the court where the fines could be higher than the requested bribes. My informants believed, in fact, that officers who took bribes to free them were being compassionate, but many officers, upon collecting the bribes, would still demand sex from the women. Most sex workers, while on the street, carried *musimamo*, "eventuality money," which they often hid in bras, underwear, stockings, shoes, or wigs, to use as a bribe when the need arose.

Sex workers suffered particularly malicious forms of harassment in detention. They often were held in overcrowded cells that lacked sanitary conveniences. One sex worker did not bathe during the two days she spent in detention. Detained sex workers were sometimes also forced to engage in sex or domestic work in officers' homes. During her three-day detention at a police station near Buruburu, Wendy cleaned house and washed clothes for the station's resident commander. She was later released without ever seeing a magistrate or being fined. One sex worker was denied medication following her arrest, during which officers gleefully told her that they would be happy to see her die in front of them. In detention sex workers lost jewelry and other personal effects, including shoes, belts, bracelets, wigs, handsets, and watches. Officers also entertained themselves by demanding that sex workers fight with one another, compete in races, participate in nude parades, or simulate sexual congress. During her detention, Sikala was made to perform erotic dances, simulate orgasm and the sex act, and even fondle her own breasts.

Police officers also rape sex workers, frequently forcing them into unprotected oral and anal sex. One respondent maintained that HIV/AIDS remains very high among the police in Kenya because "they like to force sex workers to have sex with them. Policemen do not bother about condoms. They just force you to bend over in the dark or push you into their patrol vans, pull their trousers down, and have sex. They do this a lot." This particular interlocutor admitted personal knowledge of several sex workers who had been forced into unprotected sex by patrol officers.

Acknowledging both the difficulties of working in a hostile environment and sex workers' own determination to defy state regulation, Rosemary declared: "Hata watufanyeje, kazi itaendelea[No matter what they do to us, work must continue]." Generally my research suggested that Nairobi's sex workers used novel strategies to defy arrest and control by law enforcement agents. As I will show, however, these strategies were accompanied by significant risk, disempowerment, and vulnerability for sex workers.

One means by which sex workers addressed state regulation was through membership in information networks, informal channels through which sex workers continually seek and transmit critical information about the current situation on the streets and in other work settings. Simply by exchanging phone numbers with other sex workers, a woman becomes part of an existing network or develops her own. Illustrating the dynamics of one such information cell, Jewel told us:

> You simply take the numbers of others girls you meet on the street and give them yours. You can call them the following day and say "I am at Black Diamond [a pub in Nairobi] already, are you coming out tonight? Don't use this or that road, there is police or the traffic is heavy." She will know you care for her safety. Or you can call to ask her whether she is already in town and whether a particular road or pub is safe to go to.

Membership in information networks is critical for sex workers who want to avoid encounters with law enforcement officers. Through these cells, sex workers stay abreast of news about police activities in the city or near a bar; they may learn that a raid has just ended or that a street or bar has returned to normalcy after a raid. These cells also allow friends to know one another's whereabouts and whether someone is in danger. Sometimes non–sex workers, especially night guards, street men, bartenders, and taxi drivers, are also part of the cells. These persons act as lookouts for sex workers and monitor the tempo of various parts of the city, night and day. Tim, a taxi driver who works at night around Koinange Street and is a lookout for sex workers, told me he had the phone numbers of more than forty sex workers. Besides using these numbers to link sex workers with male clients, who might ask him where they might find women, sex workers also called him most nights on his phone to find out if the city was safe for them. Tim reported: "Once I sight the police I let them know. I will tell them what I have seen and where it is happening." Tim also told me that sex workers paid him by providing airtime for his mobile phone and sometimes with sex.

Membership in information cells also puts sex workers at a disadvantage, however. When police arrest sex workers, they often threaten them into using their phones to lure out their friends, who are then also arrested. Another disadvantage of belonging to a cell is that one could be called to bail out an arrested friend or to pay a bribe to secure a friend's release. When sex worker Naomi's friend was arrested, she did not have bribe money with her. The police thus detained the friend, threatening to arraign her in court the following morning. To raise money to free her friend, Naomi gave unprotected oral sex to one of her long-standing clients in a dark alley. Sometimes the night guards and taxi drivers who act as lookouts for sex workers also demand unprotected sex as payment from them. Lookouts demanding cash payments played on sex workers' desperation for money, increasing their vulnerability for abuse and unprotected sex.

Striking deals with law enforcement agents was a second major strategy that Nairobi's sex workers used to prevent arrest. This tactic involved various activities that led law enforcement officers to ignore sex workers during patrols, alert them to impending raids, avoid the areas where sex workers operated, or secure their release when arrested. Deals could be secured with both junior and senior law enforcement officers. Several means were used to get the police and law enforcement agents of the municipal councils to cooperate with sex workers, including protection fees given to officers through sex workers' organizations or through proprietors of pubs and bars where sex workers operated.

Sex workers in one of the pubs covered during this study contributed money weekly to secure police protection. Reports of granting police officers sexual favors to secure their protection and cooperation were also elicited. For example, Martha had befriended a high-ranking policeman as a precautionary measure, and Joan, an informal leader of sex workers, sent a different sex worker every week to a patrol commander as a protection fee. In Joan's words: "Last time he called that . . . he wanted two girls for himself and his friend. He will sometimes call off a patrol because of us or tell us where to operate."

As with membership in information cells, pacts with law enforcement officers had their unique problems. In order to get the money to pay conniving officers, sex workers sometimes resorted to risky sexual practices. Sex workers who paid officers with sexual favors also often did so under dangerous conditions, and such encounters usually involved unprotected sex. Joan told us that the commander to whom she sends girls always asks for "clean girls." "He will tell me, 'Hey, you know I do not use condoms at my age, so send me very clean girls or you will regret [it]; send me your new girls.'" Sex workers often paid dearly when they failed to meet the expectation of officers or fell out of favor with them. Kitty's pub was ransacked because of a quarrel she had with a high-ranking officer who had been offering her protection. Following the raid, Kitty attempted to reconcile with him.

Sex workers also dealt with the risk of arrest by working in groups, avoiding alcohol while at work, working in well-lit areas and familiar places, and using male scouts, called *mabeshites*. The sex worker raids, which I witnessed, drove home the importance of sex workers using these methods to deal with the problem of policing. Law enforcement officers in Nairobi often worked in groups of three to five plainclothesmen. Because government or police vehicles are easily identified when they pull up in the well-lit areas of the street where sex workers operate, undercover agents often used privately registered vehicles. When using official vehicles, they would park them a distance away. They would then approach the street where sex workers were soliciting clients, some from one end of the street and some from the other. Usually they walked casually, pretending to be clients, passersby, or even drunken vagrants. Law enforcement agents also often left their guns or batons in the vehicles, as those easily gave them away. Because they worked in well-lit streets and corners, sex workers were often able to evaluate persons approaching their work sites from afar and flee if suspicious. Many of my respondents admitted that they could tell whether an approaching man was an enforcement officer, even when the person pretended to be drunk.

Using private vehicles to raid sex workers also makes patrol officers easily identifiable. When a bus or van occupied by three or four men pulls up near sex workers, they flee. Working in well-lit areas enables sex workers to identify suspicious private vehicles before they reach them. "Often, they hire *small* buses, and we . . . know that men who come to pick women do not normally come in buses, so once a bus comes around where we work, we know there is something fishy." Working in groups thus enables sex workers to pool their skills and street-related knowledge to assist one another in avoiding violence and arrest.

Operating in familiar and strategic places ensures that sex workers are in areas they know well, where they can hide or easily escape. Crossroads and areas where taxis gather are among the strategic places where Nairobi's sex workers like to operate. When raided at a crossroad, sex workers can escape arrest by running in different directions. Where taxis gather, they can disappear into taxicabs, with drivers they already know. *Mabeshites* also alert sex workers to the presence of patrol officers or suspicious persons. Sometimes, when sex workers are arrested, *mabeshites* will emerge and claim to be their husbands or boyfriends. In one raid I witnessed along Koinange Street, a plain-clothed officer snuck up behind a sex worker and arrested her. Her shouts attracted two *mabeshites* who physically forced the officer to release the sex worker.

Still, all these strategies have their downside. Working in groups increases competition among sex workers, which is worsened by a reported disinclination among men, especially those who are wealthy and well known, to come to brightly-lit areas where sex workers prefer to operate. "What if you go there and your fellow church member or workmate sees you?" one male client asked me. Further, when sex workers operated in groups, many returned home without clients or were forced to accept cheap and often risky propositions from clients. *Mabeshites* were also paid, sometimes with unprotected sex, increasing sex workers' vulnerability to STI transmission.

Conclusion

Theories of agency extol the human capacity for inventiveness and resistance, assuming that people's agentive strategies most often present them with real possibilities for increased life choices and opportunities. This chapter demonstrates that this assumption is simply irrelevant in Nairobi, where sex workers' practices for negotiating policing only add to the risks and vulnerabilities they face. The By-Laws of the City of Nairobi of 1960 criminalize sex work, exposing sex workers to harassment and mistreatment by law enforcement officials. To navigate the activities of law enforcement agents, Nairobi's sex workers joined information networks, made deals with and bribed police officers, worked in groups and in well-lit areas, avoided unfamiliar places, and contracted male scouts. But these strategies ultimately heightened their vulnerability, increased their desperation, and pressured them to engage in risky sex.

A dynamic of the agentive strategies of Nairobi's sex workers for defying arrest, which rarely receives appropriate attention in the contemporary literature, is the potentially harmful consequences of such strategies. The tactics sex workers in Nairobi employed to resist state control actually increased their vulnerability to risk and harm, and also exposed them to further exploitation. Clearly agency offers a critical tool for understanding the resistance practices of politically vulnerable groups, but, contrary to the common refrain in the literature, agency may not always benefit those who express it.

NOTES

1. *Malaya*, meaning "worthless," is the Swahili word for a sex worker and is always used derogatorily. The term may have been derived from the dark brownish-red garnet stones found in Eastern and Central Africa that were once considered valueless and were discarded in favor of the more richly colored pyrope and rhodolite garnets. *Umalaya* refers to the act of selling sex.

2. Pumwani, one of the oldest settlements in Nairobi, was established in 1922 by the colonial government as a "Native Location." Colonial records state that the settlement was established as a first measure to curb native prostitution (White 1990).

10

Prostitution in
Contemporary Rio de Janeiro

THADDEUS GREGORY BLANCHETTE
AND ANA PAULA DA SILVA

A Trip Down Rua Buenos Aires

One way to appreciate the diversity of prostitution in Rio de Janeiro is to walk through the downtown area. Starting near the beginning of Rua Buenos Aires, one can find five *termas*—heterosexual saunas catering to the day trade of foreign tourists and carioca[1] businessmen. Each *terma* is typically composed of a sauna and bathing area, a *whiskeria* or bar, and a discotheque. The men pay 20–50 Reais[2] to swap their business suits for bathrobes. Inside, anywhere from fifteen to sixty young women are available for sex in rented "cabins" at 100 to 300R$ for forty to sixty minutes of sex. One-third to one-fourth of this money is taken by the house as "room rental fees." There are better and worse *termas* in the business district, but all of them are clean, safe, and relatively expensive.

Crossing over Av. Rio Branco, the "Wall Street" of Rio, one comes to a commercial district similar to the immediately preceding area. Here one finds small *privés* and massage parlors—rented apartments or offices in which two to six women offer forty to sixty minutes of sexual services for about 55–150R$. The clients are middle-management and skilled workers looking for sex on their lunch break or after work. The *privés* are small but quite clean and safe. They charge no entrance fee and do not have bars or other diversions: clients come for sex only.

This stretch of Rua Buenos Aires, however, also has a series of places which carioca clients call, in a pun on the English term "fast food," *fast fodas* [fucks]: small brothels generally situated in decrepit nineteenth-century townhouses that cater to working-class men. These houses typically charge 1 Real per minute for fifteen to twenty minutes of hot, sweaty sex in tiny cubicles without air conditioning. *Fast fodas* range from surprisingly good to hellishly bad in terms of their safety and sanitary conditions, but they all tend to be crowded in the late afternoon, with five to ten women on duty and twice that number of clients waiting their turn. Sometimes a single building will contain several *fast fodas*.

Continuing on down Rua Buenos Aires and crossing Rua Uruguaiana, one leaves the business district and enters the SAARA popular market: sixteen square blocks of commerce crammed into tents and the *Centro's* ubiquitous decaying townhouses. Here one finds *fast fodas* and *privés* but also encounters more traditional *casas*, or brothels. These are relatively spacious and often offer strip shows for clients, who are young, working-class men and middle-aged merchants. Prices hover around 40–80R$ for forty minutes of sex, though the *fast foda* option is often available. *Casas* have anywhere from five to fifteen women on duty and, although they are less crowded than *privés*, they also tend to be more precarious structurally. Recently a downtown *casa* had to close because the facade of its 150-year-old building collapsed.

In the SAARA one also finds prostitutes on the street in three main concentrations: near Praça Tiradentes, in the Praça da República, and around the Central do Brasil railroad station. These women are typically thirty years old and older and alternate between streetwalking and sitting in front of bars, drinking and chatting with friends. When they find clients, they retire to nearby rundown hotels, where rooms can be rented by the half-hour. The women charge from 30–60R$ for thirty minutes of sex. Clients tend to be the same sort of men who frequent the *casas* and *fast fodas*, though the women of the Praça da República specialize in selling sex to senior citizens.

Finally, at the margins of the SAARA one can find a new sort of establishment in Rio de Janeiro: the swingers' club. Only one of these has been established in the region, but its popularity indicates that others may soon appear. The swingers' club is the BYOB of commercial sex. Men show up with "dates": generally prostitutes contracted via call girl services or off the streets. The couple pays around 40–60R$ to enter the club (which sports a disco, bar, showers, and several small bedrooms) and can have sex with anyone who is willing.

Rua Buenos Aires ends at the Praça da República, but if one were to cross the park and continue in a straight line, other interesting places come into view. One kilometer further on is the Cidade Nova, Rio's administrative center, built in the 1970s and 1980s on top of the Mangue, the city's traditional working-class red light district. In the 1970s and 1980s the Mangue was leveled to make room for the new municipal government complex and a subway station. Today no prostitutes walk its streets, but Rio's imposing City Hall and attendant Annex are known as the "Big Whore" (*Piranhão*) and the "Big Pimp" (*Cafetão*).

Part of the Mangue relocated to Vila Mimosa (VM) in 1987 (Pasini 2005). VM is located an additional kilometer ahead and slightly to the north of our imaginary line extending from Rua Buenos Aires. It is a warren of small *casas*, strip joints, and cut-rate *termas* established in and around an abandoned warehouse. Some three thousand women work there (Simões 2010), although only about three hundred to five hundred are present at any given time. Unlike downtown, VM comes alive in the evening, frequented by men looking for cheap entertainment. Prices are around 25R$ for fifteen to twenty minutes of sex in tiny cubicles, with 5–10R$ of this going to the bar or club owner for a rental fee and a condom. VM is often considered to be one of the least hygienic and most dangerous commercial sex venues in town, but several street scenes, *fast fodas*, and *casas* downtown are even worse.

But Vila Mimosa is not the last stop for commercial sex. Continuing on a few more blocks, one comes to an area where interstate highways merge with the municipal road network. Here, near the Quinta da Boa Vista, street-walkers converge in the early evening to meet the needs of taxi drivers and long-distance truckers. This is a street prostitution scene that is considered by sex workers and clients alike to be one of the most dangerous in the city. Recently a police raid caught three children selling sex near the Quinta, allegedly under the control of drug gangs from nearby shantytowns ("Tráfico prostitui menores" 2009). It would be a mistake, however, to believe that sex here is necessarily cheap. Though tricks can be bought for 30R$, women can charge as much as 100R$ for an hour in nearby hotels.

Our imaginary jaunt should give the reader an appreciation of the size and variety of Rio de Janeiro's commercial sex market. The downtown area and the associated port district, however, contain only about a third of the prostitution venues that we have discovered in the city. Another large concentration can be found in the beach neighborhoods of Ipanema and Copacabana. Here the *privés*, massage parlors, brothels, and streetwalkers that meet the sexual needs of local clients are intermixed with *termas*, nightclubs, and restaurants geared toward the tourist trade. Meanwhile, out in the suburbs, cut-rate brothels and *termas* abound, and a growing series of Internet-based agencies send call girls all across the metropolitan region.

Rio de Janeiro boasts a large and complicated commercial sexual scene, but the reports that have been written about it (Ribeiro 2002; Blanchette and DaSilva 2005; Pasini 2005) tend to concentrate on one particular aspect or area of sex work in the city. Rio de Janeiro, by any definition, is not just a singular and homogeneous sexscape (Brennan 2004, 16) but is better conceived of as a series of overlapping and intertwining commercial sex scenes of almost bewildering variety and complexity.

As pointed out by urbanists such as Mauricio de Abreu (1997), Gilberto Velho (1994), and Lícia Valadares (2005), Rio de Janeiro has long contained structural inequalities along various axes of identity (race, class, and gender). It also hosts multiple migratory movements encompassing foreigners who come to Rio, Brazilians who leave it for overseas destinations, and Brazilians who arrive in the city from elsewhere. The result has been the creation of prostitution venues for every type of consumer imaginable and the maintenance of these venues over the long term, in some cases over generations.

The age and persistence of the commercial sexual market in Rio, as well as its penetration into the city's nightlife and politics, has given sex work an intergenerational character. Older prostitutes often retire to become madams, or "agents" for younger workers, and the general fund of sex work knowledge grows and is passed on from one generation to another. It is notable that the city's two main sex work organizations have been created by madams and prostitutes, both groups over the retirement age. Although this in no way resolves the inequalities that make up Rio as a sexscape, it does create a situation in which sex workers are relatively well informed and pragmatically equipped to deal with such inequalities—and often bend them to their favor.

Prostitution as Option

Why do women in Rio de Janeiro work as prostitutes? Our informants give one main reason: it is the best way to earn enough income to survive and improve their socioeconomic status. All our female informants report having access to other forms of labor, often with retirement and health benefits. Many of these jobs, however, pay the equivalent of a Brazilian minimum wage for forty weekly hours of work. Prostitution pays more, sometimes much more.

Three types of jobs are constantly cited by our informants as common alternatives to prostitution: paid domestic labor as a maid, unpaid domestic labor as a housewife, or work as a supermarket checkout clerk. These jobs are readily available, but our informants describe prostitution as more lucrative and often more agreeable. Two other advantages of prostitution, we were told, are the relatively flexible hours and the possibility, though remote, of making a large amount of money from wealthy clients. We thus believe that one motivation behind prostitution is *ambition*, given that, of all the typically feminine forms of labor in the city, only prostitution and marriage hold out hope for socioeconomic ascension. In this sense, as anthropologist Dawn Pankonien has pointed out (2009), prostitution holds a distinct advantage over marriage in that it does not tie a woman's future to any one man in particular but let's her "play the field."

Many of our informants are married or have been married. Still, they do not see marriage as a substitute for prostitution. One reason is that they distrust men's capacity to sustain them. In the words of Wilma, a thirty-five-year-old white prostitute in a Copacabana nightclub, "Men promise a lot of things, but can't keep their promises."

> What I do out here in the street isn't any bit different from what I did at home when I was married. . . . It was a job, just like this here. Actually, that's a lie: it was a *duty*. And you don't make money off of a duty. Here, at least I get paid for what I do.

Women also recognize that a single wage is not enough to support a family. This leads some women to engage in sex work when they are married. According to Dara, a forty-year-old black streetwalker in Praça Tiradentes, "My husband can't cover all our bills on his own":

> The days are gone when a man made enough for a woman to stay at home and take care of the kids. . . . At least [working] like I do, I earn enough to help out at home and I still have enough time to take care of my daughter . . . [My husband] knows what I do and knows I do it not because I enjoy it. I've already told him: I'll stop whenever you want, but you better be able to carry this whole thing by yourself, because I'm not going to be able to find another job that pays as well as this and lets me stay home six days a week.

For Dara, prostitution complements family life; it is the only way that she feels she can adequately enjoy a "traditional" domestic existence. Many of our informants have offered similar observations.

Even well-paid, conventional employment may not compare favorably with prostitution. For example, Dara and Wilma turn tricks at the basic rate of 1 Real (U.S.$0.50) per minute and generally earn 20R$ per trick, with twenty-five tricks—slightly more than eight hours of work—earning them the equivalent of a monthly minimum wage. Thirty-one-year-old Vânia, on the other hand, has been in the sex trade for nine years and works downtown at the Wagon Wheel *termas*, having quit her job as a real estate agent to work as a prostitute:

My old job paid well, when it paid. . . . But there were periods in which nothing came in. A friend told me about the Help disco in Copa[cabana]. I'd go there and make 200R$ per trick. It helped a lot and I could still work as an agent . . . Then I was offered a job at the Unicorn *termas*. I only made 160 Reais a trick there and had to work every day, but it was safer. Three years later I came here [to the Wagon Wheel] because I fought with the owner [of the Unicorn]. Now I'm thinking of quitting whoring and going back to real estate because I'm getting to be too old to be a whore. Except this time, I have my apartment and my car, everything paid for by whoring. Now, I can get through the bad times.

Vânia's account testifies to the economic logic of prostitution and its configuration as a career. Vânia is middle-class, white, and holds a university degree. She initially engaged in freelance sexual work at Help discotheque in order to meet economic crises caused by the irregular income flow of her job as a real estate agent. She later abandoned her freelance and regular jobs to work full-time in a *termas*, the Unicorn, making less per trick but gaining in security and client turnover. Vânia decided to leave the Unicorn because of an argument with her boss. The misunderstandings between Vânia and her boss may have been affected by Vânia's relatively advanced age for *termas* work, as the Unicorn is among the most expensive *termas* in Rio and has a constant turnover of young female employees.

Vânia's tale seems to follow the pattern of a decadent career, as described by sociologist Paul G. Cressy (2008 [1932]). According to Cressy, age exercises a downwardly mobile pressure on individual careers in occupational fields that value youth. An older woman among younger women will thus have to work harder to attract the same number of clients. This dilemma has two solutions: change careers or move to a less exclusive venue. The final result of this process is "reduction" to employment in the cheapest houses. In the context of carioca prostitution, this process may lead to work in the streets around the Central do Brasil or the Quinta da Boa Vista. Vânia contemplates a return to her former profession as real estate agent, but this time she feels that the agency career will be viable because prostitution has allowed her to stabilize her economic situation.

Neither marriage nor other employment can thus necessarily substitute for sex work as a means of earning a living in Rio de Janeiro. Vânia's case is relatively rare among our informants, who normally do not leave middle-class jobs for prostitution. But we have encountered numerous middle-class women at the bottom rungs of ascending professional careers who also work as prostitutes. During the week before Carnival 2010, for example, we met three university students, a secretary, and an intern at the Bank of Brazil turning tricks in Copacabana.

The majority of the women we interviewed live in the working- and lower-middle-class carioca suburbs and not the city's many shantytowns. They are often engaged in long- and medium-term plans for social mobility that include acquiring property or achieving a professional education. Prostitutes in Rio de Janeiro are demoralized as a class, and current legislation regarding sex work is contradictory: adults can prostitute themselves, but "sexual exploitation," understood as third parties profiting from prostitution, is prohibited. What this actually means is debatable. For example, a traditional *casa* where women work while giving a set percentage of their earnings to the madam is illegal. A bar used by prostitutes to meet clients prior to retiring to other places for sex is not considered illegal. In practice, however, the *casa* may have police partners among its owners, whereas the bar does not. Alternatively, the *casa* may be located in a rundown commercial or industrial district, whereas the bar may be in a middle-class, beachfront neighborhood. These conditions mean that pressure to crack down upon "sexual exploitation" will probably result in raids on the bar rather than on the *casa*. Simply put, the city and police rarely define "sexual exploitation" in accordance with concern over violations of prostitutes' rights.

Effective regulation of the conditions under which sex workers operate thus becomes very difficult in Rio de Janeiro. Sex workers' rights are routinely violated by the owners of the clubs, *termas*, escort agencies, and *casas,* all of which profit—directly or otherwise—from the sale of sex. Although pimping is illegal in Rio and its more brutal manifestations seem to be repressed by the police, a series of agents manage to extract a surplus from sex work.

Because of the legal restrictions on profiting from the sexual labor of others, prostitutes in Rio de Janeiro are formally defined by their employers as performing a different kind of work or, in fact, as independent. In either case, the prostitute has control of her body and of the decision whether to have sex or not. The production of a commercial sexual act, however, implies the use of means of production that are typically not controlled by the prostitute. For example, a prostitute needs a place where she can meet with clients. This involves the creation of what Robert Park and Ernest Burgess (1984 [1925], 45–48) call a "moral region," a space where a distinct moral code prevails. Such spaces must minimally attract clients, offering anonymity and some degree of choice in sexual partners; they can be virtual, such as an Internet site, or even interspersed with other spaces, as is the case of much of Copacabana, where "normal" bars also serve as meeting places for prostitution, but they must exist for prostitution to occur. In Rio de Janeiro, surplus is generally extracted from prostitution by third parties through the control of these moral regions where prostitution is tolerated or permitted.

Our research has revealed 278 prostitution venues in the city of Rio de Janeiro, 58 of which we have personally visited. For the purposes of this chapter, the term "venue" is understood to mean a single address or cohesive moral region. Thus Vila Mimosa, which has some twenty-five separate clubs, houses, bars, and *termas* qualifies as a single venue. If we were to consider each discrete prostitution space that exists in venues like these, our total count of prostitution venues would rise above 500. These venues are generally "hiding in plain sight," as that can easily be found in normal, everyday neighborhoods. With the exception of VM, they are not segregated into their own specific spaces.

Prostitution venues in Rio are grouped into seven main regions. Region I is virtual and composed of call girl services and agencies operating over the Internet. Region II is clustered around the North Zone suburb of Madueira. Region III takes in another cluster in the neighborhoods of Tijuca, Saens Pena, and Maracaña, and this region runs into Region IV, grouped around Praça da Bandeira, Vila Mimosa, and the Quinta da Boa Vista. Region V includes downtown and the port district, and Region VI is composed of the neighborhoods of Copacabana, Leblon, Ipanema, São Conrado, and Jardim Botânico. Finally, Region VII is made up of the southern coastal neighborhoods of Barra da Tijuca and Recreio, plus adjacent areas. Table 1 gives a breakdown of the venues by region, subregion, and type.

Sex Work and the State in Rio de Janeiro

State intervention in prostitution in Rio has a long history. Historian Magali Vainfas (1985) outlined the nineteenth-century discourses that led to attempts to confine "common" prostitution to the old Mangue district. Historian Sueann Caulfield (1997) detailed the resulting division in the organization of sex work in the city, with the Mangue established as the working-man's red light district and Lapa, the "Montemarte of Rio de Janeiro," enshrined as the Bohemian and tourist alternative. As Caulfield reports, the social boundaries of both areas were patrolled by the city's police, who took it upon themselves to determine which women fit where:

> Police may have been unable to control prostitution completely, but they were able to concentrate some of the most conspicuous sex workers to

TABLE 1
Prostitution Venue By Region, Subregion, and Type

Region (Subregion)	Total	C. Girls	Termas	Privés	Massage	Brothels	Closed	Bar/ Rest.	Beach	Street	Open	Mxd	N. Class
I. Virtual	54	54					54				0		
II. Madureira	9		5			4	9				0		
III. Tijuca	7			5	2		7				0		
IV. Pça Bandeira	8		5	1		1	7			1	1		
V. Downtown	90												
Port	18		7	3	2	5	17			1	1		
Cent. Do Brasil	5		2			2	4			1	1		
Tiradentes	17		2	3		7	12	1		2	3		2
Rio Branco	40		10	9	13	8	40				0		
Lapa	10		2	3			5	2		3	5		

Region (Subregion)	Total	C. Girls	Termas	Privés	Massage	Brothels	Closed	Bar/ Rest.	Beach	Street	Open	Mxd	N. Class
VI. South Zone	70												
Copacabana Prado Jr.	28		9	6		1	16	11		1	12		
Copa. Siq. Campos	21		7	2	4	1	14	3		1	4		3
Copa. Posts 5 e 6	6				1		1	2	1		3	1	1
Ipanema	10		1		1		2	7	1		8		
Leblon	3						0	3			3		
JD. Botânico	1		1				1				0		
São Conrado	1						0				0		1
VII. B. da Tijuca	12		5	2	2		9	3	1	1	2		1
Unassigned	29		9	5	2	5	21	3	1	3	7		1
Total	279	54	65	39	27	34	219	32	4	14	50	1	9

areas designated for "tolerated prostitution," such as the Mangue. . . . Prostitutes who were considered less coarse, "whiter" and more attractive gained a firmer hold on higher income markets, and generally chose to avoid Mangue. They worked instead in the more discrete brothels or private apartments or houses known as *rendez-vous* in Lapa or Glória, an adjacent upper crust zone. Most prostitutes, however, continued to work clandestinely in "moralized" areas, hiding from or bribing patrol officers or waiting out the short-lived morality campaigns. (Caulfield 1997, 91–92).

During the 1940s and again in the 1950s both the Mangue and Lapa were raided (Leite 1993) and finally were leveled by urban renewal projects during the military dictatorship in the 1970s and 1980s (Abreu 1997). Working class prostitution moved to the port region and the area around the Central do Brasil railway station. Vila Mimosa was also born out of the ashes of the Mangue. Meanwhile, Lapa's "chic" prostitutes followed the bohemians as middle-class nightlife shifted to Copacabana during the Bossa Nova era of the 1950s and 1960s.

Today we can still discern the general outlines of the split caused by state intervention in the division of most of the city's prostitution venues into two main zones based around downtown and Copacabana. A look at Table 1 confirms that the majority of "open" venues are situated in the South Zone, whereas the Central Zone is mostly made up of "closed" venues. The class and ethnic divisions between these two sides of the market no longer apply, however. Women of all ethnic groups work in the downtown venue, for example, which contains some of the city's most exclusive and expensive *termas,* and also in the South Zone with its cheap *privés* and street scenes.

From the 1980s on, the military dictatorship then ruling Brazil was in retreat and liberal movements were in full flower. Sex workers themselves were resisting police repression (Leite 2009), but as anthropologist Adriana Piscitelli remarks (2008, 38–39), prostitution was not on the feminist agenda in Brazil. Rio's sexual market thus thrived in relative peace, obtaining the general configuration described above, with all venues attempting to avoid the legal definition of "exploitation of prostitution" and stay within the bounds of the legally permissible. We can thus say that although "pimping," in its more sensational and brutal aspect, certainly still occurs in individual cases, it is not a structurally significant component of the market in general. In fact, prostitution activist Gabriela Leite explained in an interview with the authors that "traditionally, nothing is more likely to get a carioca cop motivated to arrest someone than the accusation that there's a pimp who's abusing a prostitute."

Today, however, things seem to be on the verge of change. Interest in the repression of prostitution has been renewed by political pressure resulting from social panic (Cohen 1972) over the trafficking of women (see Piscitelli 2008; Grupo Davida 2005), by the sexual exploitation of children (Amar 2009), and by the subsequent conflation of sexual tourism as synonymous with these two crimes (Blanchette and DaSilva 2005, 2008). Although the sale of sex continues to be legal (or, more apt, "not illegal"), governments have increasingly used zoning ordinances, eminent-domain law, and police harassment to curb prostitution or channel it into areas where it will not intermix with tourism and middle-class life. As anthropologist Paul Amar (2009) pointed out, these political pressures have resulted in an expanded notion of "sexual exploitation" and the creation of the first official vice squad in Rio in the last seventy years.

Prostitution was a hot issue in the 2008 mayoral race, with winner Eduardo Paes comparing the legalization of sex work to the institutionalization of pimps ("Paes se diz contra a legalização da prostituição" 2008). This climate has been exacerbated by the fact that Rio will host the 2014 World Cup and the 2016 Summer Olympics. Recent declarations by federal tourism minister Marta Suplicy (Fussy 2008) indicate that Rio's preparation for the games will include the repression of prostitution. Sex workers in Rio thus face a situation where both local and federal government see the sale of sex as a "problem" that must be eliminated or, at the very least, discretely managed. Rio has even gone so far as to contract former New York mayor Rudy Giuliani as a security consultant for the Olympic Games (UOL 2009).

Part of this campaign has been the systematic harassment of visible prostitution venues, especially those in middle-class areas or regions targeted for games-related urban renewal. Café Dunas, a beachside *termas* in Barra da Tijuca, repeatedly has been closed for alleged "health code violations," which include the discovery of a cockroach in its kitchen. Meanwhile, the eighty-two-year-old Alhambra in Praça Mauá has been fined heavily for maintaining an illegally large neon marquee (in place now for close to a decade). Several *privés* along Avenida Rio Branco have been raided and closed for not operating in accordance with their rental contracts. In all these cases, none of the laws regarding prostitution and sexual exploitation has been applied; instead, minor code violations, normally ignored in other businesses, have been cited in order to close down commercial sex venues. Another front in the antiprostitution campaign involves the use of eminent-domain law. Praça Mauá is scheduled to be transformed into an entertainment and museum complex, removing some fifteen *termas* and *casas* (Goes 2010). Vila Mimosa and Praça da Bandeira will be leveled to make way for a bullet train station, eliminating in one blow the last vestiges of the old Mangue and the largest remaining commercial sex venue in the city ("Vila Mimosa no caminho do trem" 2010). The State of Rio de Janeiro's recent expropriation of the Help discotheque, however, has been a paradigm of the kinds of changes "urban renewal" will bring about.

The Help discotheque scrupulously followed the law regarding sexual exploitation. Minors were not allowed in the club nor were drugs or sexual activities. The women who frequented the disco were treated not as employees but guests, exactly like the men. House security was tight, and fights were immediately stopped and the instigators expelled. The hundreds of women we have talked to over the years who used Help to meet clients were universal in their praise for the establishment and in their claims that management did not touch prostitutes' earnings. Close to five hundred women a night would show up at the disco during high season, and thousands of women used the facility.

Help, unfortunately, was also sitting on prime beachfront real estate. Claiming that he was "transforming a brothel into a temple of carioca culture" (Revista Terra 2009), Governor Sergio Cabral employed eminent domain law to confiscate the lot for a new Museum of Sound and Imagery. On January 7, 2010, the disco closed its doors after twenty-five years of business. Within weeks, the building was leveled, but construction on the new museum has yet to begin.

Since Help closed, prostitutes have migrated to other venues in Rio and elsewhere. Some have gone to São Paulo; others have crossed the bay to Niteroi or have gone two hours up the coast to the petroleum boomtown of Macaé. A greater number have moved down to the Prado Junior region of Copacabana and, in particular, to the Veranda Bar where, during Carnival 2010, more than 600 prostitutes and tourists congregated nightly. The bar's capacity is 150, and crowds would pour out onto the surrounding sidewalk, causing public disturbances. The crush was so thick that the waiters and bouncers often could not move about. In contrast to the calm and controlled scene at Help, Veranda Bar was utter chaos. Drug dealing took place on the nearby street, and child prostitutes worked the crowds. A few child prostitutes have always been present on Copacabana, but they were kept away from Help by the disco's security staff. At Veranda, during Carnival, bouncers could barely get out of the bar, let alone police the area around it. The situation became so bad, with so many women fighting for so little space, that by early March many of the immigrants from Help were already looking for other venues. In this endeavor they have been "assisted" by people whom the prostitutes qualify as "pimps" and who began frequenting Copacabana months before Help's closure. As one of our informants put it:

There are a lot of pimps on Copa now. Militia types. Two nights ago, an off-duty civil policeman drew his pistol on an off-duty fireman and shot a bunch of holes in the bar awning. The sharks are circling.

The unusual juxtaposition of the terms "pimps" and "militia" is relevant. Rio's "militia" are vigilante gangs based in the city's outlying working-class suburbs and shantytowns who charge protection fees from local merchants and become the ipso facto rulers of their region. Militia members are often off-duty, retired, or fired members of the city's public security forces. In many cases they run nightclubs and bars in their areas, and rumors circulate that militia-run brothels are being established along the main highways leading into Rio. On several occasions since Help has closed, we have seen Brazilian men (who until then had been an almost negligible presence in the Copa tourism prostitution scene), sporting clothing styles and tattoos typical of the security forces, talking to women at the Veranda. It is these men whom our informants point out as "pimps" and "militia," and it is in this context that the informant's comment above regarding "circling sharks" must be understood. Apparently the post-Help exodus from Copa has caught the attention of recruiters for gang-run commercial sex venues.

Post-Help Veranda, in other words, is a good example of the chaotic and exploitative commercial sexual scene that the city and state governments say they wish to avoid but which has been created almost entirely by the forced closure of Rio's largest, safest, and least exploitive commercial sex venue. With the World Cup and the Olympics on the horizon, Rio now seems poised to repeat the past. Sueann Caulfield's remarks about the birth of the Mangue in the 1920s seem to prefigure the situation that the city faces today:

Brazil's desire to portray itself as a modern nation involved obscuring prostitution control in its capital city, Rio de Janeiro. How could Brazil regulate prostitution and still be considered modern? While prostitution became an astonishingly frequent topic of debate among diverse groups of public officials and professional elites, control measures in Rio were never clearly delineated. Official regulation was considered by legislators to contradict both Catholic morality and civil liberties guaranteed by Brazilian law. Nevertheless, pressures to clean up the city so that elite families and foreign visitors would not have to view prostitutes forced the police to follow extralegal policies. Their actions, including the relocation of some prostitutes to less visible and less desirable parts of the city, reflected the racial, ethnic, and class prejudices that informed elite ideals for the nation. (Caulfield 1997, 86)

That the new wave of repression and urban renewal will eliminate prostitution in Rio de Janeiro is highly unlikely. It is, however, apparently forcing it out of many long-established venues where sex workers had achieved some degree of autonomy and an enviable market position. The result of these policies, if the experience of Help is anything to go by, will be the reorganization in the city's commercial sex market. As obvious sex venues in middle-class and tourism areas are labeled an embarrassment to the city, sex work will be pushed to the margins of town and into less tourism-oriented areas, reducing profitability and forcing women under the control of new club owners in areas where they are isolated from the population at large. Prostitute-rights activist Gabriela Leite (2009, 64) sees this as a very worrisome tendency:

> For decades, prostitutes have been part of the carioca urban scene, mixing freely with families and bohemians alike. Different from many cities in Brazil, Rio has never had a delimited red light district. Vila Mimosa and the Mangue are the exceptions that prove the rule because they were never able to keep us confined to those areas. When prostitutes are pushed out of public sight and mind, however, it becomes easier to stigmatize and control them. A woman who works a downtown *privé* is literally six meters away from help: a woman in a closed club set out along the highway or segregated in a shantytown has little contact with anyone but pimps, clients and other whores. She's easily eliminated if she becomes a problem.

By pushing commercial sex venues out of the public eye, the government of Rio de Janeiro seems to believe that it is "making the city safe for families and tourists"—two groups that have never before been threatened by the presence of prostitutes. The practical effect, however, is that the government is intensifying the stigmatization of sex workers and forcing the sexual market to consolidate under the tighter control of third-party exploiters (namely, "pimps) in venues farther removed from public oversight. If current trends continue, we can expect to see another division of the carioca sexual market, with the upper-end and tourist-oriented call girls driven to virtual venues on the Internet or to a handful of discrete, expensive *termas*, while lower-end, working class prostitution is driven into the city's margins and shantytowns.

Fortunately for prostitution rights activists, this process has just begun and may yet be resisted.

NOTES

The authors thank Steven Berg, Sherri McCutchen, and Drs. Susan Dewey and Sean Mitchell for their work in reading through the rough draft of this article and providing useful suggestions. We also thank Sexual Policies Watch for funding the production of the original version of this chapter.

1. "Carioca" is the adjectival form of "Rio de Janeiro."

2. For the period between 2006 and 2010, the exchange rate has hovered around 2R$ per USD. The prices quoted here are current for June 2009.

11

Prevailing Voices in Debates over Child Prostitution

HEATHER MONTGOMERY

In the early 1990s child prostitution became a central focus of worldwide concern. Concentrating on South East Asia, especially Thailand, the issue was analyzed in a particular way, which blamed the problem on Western men traveling abroad to countries with lax law enforcement and taking advantage of the poverty and gullibility of local children and their parents. A consensus on the nature of the problem was quickly reached between the Thai government, which was horrified to see the country described in the Western media as a "Disneyland for pedophiles" (Ehrlich 1994), Thai nongovernmental organizations (NGOs), which campaigned on behalf of the children, and their Western counterparts. Eventually, too, Western governments would come to support anti–child prostitution campaigners by bowing to pressure and passing extraterritorial legislation allowing the prosecution and imprisonment of men in their home countries for sexual crimes committed against children abroad (Montgomery 2010).

Such unanimity of purpose and understanding was both intellectually and morally satisfying and, indeed, in the face of some of the horror stories coming out of Thailand, completely justified. Yet the image of the child prostitute presented in these campaigns did not tell the full story, and other children, whose lives and experiences did not fit into the prescribed pattern, were overlooked, ignored, and silenced. This chapter examines the way in which the image of the "perfect" child prostitute was constructed in Thailand and the West, comparing this to a group of children, with whom I did research, who worked as prostitutes and whose lives did not fit the ideologically expedient stereotypes.

Creating the Context

Despite its reputation for sexual license, all forms of prostitution are, in fact, illegal in Thailand (Montgomery 2001a). It is also evident, however, that prostitution is implicitly condoned, and various red light districts, such as

Patpong in Bangkok or The Strip in Pattaya, exist as proof that law enforcement is not so much lenient as nonexistent. Outside the tourist areas the sex industry is even more endemic, and it is rare to find even the smallest towns or villages that do not have a brothel (Fordham 2005). The reasons behind the pervasiveness of the sex industry have been a source of much debate. Some NGOs prefer to see prostitution as a foreign problem, imported into Thailand by outsiders with minimal Thai involvement. Others have argued that foreign influences have simply been mapped onto preexisting social institutions and that prostitution was long regulated, taxed, and implicitly condoned by the Thai authorities before becoming criminalized in 1960 as part of a wider plan to rid the country of "undesirables" such as beggars and prostitutes (Montgomery 2001a).

Evidence strongly suggests that a thriving indigenous market for sex dates back hundreds of years in Thailand (Boonchalaksi and Guest 1994), but also undoubtedly true is that the influx of large numbers of foreigners into Thailand in the 1960s dramatically changed the nature of the Thai sex industry. During the Vietnam War the Thai government allowed the United States to station troops in Thailand where American servicemen were permitted to use Thailand as a base for "R&R" (rest and recreation). The large numbers of young Western men with money to spend quickly led to the creation of bars and brothels catering to foreigners, and it was during this period that a recognizable industry was first established to sell sex to foreigners. After 1975 the troops were gone, but they had left behind the sex industry's infrastructure in the form of clubs and bars, as well as the stereotype of beautiful, pliant, and docile Thai women who would fulfill every sexual fantasy for a small price.

This infrastructure was easily harnessed to the needs of the Thai state, which wanted to develop and modernize the economy. With money no longer coming in from the Americans and with a very limited manufacturing and industrial base, Thailand needed other sources of revenue; like in other developing countries in the 1970s, tourism was viewed as the way forward, and, despite the illegality of prostitution, sex tourism was seen as part of the development strategy. The Thai deputy prime minister stated this quite explicitly in 1980 in a statement to provincial governors:

> I ask all governors to consider the natural scenery in your provinces, together with some forms of entertainment that some of you might consider disgusting and shameful because they are forms of sexual entertainment that attract tourists . . . we must do this because we have to consider the jobs that will be created for the people. (Quoted in Ennew 1986, 99).

By the 1990s however, the policy of condoning sex tourism was coming under attack. Women's groups and anti-tourism groups started to campaign against the use of sex tourism as a way of promoting the tourist industry and launched a series of high-profile publicity stunts in which they attacked the image of "brothel Thailand." Activists picketed Bangkok airport and targeted tourist flights with placards that read "Thailand not Sexland" and "Gonorrhea Express" (Montgomery 2008, 907). Furthermore, the international image and reputation of Thailand began to come under scrutiny and, if anyone had any doubts about how Thailand and its tourism industry were perceived in the West, in 1993 *Time* magazine published a special report on the sex trade and featured on its cover a picture of a young Thai prostitute (Hornblower 1993). A week later a new edition of Longman's *Dictionary* was published in the United Kingdom that described Bangkok as "the capital city of Thailand. It is famous for its temples and other beautiful buildings, and is also often mentioned as a place where there are a lot of prostitutes" (Sakboon 1993, 8). These two images of Thailand were widely publicized within the country, causing great controversy and alarm that Thailand had become so synonymous with sex tourism that the words "Thailand" and "prostitution" were interchangeable.

Despite the protests, however, the campaigns against sex tourism had minimal impact. Tourism was perceived as necessary to the Thai economy and was supported by the government. Furthermore, the demonstrations were being held at a time when feminist writers in the West were moving away from a complete abolitionist perspective when discussing sex work. While some authors remained opposed to all forms of commercial sex, viewing it as inherently oppressive to women, others began to explore issues of force and choice, voluntary and involuntary prostitution, and the agency that sex workers could deploy in prostitution (Day 2007). Thus, although launching a battle against male sex tourists in Thailand generated some headlines, it provoked limited action, and even though several Thai NGOs battled hard to keep the issue on the agenda, only the discovery of large numbers of young girls and boys working as prostitutes with Western clients provided an issue that could unite various vested interests (Saunders 2005).

Child Sex Tourism

The issue of child prostitution galvanized public opinion nationally and internationally. Although the morality and necessity of adult prostitution continued to be debated, child prostitution was seen as beyond the pale and the lurid stories that emerged around this time reinforced the notion that child prostitution was quite separate from adult prostitution and of a different magnitude of horror. Discussions could only concern the scale (already huge and always increasing) or the terminology, whether or not to call these children child prostitutes, prostituted children, abused children, or commercially sexually exploited children (Saunders 2005), but issues such as agency were off the agenda for debate. At the forefront of these campaigns were ECPAT (End Child Prostitution in Asian Tourism, later End Child Prostitution, Child Pornography, and Trafficking of Children for Sexual Purposes) and ECTWT (Ecumenical Council on Third World Tourism), both of which drew very explicit links between tourism, child rape, and child trafficking (Montgomery 2001a).

In its earliest days ECPAT relied on extremely compelling personalized testimonies and accounts of innocent children being horribly abused by Westerners. One campaigner told the *Bangkok Post*, "I still remember vividly the tears in the eyes of the child rescued from a Bangkok brothel who told me how she begged a customer not to harm her, only to have her pleas mercilessly rejected" ("Tourists Pay Dearly for Underage Sex" 1993). The media quickly picked up on these stories and began to publish heartbreaking accounts of individual children's lives that had been ruined by abuse and HIV infection because of Western men's selfishness. These stories tended to follow a reliable pattern involving a young Thai girl tricked into leaving home or sold by impoverished parents into a brothel, where she was repeatedly raped and terrorized into servicing many foreign clients a night before being rescued by a charitable organization, only to be discovered to be suffering from HIV (Montgomery 2001a; Murray 2006). By the early 1990s journalists had a clear image of the "right" sort of child prostitute as well as a narrative that always repeated the familiar patterns of betrayal, abuse, rescue, and death, with the foreigner the ultimate cause of the misery (Montgomery 2001a; Fordham 2005). Child prostitution had become, as one newspaper article put it, a "scandal which has left youngsters of only 10 available as prey for charter-flight tourists" (Drummond and Chant 1994, 20).

There is no doubt that terrible cases of child abuse did occur and that it was possible for Western men to buy sex from children in Thailand with impunity.[1] Such stories, however, were not necessarily typical of all child prostitutes in Thailand, even though they were presented as such, and the situation was far more complex than these rather formulaic cases would suggest. For a start, although the concern was focused on children with Western clients, such children actually formed a minority (Black 1994). The overwhelming majority of young prostitutes were not found in the tourist bars of Bangkok, Pattaya, or Phuket but in the brothels of rural Thailand or the backstreets of Bangkok, where they serviced local clients for low wages. It is sometimes assumed that because buying sex from children is so heavily condemned that it must be the most expensive and forbidden form of prostitution, but this is not always the case and children may also be at the bottom end of the market. It was very rare for such children to have foreign clients, and suggestions that all child prostitutes had Western clients and that the problem of child prostitution in Thailand was caused primarily by tourism seriously warped discussions and made research into actual prostitution practices extremely difficult.

One example of the effect of this representative straightjacket was the way a fire in 1984 at a brothel in Phuket was reported. Newspaper accounts told how, on entering the building, fire fighters discovered the charred remains of five young prostitutes who had been unable to escape the blaze because they had been chained to their beds. This case generated a public outcry, and the pimps and procurers of these girls were prosecuted and made to pay compensation to the victims' parents (Rattachumpoth 1994). It was a gruesome story that has been endlessly repeated to show the "typical" horrors of brothel life. Yet there is no evidence to suggest that these girls had Western clients or that the brothel catered to tourists. The pimps and procurers were local men and, in all probability, so, too, were the clients. This, however, did not stop the incident from becoming part of the child sex tourism mythology. The story found its way into an ECPAT book, *The Child and the Tourist* (O'Grady 1992, 97–98) and was also fictionalized by the Foundation for Women in the book *Kamla* (1990), which was distributed among girls considered to be at risk of becoming prostitutes, in order to warn, through the story of the eponymous heroine, of the dangers and likely outcomes of entering prostitution. This book makes the point that Kamla moved to Phuket, because "she was told by her friends that it was in the south of Thailand and that there were plenty of tourists there" (ibid., 23). Inevitably she was burned to death in a brothel fire.

It may well seem offensive to quibble over details; the abuses that went on in this brothel were indefensible, and the ten-year sentences handed out to the pimps and brothel owners were clearly inadequate. It is equally clear that lessons were not learned and similar abuses continued throughout the 1990s. In 1994 another fire claimed the lives of two other young women trapped in a brothel (Sakhon 1994). Yet in neither case were these brothels catering to Westerners, and to suggest that these children died because of their involvement in tourism is disingenuous. As development studies scholar and journalist Maggie Black has argued:

No society wants to admit that it practices "child prostitution." And where the evidence is undeniable, it is more bearable to blame the "unclean other"—decadent foreigners with their incomprehensible tastes and mis-behaviours. Where there is an overlay of North-South exploitation—the Western tourist ruining innocent paradise with his credit card and unleashed libido—this aversion plays easily in certain well-meaning ears (1994, 13).

Highlighting the abuse of Thai children by foreigners meant that other forms of child sexual exploitation, which were less politically expedient to expose, received much less attention. Chief among these was the treatment of Burmese children and young women found in brothels on the Thai side of the Thai–Burmese border. In 1993 a human rights group, Asia Watch, reported on the widespread collusion of Thai officials in the indigenous sex trade and, in particular, on their treatment of Burmese girls. Asia Watch dis-cussed at length a raid on a brothel in Ranong (near the Burmese border) in which the police found 148 underage Burmese girls. Although this case attracted some attention in the Western press, that it involved poor Burmese children having cheap sex with poor Burmese men rather than depraved Westerners indulging their tastes at high prices meant that the story quickly faded from view and no mention was made of immigration policies, racism, law enforcement, or the use of child prostitutes by local men. Yet it exposed another side of the child sex industry in Thailand, which was acutely embar-rassing for the Thai government. The exploitation that occurred in Ranong was a gross abuse of human rights taking place with the full knowledge of Thai officials. Far from being an imported problem of oversexed Westerners causing social chaos with their wallets and depraved tastes, exploitative sex involving children was shown to be commonplace, endemic, and supported by those who should have been stamping it out.

With the parameters of the problem firmly set, child prostitution was understood as being caused primarily by foreigners, and it was therefore argued that the solution was also a foreign one. Although some comments were made in the Western press about law enforcement and the corruption of the local police (Drummond and Chant 1994), the most pressing problem was understood to lie in the lax legal systems of the tourist-sending countries which meant that if men had escaped justice in Thailand then they could not be prosecuted in their home countries. One of the cases ECPAT highlighted was that of a Swedish man, Bengt Bolin, who, in 1992, was caught with a naked boy in his bed but claimed that he had been led to believe that the boy was over fifteen and therefore of legal age. Before he could be prosecuted, he applied for a new Swedish passport and left the country. Three years later, in 1995, the *Bangkok Post* reported the case of a Frenchman who had been found guilty in a Thai court and sentenced to four years imprisonment but had been bailed out in order to launch an appeal. Instead of doing so he simply left the country, having had his passport returned to him by the French Embassy ("Child Molester Flees Thailand" 1995). In both these cases, once the men involved had left the country, nothing could be done. Sweden does not extradite its citizens to non-Nordic countries, and the French government claimed that because their citizen had already been tried once for these offenses, he could not be tried again (Hirst 2003, 268).

Both Thai and international NGOs began to push for extraterritorial legislation to be passed in tourist-sending countries that would enable the prosecution of those accused of sexual crimes against children abroad. In 1994 Australia became the first country to introduce extraterritorial legislation, passing the Crimes (Child Sex Tourism) Amendment Act which brought in penalties of up to seventeen years imprisonment for those convicted of sexual crimes against children overseas. Over the next five years Norway, Germany, France, Belgium, New Zealand, Sweden, and the United Kingdom passed similar laws and successful prosecutions were quickly obtained in 1996 in Australia and in 1997 in France (Montgomery 2010).[2] Interestingly the first case to be successfully brought before the Swedish courts was that of Bengt Bolin, mentioned above, who was sentenced to three months imprisonment in 1995 for his crime of having sex with a teenage boy in Thailand.

In passing such laws Western governments acknowledged that they shared responsibility in finding a solution to the problem of their citizens traveling overseas to have sex with children. Pushing for such laws also enabled Thai and international NGOs to work together without the charge that Western NGOs were interfering in another country. There was also support from the Thai government, which had been embarrassed by the country's reputation as a place where commercial sex with children was freely available. Indeed, it would be hard to imagine anyone or any institution that did not support the aim of stopping Western men from sexually abusing young girls and boys abroad. Yet, by focusing so exclusively on the prosecution of Westerners, the troubling way that Burmese women were treated, the widespread use of child prostitutes by local men, the problems of law enforcement, and the use of tourism as a development strategy were obscured and ignored. Perhaps most important of all, focusing on the perpetrator meant that the children themselves became marginal to discussions about their own lives.

Child Prostitution in Thailand: An Ethnographic Study

When I went to Thailand in 1993 with the aim of conducting ethnographic fieldwork among child prostitutes, I wanted to ask the questions that had not been discussed by the media or the campaigning groups. Who were the children who became prostitutes? What were their living conditions? What were their relationships with their parents, their family, or the broader community? Who were their clients? What were their paths in and out of prostitution? I wanted to hear the children's own view of what they did and why, and find out if the reality of their lives matched up to the image of child prostitutes that was widely disseminated at the time.

Not surprisingly finding children who were working as prostitutes, and who were willing to talk about their lives, was extremely difficult.[3] It took several months of visiting various anti–child prostitution projects before I found a small charitable organization whose practitioners worked with young prostitutes and street children and who were prepared to let me work with them. I had to promise that I would not name the organization, its workers, any of the children I worked with, or indeed the town I worked in. This group's focus was on a community I call Baan Nua, which consisted of approximately 150 rural migrants and their children, who lived in a slum village set up on the outskirts of a larger town whose major industry, as in much of the rest of Thailand, was tourism. It was a poor community that survived almost exclusively through the prostitution of some of its children. The children's clients were Western and their parents were well aware of, and even encouraged, what they did. There were sixty-five children in Baan Nua, and around thirty-five of them worked regularly or occasionally as prostitutes; this number included both boys and girls between the ages of six and fourteen. I spent fifteen months doing this research, interviewing the children, gathering life histories, and acting as a participant observer in their lives.

As I have discussed my findings at length elsewhere (Montgomery 2001a), here I focus on the three issues I identified as central to understanding these children's lives. First, these children had not been trafficked or debt-bonded into brothels. They lived with their parents, worked part-time, and exercised some choice about which clients they accepted; second, the children never identified themselves as prostitutes; and, third, they saw prostitution not in terms of abuse and exploitation but as a filial duty and obligation. This final point is the most important. Prostitution was seen as a means to an end; by selling sex, the children kept their families and their communities together.

The concepts of filial duty and supporting one's parents are fundamental throughout Thai society (Tantiwiramanond and Pandey 1987). Whereas the generalized pattern in Western societies is that parents support their children and, if necessary, sacrifice for them, in Thailand the reverse is true. Although this is now changing and the emergence of a Westernized Thai middle class is beginning to transform understandings of the family and of parent-child relations, in many rural areas, or those far away from the metropolitan center, children's obligations to their parents remain strong and are highly valued. Children are seen as a parental investment with an anticipated return, and they are expected to work for the family as soon as they are able. This emphasis on filial duty has been a constant theme in ethnographic and other studies of prostitution in Thailand, and anthropologist Marjorie Muecke (1992) has argued that whereas girls in the past would have earned money through market trading, contemporary young women are likely to earn money through prostitution. Economist Pasuk Phongpaichit (1982) made a similar point in an early study of young prostitutes in Thailand, showing that daughters who left their rural homes to work as prostitutes were not running away, being coerced into prostitution, or discarding the principles of support and repayment; instead, they were fulfilling those principles as best as they could in a changed environment by earning money elsewhere and sending home the remittances.

These ideals of family obligation and support remained strong in Baan Nua, and it was because of the duties that kin felt toward one another that the children were able to rationalize and justify what they did. Concepts of gratitude and obedience toward parents remained important cultural reference points, and whenever I asked the children about prostitution they almost always referred to them. I was constantly told that prostitution was a way of fulfilling the filial obligations that they felt their families demanded of them. Despite the stigma against prostitution, a powerful mitigating circumstance for many was the financial support they provided for their mothers. The children felt that they were acting in socially sanctioned roles as dutiful daughters and sons, and that prostituting themselves with the "right" intentions meant that there was no moral opprobrium on what they did (Montgomery 2001a). In all the conversations I had with the children about selling sex and their feelings about it, this was the point they kept referring to. As one twelve-year-old informant put it, "[that's] only my body but this is my family" (Montgomery 2001b, 84). Such a view is not uncommon and, as other studies have shown with both adults and children, the way that a person spends his or her earnings can help mitigate the stigma of sex work.[4]

This is not to argue that child prostitution is an intrinsic part of Thai culture or that it is not abusive; it does suggest, however, that the children's view of prostitution should be understood through the cultural reference points of duty and obligation.

The issue of force and choice is central to discussions of adult prostitution, but, with regard to children, it is assumed that they have no agency and are inevitably victimized and crushed by sex work. Yet the children that I knew in Baan Nua did exercise some agency, whether this meant involving some clients in longer-term relationships, pimping for other children, denying victimhood by concentrating on filial duty rather than abuse, or by choosing prostitution above other bad options. In many cases the children in Baan Nua had tried other jobs before entering prostitution, but the opportunities for poor, uneducated slum children were limited to working in sweatshops, street vending, begging, or scavenging on a nearby garbage dump. All these options carried risks, brought in less income, and were generally unpopular with the children. Although prostitution is usually presented as the worst of all possible options, many children saw it as one of the better choices given a limited and terrible set of alternatives. Prostitution with foreigners was relatively highly paid and enabled them to eat the food they wanted, go to places they could not afford, such as amusement arcades or theme parks, and, paradoxically, enjoy some aspects of a childhood otherwise denied to them.

However misguided the children might have been, and however little they understood the wider political, social, and economic contrast of their situation, they remained adamant that they were agents who could exercise some choice. Their language also suggested an attempt to manipulate their reality. They consistently refused to admit to prostitution, rejecting the very term when I used it, calling it an ugly thing that had no meaning in their lives. They continually emphasized that they did not "sell sex," that they were just going "out for fun with foreigners" or "having guests." In their terms, only children in brothels could be called prostitutes. Given this view of the world, it was not surprising that they distinguished between different types of clients. Some, they admitted, were customers who simply bought sex, but the children disliked these sorts of relationships and rarely talked about them. They preferred to discuss the men who were "friends" who would respond to requests for help, give large lump sums when the children needed it, and had been integrated to some extent into the lives of their families. With these men it was possible to downplay, and even deny, that the relationship was about the exchange of sex for money and the children couched their descriptions in terms of love and romance rather than commercial transactions.

There was no set price for sexual acts; money given to them after sex was referred to as a gift or as a token of appreciation. Sometimes a client would not leave cash for the children but would contribute it for the rebuilding or refurbishing of a girl's house. The children in Baan Nua were not immune to romantic dreams, and they avidly watched Thai soap operas and talked about their love of certain pop stars. These views, however, were tempered by realism. The girls did not dream of true love or of being poor but happy; they dreamed instead of a rich man taking them away from Baan Nua and looking after them and their family.

But despite everything the children said about prostitution, I remained deeply unhappy about the children's denial of abuse and their rejection of victimhood. While acknowledging their resilience and admiring them greatly, I personally believe that when an older, richer man from the West is buying sex with young children, exploitation is inevitable. Even though the children claimed that their clients treated them well, this must be set against the risks they faced and certain other aspects of their behavior. There was a high level of drug and alcohol use in Baan Nua among the children; there were unwanted pregnancies and sexually transmitted infections. A child's body is too small for penetration by an adult, and some of the harm done by these men was evident in the bleeding and tearing that occurred during occasions when the children sold sex. Though almost never mentioned, the threat of HIV was ever present, and toward the end of my fieldwork one twenty-year-old, who had worked for several years as a prostitute, died of tuberculosis which I believe, but cannot prove, was AIDS-related.[5]

Given all these problems and evidence of vulnerability, why did the children still claim to see no abuse? One possible reason is that the images of child prostitution that saturated the media bore no relationship to them and their lives. By the end of my time in the field, the children had become aware that what they did was considered wrong and stopped talking about it. Even so, they never identified themselves as prostitutes; indeed, they went to great lengths to deny it. They believed that child prostitution, as noted above, only referred to those children who had been tricked into brothels and forced to sell sex to whoever wanted it. In their own minds they were very different: they lived with what in their terms were loving parents; they were not trapped in a brothel; and they had plans for life after prostitution. The image of child prostitution so prevalent at the time had the unintended effect of excluding them from believing that there were other forms of abuse and that what was happening to them was wrong. They saw no overlap between their own lives and the image of a child prostitute propagated by the media.

Conclusions

When child prostitution was first identified as a major problem, a consensus was quickly reached on its nature and what needed to be done. The solution was assumed to be extraterritorial legislation to prosecute men in their home countries for crimes against children abroad. Trying and condemning such men had a neatness to it which was appealing: it united Western NGOs and governments with their Thai counterparts, and it made a symbolic gesture that this problem was also the responsibility of the Western world. It was also intended to send a message to men who might think about using children sexually and make them reflect before they traveled to buy sex from children abroad. Yet it is questionable whose needs were really fulfilled by this legislation. For NGOs and governments there were tangible benefits to legislative change, namely, proof that something palpable was being done in spite of the legal and constitutional difficulties. Focusing on the prosecution of foreign men also allowed less palatable issues to be swept aside, such as the fact that sex tourism was developed and condoned by the Thai government and allowed to flourish with minimal regulation. Emphasizing commercial sex with foreigners also ignored the issue of patchy law enforcement and police corruption, charges that remain until this day, according to a recent U.S. State Department's Human Rights Report(Bureau of Democracy, Human Rights, and Labor 2008). Immigration policy and the treatment of illegal migrants, especially from Burma, was a sensitive issue in Thailand, and the emphasis on Western clients, once again, neatly sidestepped this problem.

In terms of its impact on the actual children who worked as prostitutes, the picture was less clear and little thought went into the issue of what would happen to children who reported abuse to the authorities or testified against abusers. Would they be placed in government or foster care, given counseling and alternatives to prostitution? Would they be stigmatized in the eyes of the government and their communities? Or would they simply be forgotten? Certainly, for the children in Baan Nua, extraterritorial laws would have been meaningless. Neither the children nor their families had any interest in seeing their clients prosecuted. In the absence of any social support or any form of welfare, these men were the only form of income and protection they had, no matter how damaging that might seem to outsiders. Obtaining a conviction against them, in either Thailand or abroad, would be close to impossible.

In 1996 a change of law in Thailand meant that parents could be prosecuted if they allowed or encouraged their children to work as prostitutes.

Given the emphasis the children placed on family relationships and filial obligations, such laws would make it extremely difficult for the children to ask for help, even if they recognized that they needed it. Keeping the family together was their primary justification for what they did and, concomitantly, the prosecution and imprisonment of their parents was their worst fear. Furthermore, laws such as this made it very easy to ignore structural causes of child prostitution, thus giving the state immunity by privatizing the issue and laying the blame at the feet of the family. Despite the presence of NGOs and the state claiming to protect such children and act in their best interests, it is the voices of children like those in Baan Nua that tend to get lost in debates about child prostitution. They were not the suffering innocents trapped in a brothel; they were well paid and had certain freedoms. They were undoubtedly exploited but, unfortunately for them, they were exploited in the "wrong" way. Ideologically out of place and challenging to accepted ideas of what a child prostitute should look and act like, these children were an embarrassment and, along with so many other uncomfortable issues concerning child prostitution, were overlooked, and even silenced, by those claiming to speak in their name.

NOTES

1. For a nuanced and balanced account of the problem, see O'Connell-Davidson 2005.
2. For a summary of the laws in each country, see the World Tourism Organisation, n.d.
3. For a full discussion of methods and ethical dilemmas, as well as issues of access, see Montgomery 2007.
4. See Kelly 2008 for a vivid example of this.
5. For a fuller discussion of the risks of pregnancy and disease, see Montgomery 2001b.

12

Organizational Challenges Facing Male Sex Workers in Brazil's Tourist Zones

GREGORY MITCHELL

Brazil's governmental policies and extensive sex worker advocacy organizations have created a rich environment for battling stigmatization and improving labor conditions for sex workers. Still, Brazil's male sex worker population (*michês*), which mostly identifies as heterosexual, remains conspicuously absent from the creative and successful efforts of the sex workers' rights movement. Although their inaction may easily be attributed to male privilege and a lack of exploitation, I argue that stigmatization interferes with outreach and organizational efforts directed at *michês* in ways both similar to and remarkably different from those involving women in the industry. This creates particular challenges for public policy makers and outreach professionals whose work affects these male sex workers.

In 2005 the Brazilian government shocked the Bush administration when it rejected $40 million from the United States Agency for International Development (USAID) that was contingent upon Brazil publicly condemning prostitution.[1] In Brazil, where sex work is technically permissible under law for women and men eighteen years of age or older, the government assists prostitutes through its efforts toward HIV prevention, education, and treatment. By taking such progressive and comprehensive approaches, Brazil cut its expected HIV infection rate by an impressive 50 percent between 1992 and 2002 (from 1.2 million anticipated cases to 660,000), while also prolonging lives by providing free antiretroviral medications. So while Brazil went from a 1.0 percent to a 0.5 percent infection rate, South Africa jumped from the same 1.0 percent rate to percentages reported to be as high as 20.0 percent in the same time period (Phillips 2005). Brazil is rightly proud of its record and did not intend to change its policies to suit U.S. neoconservatives' religious beliefs.

Far from condemning prostitution as demanded by the U.S. government, Pedro Chequer, director of Brazil's National HIV/AIDS Commission, instead called prostitutes the government's "partners" and condemned the mandate issued by Bush and the Republican Congress as a "theological" and "fundamentalist" blow against "ethical principles and human rights" (Rohter 2005).[2] Although Brazil is widely regarded as a rising star with increasing geopolitical influence in the global economy, no one expected this scathing rejection from its government. In siding with prostitutes over the U.S. president, Dr. Chequer endeared himself to sex worker rights activists worldwide. But in a country with such progressive views on prostitution, what more could sex workers there want? As it turns out, quite a lot.

Following the rejection of the USAID offer, funding for sex work–related projects became scarce, yet the sex workers' rights movement flourished, including innovative programming such as the launching of the fashion line Daspu by the sex workers of Davida and the national candidacy of its founder, Gabriela Leite, for Brazil's congress. Yet *michês* generally remained skeptical and dismissive toward sex workers' rights movements, and apathetic about the funding controversy. Drawing on ethnographic research conducted between 2006 and 2010 I examine processes of stigmatization among men who sell sex to comparatively wealthy Brazilian and foreign men in areas popular with tourists, both on the street and in indoor commercial sex venues.[3] I contend that the men do not openly identify with the profession not only out of a desire to remain "closeted" about their work, but because they do not want to be categorized as sex workers at all. Although they often do frame their commercial sexual activities as "work" (*trabalho*), they do not label it as such when it comes to legal and social professionalization. This is difficult to reconcile with the movement's emphasis on professional pride and labor rights, and creates unique challenges for persons both in and outside the movement who are charged with crafting and implementing public policy that deeply affects this population. This problem may be true of both male and female sex workers, but I focus here only on the challenges specific to these men, such as their intense fear of being wrongly categorized as gay, their view of "sex work" as a feminized occupational category, and the reality that their machismo impedes communication and solidarity with one another and other stakeholders (see also Aggleton 1999).

Past Efforts

In 1991 Rio de Janeiro was already home to two thousand boys and men who supported themselves or their families by selling sex to other men, including gay tourists (Longo 1998a). Just as the gay travel industry began to boom worldwide in the 1990s, Brazil's inflation soared to an astonishing annualized inflation rate of 6,100 percent in 1994 (Tullio and Ronci 1996). Thus Brazil became exceptionally affordable for foreigners at a time when many young Brazilians were desperate for money and excited by the additional opportunities that relationships with foreigners could provide, including travel and even immigration. Immigration is difficult for men, however, as they cannot marry their male clients, nor would many choose to. However, they do sometimes vacation in Europe with clients or through networks of friends and sex worker colleagues.

Male prostitution certainly thrived prior to this time, but by the 1990s it was moving increasingly indoors to bars and *saunas*, the latter term used for bathhouses featuring brothel-style prostitution (Parker 1999; Green 1999). What had often been a confusing network of informal sexual economies during Brazil's military dictatorship (1960–1984) became increasingly formalized in the 1990s, especially in urban centers such as Rio de Janeiro. This transformation eventually accommodated the increasing popularity of Brazil in gay travel circles, gay magazines, and online gay communications networks. With the formalization of the gay tourist industry into a lucrative market that included package tours organized exclusively for gay men *Michês* filled out the rapidly segmenting market, which included high-end escorts advertising in newspapers (and eventually online), cheap and seedy to expensive and ultra-modern *saunas*, low-wage street (or beach) prostitution, and, of course, more informal exchanges made in various venues. This diversification is not particularly unique in and of itself, but its cumulative effects created Brazil's contemporary gay sex industry.

Ironically the contemporary gay tourist industry would not exist without the outreach and HIV prevention efforts of Projeto Pegacão, which first emerged in 1989 under the leadership of Paulo Longo and draws its name from a slang expression alluding to "cruising" for sex. Several of my tourist interlocutors explained that they and their friends had stopped visiting the Dominican Republic and Mexico over concerns about HIV but that Brazil's lower HIV rates made it appealing. When the project began, only 15 percent of *michês* surveyed reported using condoms, but that figure increased to a reported 80 percent within a year (Larvie 1999, 1997; Longo 1998b). *Michês* consistently referred one another to Longo and his three-person staff, and several began distributing condoms to colleagues themselves. Despite some successes and recognition, the project was effectively bankrupt by 1998, and Longo died in 2004 at the age of forty. Longo complained that funders preferred distributing educational pamphlets and "did not seem to be interested in financing a project whose methodology is based upon the relationship between street educators and the target audience" (Longo 1998b).

The sexual landscape of the city has shifted considerably since Longo's outreach work, but street hustling still exists, as does noncommercial and quasi-commercial gay cruising for public sex. Because Rio also has a well-deserved reputation for crime, poverty, and violence, the city's safe, convenient, and legal *saunas* became an appealing alternative for gay tourists. Many—though not all—of these *saunas* feature *michês*. Here, gay tourists and locals can cruise several floors of bars, video rooms, wet or dry saunas, showers, hot tubs, workout centers, and stages featuring entertainments such as go-go dancing, drag performances, and even bingo games.

Michês, who often wear a colored towel to differentiate them from clients in white, stroll throughout the *saunas* casting provocative glances and flirtatiously revealing their genitals to prospective clients. Clients negotiate prices with and pay *michês* directly, whereas *sauna* management profits from the sale of drinks and food, as well as the entry charged to the *michês* (U.S.$5) and clients (U.S.$15). Management also collects U.S.$15 or more from clients who rent *cabines* (private rooms) for forty- to sixty-minute sexual sessions, known as *programas*, that often include clean linens, condoms, and lubricant. In order to bypass laws against pimping, *saunas* cannot profit directly from the *michê's* sexual labor. Despite this prohibition, some interlocutors reported that a few establishments make clients pay the house, which then pays a portion of the money to the *michê*.

Saunas also employ staff members (some of them former *michês*) as doormen, bartenders, or locker-room attendants. Although rigid divisions exist between staff and sex workers, some staff members envy the money *michês* make and make themselves available for post-shift *programas*. *Michês* do not have set schedules and tend to work only when they need money, and they are quick to admit that they spend their earnings on clothes, electronics, going to clubs, or on gifts for girlfriends. *Michês* sometimes work for more than one *sauna*, especially in Rio, as typically no exclusive agreements are made between management and *michês*. Upon entering a *sauna* for the afternoon or evening, however, they must commit to a stay for a set number of hours. Leaving early, either alone or with a client, necessitates paying a fee or a bribe to the manager.

Various nongovernmental organizations (NGOs) and government workers have targeted *saunas* for safe sex education and outreach efforts. The *Michês* I know appreciate the information and the effort but told me they had little interest in getting deeply involved with these organizations, which they sometimes describe as condescending, or in forming their own. "There is no NGO to really help the *boys*. They just want to find out if you have a disease," Jonaton complained. "I don't want [any contact] with them." Others said the information was unnecessary because they already have a thorough knowledge of safe sex practices and extremely high rates of condom use. Relying on self-reporting can be dangerous, as male sex workers sometimes say what they think researchers want to hear (Padilla 2007, 10), but I have observed many casual conversations between *michês* regarding the best strategies for determining when one ought to use condoms for oral sex. They show no such ambivalence regarding condoms and anal sex, and are quite emphatic on this point. Indeed, mutual suspicion between clients and *michês* seems to have resulted in the normalization of condom use. Thus, in at least this one regard, bias against gays and sex workers appears to be keeping people safe.

Challenges

Despite my optimism about certain aspects of sexual health, very few of the *michês* use condoms with their intimate female partners. Some of the men say they get tested regularly at the local clinics, but only a few ever offered convincing details. Substance abuse is high, especially of alcohol, marijuana, and cocaine, and some use these drugs as a form of self-medication either to deal with aspects of the work they do not like (see also Mimiaga et al. 2009, 62) or at the client's request. The men also frequently purchase inexpensive counterfeit versions of an erectile dysfunction drug called Pramil from *sauna* staff or other sex workers. Antonio, a *sauna michê* in his early twenties, noted the undesirable but necessary nature of the drug: "When the house is very full and there are lots of clients wanting to go upstairs [to a *cabine*], then I have to take Pramil, you know? And then you do four or five *programas*. Without Pramil I can only do one or two." Because of the unreliable quality and results of these counterfeit drugs, some men take them by the handful, resulting in painful side effects such as headaches and heart palpitations. Nineteen-year-old Carlos described his only experience with it as frightening, noting, "Your veins swell, your ears get hot, your face gets hot, you turn red . . . I've already learned the dangers of it."

Although it is true that working in a *sauna* is far safer and more lucrative than working on the streets or beaches, *michês* find it difficult to stay competitive. Seasoned *michês* in their mid-twenties wax nostalgic about the days when there were fewer *saunas*. Twenty-five-year-old Anderson complained, "Nowadays, even without advertising, every day five or ten [guys] knock on the door without even calling the *sauna* beforehand. . . . [It used to be that] a *boy* would knock on the door to enter and there was a test to see if the *boy* was any good . . . Now, whoever comes in, comes in." Because many clients who visit Brazil are looking for stereotypically masculine Latin "machos" rather than young, slender "twinks," men can work well into their thirties, especially if they avoid drug and alcohol use and the sun's deleterious effects. As men age, they tend to move to seedier, lower-budget *saunas* and then to known hustler bars and street corners.

The working conditions in *saunas* are hardly ideal for younger *michês*, who complain that some *saunas* overcharge them for a towel large enough to wrap around their waist, forcing them to use a single hand towel too small to fasten. Some *saunas* feature "no towel nights," which are as unpopular with *michês* as they are popular with clients, who receive large towels, and can rent bath robes and even wear street clothes in some establishments. *Michês* complain that they feel vulnerable when nude and dislike being unable to decide how most effectively to reveal intimate parts of their bodies to prospective clients. As nineteen-year-old Naldo said of his experience working in a low-end *sauna* for nine months:

> My first impression of "the life" was harsh because I started in this *sauna* that forced me to work naked and being naked was very difficult because I was not ready to be naked in front of everybody! Just walking around normally. In other saunas you can get a towel . . . but this *sauna* is nude [some nights]. Here it was the most difficult, but later I got used to it. [Sometimes] they make you pay between 5 and 10R$ [U.S.$3–$6], depending on the towel that you are going to use. [For] 5R$ you get a small towel, and [you have to stay at least] five hours inside the house. And for 10R$, [you stay at least] three hours inside the house with a bigger towel. The point [of the pricing] is to get you to use a small towel so the *boys* are naked.

While few *saunas* directly pressure *michês* to accept clients against their will, *michês* do complain that *saunas* do not allow them to leave early without paying a penalty. The fact that they are unable to easily leave the *sauna*, especially on a slow night, also means that the *michê* is in a more difficult bargaining position. He may have to accept a client he does not like, accept less money, or agree to provide sexual services that he usually prefers not to, such as being anally penetrated. Those who work outdoors have even more grievous complaints, as they have no real recourse when a client tries to change the terms of their agreement. Indoor and outdoor *michês* both struggle with stigmatization at non-erotic establishments in the areas where they work, where they are subjected to poor service, dirty looks, snide comments, sudden and inexplicable bathroom closures, and unforeseen changes to hours of operation. It is in these most quotidian moments of marginalization where the sting of being stigmatized is felt most acutely.

When stigmatization is manifested in discrimination, the subject is reduced from a complete and valued person and rendered as a partial or incomplete subject (Goffman 1963). For many of the men, being stigmatized was so much a part of their lives that they had difficulty recognizing when a slight was not actually directed at them. For example, one time when a toilet was genuinely broken, a *michê* insisted that the manager probably broke it himself to prevent him from using it. Here it is worth remembering that examples of "felt stigma" are a result of the internalization of real stigma and are damaging in their own right (Halgrimsdottir et al. 2006).

Michês who work in areas where there is not much tourist traffic are at even greater risk and constitute a very different population. The organization Garotos da Noite, based in the Amazonian city of Manaus (population 1.8 million) has very few resources and relies almost exclusively on the work of a few volunteers to do outreach to *michês*. Outreach project manager Dartanha Silva reviewed his current research and work with me, and the results are frightening:

> When we reached out to the *michês*, they pulled away. But the biggest problem was in relation to public policy, which for male prostitution is almost nonexistent . . . and when we pass information on to [*michês*] about [STI] prevention [and] human rights, they don't want to know, unlike the girls . . . The fact that the prevalence of STDs in Manaus is 7 percent more than the national average is very worrying. And they aren't in the habit of using condoms. We talk, do the workshops, but . . . sometimes the client provides the drugs in exchange for him agreeing not to use condoms or they offer more money for the *programa* . . . some of the eighty-nine *michês* we interviewed [in our latest study] were minors . . . [But if we contribute to] police rounding them up, then we've created a problem with the kids because the next time they won't take our material. [We try to tell them] that they shouldn't do *programas* in the client's house or in their own house. Many killings occur for this reason. When it's the client's home, there are *boys* who steal and kill. On the other hand . . . last year there were five *garotos de programa* [rentboys, another term for a male sex worker] murdered by clients because the *garotos* stole from them. We've

been working with *michês* for two years and we still can't get them past the need for prevention . . . The *garotos de programa* have no interest in getting organized.

Whether working in *saunas* or on the streets, with tourists or locals, it is perplexing why the *michês* are resistant to participating in sex workers' organizations. It is true that these men operate from a more privileged position, because they do not face the same severe forms of client violence as female sex workers (Chacham 2007); indeed, Brazilian popular media shows the reverse, as *michês* are often cast as dangerous aggressors (e.g., Kaye 2007; Mott and Ferreira de Cerqueira 2003). Although *michês* are economically subordinate to nearly all their clients, they often do not have (or at least do not choose to honor) the same responsibilities as women sex workers toward children, parents, or other family members, which can make it easier for the men I spoke with in Rio and Bahia to turn down clients or take a few days off. Despite these distinctly male privileges, *michês* continue to insist that they are actually *more* stigmatized than women sex workers.

Most *michês* worried that their families, friends, and girlfriends would think they were gay. As one man noted, "there is more prejudice against men. People think that everyone who works in the sauna is gay. They know the women work because they need to. They think men are there because they like it." Another *michê*, João, cited the temporary nature of the work as another reason for this lack of organization, noting, "With men there's much more prejudice. *Michês* don't organize because nobody is there for life . . . People work there just to get some extra money so there's never going to be an NGO for *garotos de programa*." Note that João makes an important assumption that women enter the profession "for life," even though this is plainly not true.

Yet João, like many men who think of themselves as selling sex temporarily, finds that he cannot afford to stop selling sex. It is the best job available to him that he is willing to accept, and he considers it a far better option than the menial labor available to him. So while the *michês* are genuine when they say selling sex is temporary, consistently choosing to stay in "the life" is a rational (albeit repetitive) decision. The perceived impermanence of their work thus makes organizing irrelevant in their view, as any unpleasant aspects can be tolerated on the grounds that they are temporary. As one *michê* explained with deliberately self-conscious irony when I asked if he was still doing *programas*, "No, I quit." Then he smiled. "Every week, I quit."

(Dis)identities

Michês spend a great deal of time deflecting intimations that they are gay. It is commonly accepted among this population that a straight men can anally penetrate another man and retain his heterosexual status (e.g., Parker 1999; Carrillo 2002; Green 1999). However, being passive in anal intercourse is usually seen as something that no straight man - not even a *michê* - would do. Consequently, many *michês* deny that they engage in this activity. The truth, however, is that the majority of *michês* will accept anal penetration for the right amount of money, and some will even do so at no extra cost (or a small extra fee to keep up appearances.) Some clients take this as a sign that the *michê* enjoys the activity, finds the client attractive, and/or is "really gay after all." What these clients fail to realize is that when a *michê* has done multiple *programas* (especially if he ejaculated during any of them), or if he is faced with a client for whom he does not think he will be able to sustain an erection, he can be anally penetrated without worrying about his performance or losing money.

Michês prefer to keep such details "*entre quarto paredes*"("between four walls") and dislike discussing their *programas* with one another. This is an additional way of managing stigmatization and compartmentalizing their sexual behavior as distinct from their sexual identity. Sometimes, *michês* will even get angry at one another if they know or suspect someone is engaging in passive anal sex, especially at a reduced rate. This increases the risk that clients will expect similar services and pricing. Consequently, when gay-identified *michês* begin working in a *sauna* or public area, they can disrupt the social order and cause tension.

The concern with being mistaken for gay is a primary reason why many choose to lead a complete double life. They are less concerned about the stigma attached to being sexually promiscuous, which is disproportionately (and unfairly) applied to women, than they are worried that friends, family or intimate female partners might suspect them of being a "faggot" (*viado*). The priority given to warding off the stigma of homosexuality reveals a great deal. These men have internalized homophobia and experience the same shame that gay clients may experience in their own lives, and yet they react to this experience in different ways. A few become extremely homophobic and describe their existences as miserable objects suffering at the hands of perverts. Nearly all the men I know, however, emerge from their own experiences of being stigmatized with sympathy for (rather than empathy with) their clients. They tended to describe them as "sad" and "pathetic," but said these words with no tinge of malice. "I pity them. Most of them are so lonely. Look, they say you need a big dick [*mala*] to be successful as a *boy*," Anderson explained to me one afternoon as he sipped a beer. "But you know, really, you just need to be able to hold them. Many *boys* don't understand this, they can't do it . . . A big dick helps, but the main thing is that there is no one in the world for them. It's very sad."

Women's Work

It is telling that Anderson positions the job of the sex worker as a caregiver. The labor is affective as well as sexual. Affective labor is often discussed in regard to care industries in which individuals, usually women, engage in these economies, even though their jobs are actually (or should be) about tasks other than affect (Hochschild 1983). Many *michês* who spoke quite casually about "fucking," "sucking," and other acts were much less comfortable discussing the intimate behaviors that clients often requested, such as cuddling or kissing, but these activities speak to the caregiving role that men such as Anderson often had, and their uneasiness with what they perceived as an emasculating form of labor. Even those who did not want to discuss cuddling with clients had stories about clients who cried. This was especially true of older, Brazilian clients. I heard of lonely Brazilian bachelors, married men, and numerous priests who often wept during or after sex. Some would even pay for a double session, sitting contemplatively there with the *michê*. Several times I entered bar areas of *saunas* and saw *michês* I knew sitting stoically with an arm over a Brazilian client's shoulder after a session, as the client stared blankly across the smoky room downing the corrosively high proof liquor known as *cachaça*.

Other clients who desired affective labor from the *michês* included tourists who took them sightseeing and to dinner, a notable event given that many Brazilian tourist sites, such as the famous Christ statue, are far too expensive for poorer Brazilians to visit. In these instances, they expected the *michês* to function as tour guides and entertaining companions. Such arrangements allowed *michês* to speak euphemistically of "working with tourists," describing themselves as tour guides or venders regardless of how much of their income was derived from that activity or the amount of time spent on it. This kind of disidentification is not surprising for anyone who has spent much time around or working with people in informal sexual economies (Kong 2006; Munoz 1999), but many of the *michê*, primarily in Bahia, had girlfriends or wives who were also sex workers. Although they understand sex to be work (*trabalho*) and understood themselves to be selling sex, they would often reject words like "sex worker," "prostitute," "*michê*," and even "*garoto de programa*," and identify with other job categories even when they derived comparatively little to no income from those jobs.

Considerable effort has been put into creating effective sexual health prevention programming for men who have sex with men precisely because of the importance of recognizing the separation of identity and behavior, but it is also important to understand that this principle must be extended in other ways if one is to comprehend the reluctance of straight-identified men who sell sex to enter into projects that they associate with sex workers' rights movements.

Notably *michês* often denied that they functioned as a supportive community or that they worked collectively, although they do work together to keep prices up, to drive pickpockets or aggressive panhandlers and street children out of their territory, and to keep the immediate area of the beaches and streets where they worked safe enough for their work. They also alerted one another when there was free food to be had from a church group and warned one another of bad clients. Beyond general recommendations, however, they rarely spoke about the specifics of their work life and were cautious about revealing details about their home lives to one another. For *michês*, it is important to withhold information that could make them vulnerable to being dropped to the bottom of the *michê* hierarchy. This includes not only hiding details about what acts they are willing to perform but also over-reporting their prices (to emphasize their distaste for sex with men), over-reporting both their penis size and their numbers of female sexual partners, and using homophobic epithets to describe clients or *michês* who are suspected of being gay. By reasserting their own masculinity while decreasing the amount of honest communication they have with one another, they are better able to manage stigmatization.

Another important communication strategy that places them in a favorable position in the *michê* hierarchy is to assert their status as an honorable person. In interviews as well as in interactions with one another, they are quick to point out that they do not cheat or steal from clients but that others do. They often insist that they do not use drugs or that they only use marijuana, even though this information is frequently false. They emphasize their status as committed and involved fathers who are selling sex to provide for their children. This claim is true for several of the men I know well but is doubtful in other cases. Regardless of the truth of any of these claims, the important point is that they use these conventional markers of good men to emphasize that they are not like other *michês* they know and definitely not like the violent portrayals in the popular media. By presenting themselves in this manner, they use normative ideas about masculinity to lessen the stigma they experience. The combined effect of these omissions, additions, and reframings is that they re-create themselves along the lines of another stereotypical figure: the prostitute with the heart of gold.

Conclusions

The hesitancy, apathy, and hostility *michês* express regarding sex workers' rights highlight the fact that they often feel patronized or feared as a vector of disease by certain service providers. Evidently *sauna* labor conditions also need to be reformed, which is unlikely to happen without *michês'* engagement in collective bargaining. My research findings also suggest other recommendations for substantive policy change concerning *michês*. In the area of service provision, many *michês* are eager to learn skills either to leave the sex industry or to improve their skills as a sex worker. Providing these services, however, in keeping with the men's stated interests, may be less appealing to providers who prefer to remain focused solely on sexual health issues even though sexual health is inseparable from other facets of the men's lives (e.g., Parsons, Koken, and Bimbi 2007). Many *michês* want to learn English and computer skills (especially how to build their own websites), to acquire legal resources and advocates, to better understand how to navigate bureaucracy, and to improve their Portuguese literacy. They also want greater access to other career paths, including microcredit loans to start businesses, such as fruit carts and magazine kiosks.

Another area needing improvement is education for their clients; some clients do and say horrible things, and businesses such as *saunas* as well as governments do little to tell sex tourists what is expected of them as consumers. *Saunas*, for example, should post a sex workers' bill of rights developed together with the *michês* and including precautions that clients should observe proper hygiene and respect the terms of their agreements (both acts and prices), as well as information on payment. Significant disagreements among sex tourists involve the issues of tipping, the importance or insignificance of overpaying, and the ethics of using large amounts of cash to leverage men they meet in public into performing sexual acts.

The central challenge for organizational efforts is that they take into account the effects of stigmatization on different sex worker populations. For *michês*, existing models of sex workers' rights that hinge on the pride of professionalization may be doomed, as these men reject sex work as an identity-forming practice. One must therefore look to sexual health models designed specifically for men who have sex with men (MSM). The fusion of these two models—sex workers' rights activism and MSM-based outreach, each already successful in Brazil—could provide an organizational structure with the wider appeal that it is geared toward "men who sell sex to men." Until such time as such efforts get started, however, a more thorough understanding of the processes of stigmatization should inform current legislation, activism, and advocacy projects.

NOTES

1. The statement condemning prostitution can be found in United States Congress 2003; United States Leadership Against HIV/AIDS, Tuberculosis, and Malaria Act of 2003; and House Resolution 1298/Public Law 108-025.

2. Brazil's Ministry of Labor provides a useful model for the classification of "sex professionals" (*Profissionais do sexo*). It is referenced in the Classification of Occupations (CBO) as #5198-05.

3. Men and boys (including street children) also sell sex to local men in other neighborhoods and locations, including downtown streets, slums, and rural communities. For more on sexuality among street children in Brazil, see Richards 2005.

13

"What is the use of getting a cow if you can't make any money from it?"

The Reproduction of Inequality within Contemporary Social Reform of Devadasis

TREENA ORCHARD

Devadasis, from the Sanskrit terms *Deva* ("God") and *dasi* ("servant or slave"), were generally women dedicated through ritual marriage to a deity or an object (i.e., a sword) who serviced local temples and their citizenry in various ways, depending on their ritual status. The *Devadasi* system originated between the third and sixth centuries throughout India, predominantly in the South (Shankar 1990). These women sang, danced, and performed significant religious functions (Kersenboom 1987; Marglin 1985), including begging to temple patrons and people in their home communities in the name of the deities with whom they were associated. They also adopted roles as sex workers who, ordained by their union with the Gods, were believed to transfer good fortune and spiritual harmony through sexual intercourse (Tarachand 1991). Corrupt temple administration and priestly conduct, the rise of androcentric forms of worship, and temple rivalry for tourists who were attracted by "dancing girls" during the prosperous Chola Period (850–1300) began a process of marginalization among *Devadasis* that came to a head during colonial times (Orr 2000), beginning in the mid-nineteenth century. During debates over Indian independence and cultural integrity, *Devadasis* were labeled either as tarnished remnants of a "golden age" or "fallen women" of a barbaric tradition, with the latter taken to decisively mark a nation as unfit to rule itself (Kannabiran 1995).

The system of dedicating young girls to deities for the purpose of sex work and temple service continues today in northern Karnataka and neighboring states; approximately one thousand to ten thousand girls (predominantly of the lower castes) are inducted into the system annually (Giri 1999; Jordan 1993). Upon attaining menarche, a "first client ceremony" is held where the girl is deflowered by a client who offers gifts to her family (e.g., sarees, gold, money, bed sheets, jewelry), and after one or two years she begins conducting sex work. *Devadasis* generally live with their families and work in their home communities, sometimes with sisters or other female relatives (O'Neil et al. 2004). The basic starting pay per client is Rs 50 (U.S.$1) for penetrative sex, and their daily earnings range from Rs 0 to Rs 500 (U.S.$ 0–118).

Although women and girls customarily traveled to Mumbai (Bombay) or other large cities in the past, either by coercion or voluntarily to garner better income, the fear of HIV/AIDS and the higher costs of urban living have affected this pattern of migration for younger women today. *Devadasis* in the contemporary rural setting are more likely than other sex workers to migrate out of state, but this appears to be linked to their rural location rather than their membership in the *Devadasi* tradition (Blanchard et al. 2005). We interviewed a number of *Devadasi* members, most of whom expressed a desire to put an end to the *Devadasi* system, which was associated with their growing awareness of HIV. Some women and girls indicated, however, that sex work makes vital contributions to the family economy and is valued as a signifier of mature female status within their communities (Orchard 2007). These contradictory views reflect some of the complex perceptions that *Devadasis* have about their participation in this traditional system.

The *Devadasi* system is, in a real sense, a sacred cow within Indian culture. For centuries, *Devadasi* women have embodied significant cultural values and knowledge (i.e., the sacredness of sex, dance, and singing as worship), and yet their very possession and enactment of this cultural wisdom seems to single them out as somehow deviant and dangerous. Their ability to occupy definitive spaces at both the apex and margins of society can be attributed to several factors, beginning with the way in which female sexuality has been constructed in India. As in most patriarchal societies, women's sexuality is perceived as instrumental to the reproduction of the family and, as such, something that must be controlled to maintain familial purity. Indeed, in India, the management of female sexuality underpins the workings of the caste system; women must adhere to a barrage of rules in the pursuit of a "proper" sexuality which includes virginity before marriage, marital fidelity, and obedience to one's husband and his family (Marglin 1985).

Given the paramount cultural and religious importance placed upon female sexuality as something that could disrupt the foundation of the caste system and the organization of Indian society, it is also often framed as a dangerous force. Women are believed to drain men of their power during sexual intercourse through the man's loss of semen (O'Flaherty 1980; Wadley 1988), and this is tied to a system of thought where bodily fluids are important in maintaining bodily harmony and life in general. Women are also thought to have excessively "hot" bodies as a result of menstruation which involves the monthly shedding of blood, a heated substance that is taken as proof of women's overheated bodies and sexual passions (Beck 1969; Reynolds 1980). Taken together we can see how *Devadasis* were at once an anomaly and a prototype of feminine portrayals; they were set apart as wives of Gods and as women with autonomous control of their sexuality, but they were also aligned with "normal" women through their powers to weaken men through sexual intercourse.

These women's dual socio-sexual status was also affected by and played into the European imagination of Oriental sexuality (backward but bawdy) and prostitution, which underwent intense state regulation during the colonial period. In mid-nineteenth-century India, International Social Purity campaigns and rising rates of venereal disease (VD) among British troops stationed in the colony dovetailed to produce an image of prostitutes as degraded, dangerous, and a moral threat to national health, security, and modernity (Arnold 1993; Raj 1993). *Devadasis* occupied a complicated position within legislative and social discourses of that time, as they fell outside the jurisdiction of the Contagious Diseases Act of 1868, which was applied throughout the colonies to regulate prostitution because of the British policy of noninterference in religious matters. Although during this period the *Devadasi* system was understood to be connected with religious ideology and practices, the Social Purity movements and the profound cultural disruption ushered in by colonial rule inflicted significant changes in the system and it became discredited within Indian society. This led to a major decline in the socioeconomic and religious status of *Devadasi* women and their loss of temple-related revenue, as well as the dismantling of the traditional patronage relationships between the women and their clients, which often forced the women into purely commercial forms of prostitution. As a result, and despite their tenuous association with religion, many Indian and British reformers, as well as Indian society more generally, began to place all these women in the general category of prostitutes (Kannabiran 1995; Shankar 1990; Srinivasan 1985). The forces of social regulation and colonization worked to create and reproduce the idea of *Devadasis* as once sacred but now fallen, and, in most accounts from the time, this was encapsulated in what I refer to as the "divided *Devadasi*"—that is, they were portrayed as either nuns or prostitutes.

Examining the complicated, contested, and culturally divisive position of *Devadasis* within Indian society is not a new undertaking, but it is crucial now to include the perspectives of "real" *Devadasis*, whose voices are all too often excluded within the social reform and *Devadasi* literature more broadly. Their experiences belie the image—often conjured up within the social imagination, contemporary discourse, and much academic work— of victimized but also degraded participants in a backward system that has been ritually, sexually, and politically devalued to the point where it is equated with commercial prostitution. These women and girls often hold conflicting ideas about their position within society and within the evolving *Devadasi* system itself, evincing contradictions that are reasonable given the oscillating and intervening factors of state control, ritual significance and status, economic necessity, and the work of modernist discourses in the regulation and representation of their lives. In this complex world they do not simply possess a single identity or only one idea about their lives; rather, they straddle and position themselves across a variety of socioeconomic, political, and religious terrains. This multiplicity does not contradict but rather imbues their everyday existence within a unique and culturally ambiguous tradition of sex work, particularly in a time of neoliberalism and the ever intruding role of state legislation and social reform campaigns.

Methodology

We conducted an ethnographic assessment of sex workers in northern Karnataka to determine the general characteristics of the sex work environment and specifically the organization of the *Devadasi* system. Our work was facilitated with the cooperation of representatives from a local nongovernmental organization (NGO), the Belgaum Integrated Rural Development Society (BIRDS), which had been conducting HIV/AIDS education in the region since 1997.

The four northern districts of Dharwad, Belgaum, Bagalkot, and Bijapur were the focus of our investigation, because these regions have traditionally been home to the largest numbers of *Devadasis*. BIRDS counselors were the first links to women and girls in the different communities and helped to build rapport and select key informants. From February 2001 to November 2002 we conducted interviews with ninety *Devadasis* in numerous villages and small towns throughout northern Karnataka. The participants felt most at ease with group discussions, which were carried out with women and girls between the ages of fourteen and fifty in the local *Kannada* language and then translated into English. We also conducted several interviews with BIRDS fieldworkers and counselors, physicians at district hospitals, employees of other NGOs, and members of government agencies such as the Karnataka State Women's Development Corporation (O'Neil et al. 2004). A workshop was held at the end of the project, providing an opportunity to check the validity of the data and to allow the *Devadasis* present to voice their opinions on the research findings and their experiences in the process.

"Hygienic Mistake," "Social Injustice," "Moral Monstrosity," and "Religious Crime": Representation and Reform of Devadasis during the Colonial Period

As noted above, the Contagious Diseases Act of 1868 did not apply to *Devadasis* because the policy of the British Crown was noninterference in religious matters. Although the colonial government remained hesitant to intervene in the *Devadasis* issue, many Indian women's groups and social reform organizations that were formed during this time took the lead in trying to abolish the system (Forbes 1996). Established by educated and upper-caste men and women who supported Victorian ideologies, many of these early-twentieth-century organizations viewed *Devadasis* as not only degraded women who were a throwback to a lost "golden age" but as impediments to national progress. A strong foundation within reform efforts was the idea embodied in the popular national slogan of that time: "India cannot be free until its women are free and women cannot be free until India is free" (Sinha 1998). The most outspoken and politically effective proponent of this position was Muthulaskhmi Reddy, a physician and the first Indian woman legislator and leader of the All-Indian Women's Congress from 1927 to 1936 (Kannabiran 1995; Sinha 1998; Whitehead 1998).

Reddy was determined to fight the dangers posed to national health by venereal diseases, perceived unhygienic practices of Indian mothers, and the *Devadasi* system (Whitehead 1998). Following her election to the Madras Legislative Council, which governed much of South India, including present-day Karnataka, Tamil Nadu, and Kerala, she introduced the Madras Hindu Religious Endowments Act (1929). This was the key legislation that spelled the end of the traditional *Devadasi* system, as it unlinked temple service from the receipt of *inams,* which were land grants and heritable rights in revenue from temple lands that were customarily granted to *Devadasis*. Although the Act was introduced to allow these women to own property without fear of extortion of their services, it ended up benefiting the men of the community who often intervened to inherit assets formerly set aside for the sole benefit of women (Srinivasan 1985). Threads of eugenic and "scientific" discourses ran through Reddy's speeches; the following section from an address to the Legislative Council during the debates regarding *Devadasi* land grants illustrates how she tied ideas about the polluting sexuality of individual *Devadasis* with the decay of the body politic and racial purity:

> It is beyond my comprehension how in a country which can boast of innumerable saints . . . irresponsibility in vice has been ignored and even encouraged (through the devadasi system) to the detriment of the health of the individual and of the future race . . . Modern science has proven that continence is conducive to the health and well-being of the individual, family, and the future race, and that sexual immorality harms both the individual and the community. Venereal disease is responsible for fifty percent of child blindness and deafness, much insanity, and other diseases such as paralysis, liver and kidney disease and heart disease . . . and it is a racial poison capable of being transmitted to one's children, the second, or even the third generation. (Cited in Whitehead 1998, 98)

The reaction of most *Devadasis* to these reforms was categorically against the legislative and social changes. Through such bodies as the Madras Devadasi Association, the women participated in debates and lobbied hard to defeat the reforms through protest meetings and memoranda sent to governments. One of their main objections was that the reforms equated devadasis with commercial sex workers (Jordan 1993; Raj 1993; Whitehead 1998). Indeed, in their defense they adopted the cultural grammar of the "divided *Devadasi*" discourse (i.e., prostitute or nun), focusing almost exclusively on their ritual and religious duties to the exclusion of any consideration of their participation in prostitution, in which most of them did indeed participate, along with carrying out their own religious duties.

The Madras Hindu Religious Endowments Act of 1929 was an essential first step in dismantling the *Devadasi* system, but its silence on dedication and prostitution itself meant that it did not really succeed in curtailing the practice. Queries into the status of the *Devadasi* system during the late 1930s from the Association for Moral and Social Hygiene in London once again engendered legislation, and in 1938 the Madras Devadasi (Prevention of Dedication) Bill was introduced (Sundara 1993). The outbreak of World War II and persistent colonial concerns about intervening in religious matters stalled the Bill, which was finally passed in 1947. The Bombay Presidency passed its own act against the system in 1934, which is significant because most northern districts of what is now Karnataka were part of the Bombay territory at that time. Passed by the British government, it made *Devadasi* dedication a crime and included a plan for government enfranchisement of the women's temple lands and the legalization of marriages of former *Devadasis* to men (Chakraborthy 2000; Datar 1992; Jordan 1993). The 1934 and 1947 acts, both of which were applied in most of present-day Karnataka, proved ineffective in preventing new dedications, and several decades passed before the issue was again raised in parliament.

As with earlier initiatives, in the 1980s legislation and reform activities were spearheaded by various women's groups, NGOs, and voluntary organizations. The driving force behind contemporary efforts to ban the *Devadasi* system is the Joint Women's Program (JWP), a voluntary organization based in the capital city of Bangalore, that was primarily concerned with the issues of rape, dowry, and discrimination against women. In 1981, amid controversy over a rape case linked to the *Devadasi* system and the government's denial that the *Devadasi* system even existed, the JWP took up the cause (Epp 1997, 226), launching an impressive media campaign to publicize the issue and pressure the state government to pass legislation against the system. Despite the many national and local press releases, magazine pieces, and public meetings, the state government did not pass such legislation until late 1982.

The Karnataka Devadasis (Prohibition of Dedication) Bill, the first to be presented in the local *Kannada* language, nullifies the dedication of any woman to a deity, either before or after the passage of the bill (Jordan 1993). As with previous legislation, it legalized the marriage of any woman previously dedicated and declared the children of such unions to be legitimate. It makes performing, permitting, participating in, or abetting dedication a crime punishable by up to three years imprisonment and a fine of up to Rs 2,000 (U.S.$475) (ibid., 273). Parents or guardians found guilty of dedicating a girl in their care may receive a harsher penalty of up to five years in jail and a fine of Rs 5,000 (U.S.$1,180). The bill empowered the state government to make rules for the enforcement of the Bill and, unlike earlier laws, it also included provisions for the women's care, protection, and rehabilitation. Most important, whereas previous laws could only be enforced if someone filed a complaint, the 1982 legislation made dedication a crime against the state (ibid.).

Although the government envisioned that the cost of reform activities would be offset by revenue generated by the fines imposed on those found guilty of dedicating girls into the system (Jordan 1993; Shankar 1990), the exact opposite occurred. Counter to expectations, the main beneficiaries of the reforms have been corrupt police officers, religious officials, and certain unsavory organizations formed to "help" these women, all of whom engaged in monetary extortion and sometimes forced sex from the women and girls involved. The widespread systemic corruption and the fact that no one has been prosecuted under the Bill means that the income needed for reform activities has not been generated as originally envisioned. Instead, the activities of these unscrupulous organizations and individuals have spawned new economic and sexual black markets that are directly related to the perpetuation of the *Devadasi* system, despite the existence of the Bill. This problematic situation and the paucity of government funds available to fund the rehabilitation system translates into reform programs and activities that are largely ineffective and in no way offer long-term, sustainable alternatives to sex work.

Government programs for rehabilitation have four main objectives: financial assistance and incentives for men to marry *Devadasis*; rehabilitation through self-employment; scholarships and hostels for the women's children, especially girls; and assistance to institutions that will offer "moral education" to *Devadasis* (Datar 1992). Unfortunately the implementation of these programs has been incomplete. However, teasing out the guiding moral and social principles embodied in the reform discourse about *Devadasis* and the system (i.e., evil practice, cult, and victims) and their approaches to rehabilitation (i.e., short-term loans and training, and a focus on individual women) does help to expose some of the problems of *Devadasi* reform.

One of the best examples of current reform tactics in Karnataka is a voluntary organization called Vimochana. It was established in 1985 by B. L. Patil, a lawyer who became a staunch advocate for *Devadasi* reform after learning about the practice from Jogan Shankar, author of *Devadasi Cult: A Sociological Analysis* (1990). From Patil's viewpoint, the system is a "euphemism for prostitution [and is] . . . deep-rooted under the façade of dogma, superstition and religious cult" (*Hejjegalu* 2001, 5). He believes that the best way to fight "this social evil is through the children of *Devadasis*, by education, health care, vocational training, employment, [and] marriage; to ensure their rehabilitation and integration into the mainstream of society" (ibid., 6). To this end, Vimochana has adopted 1,024 children from 960 towns throughout northern Karnataka and established the Kannada Medium Residential School (1990) and Residential High School (1992) for *Devadasi* children, the first in India (ibid., 6). Vimochana has also arranged the marriages of 180 girls and provides free care (education, medical needs, and food) for all children attending its schools. Although the focus is on female children, the organization has introduced income-generating activities geared toward adult *Devadasis,* including dairy, garment, and rope-making units, as well as wool spinning and a Handloom Development Centre (ibid., 7).

Although well intentioned, the lack of funds and moralizing attitude that pervades Vimochana's activities lead to situations of greater economic dependence on charity. For instance, trainees in the garment unit receive a daily stipend of Rs 20 (U.S.$0.04), of which they may save Rs 5 (U.S. $.50) after purchasing bus fare, tea, and tobacco. One *Devadasi* who participated in this scheme sums it up well, "But we are not doing too well here, there is no regular power supply, water and raw materials. Most houses have caved in with the rains" (*Hejjegalu* 2001, 10). In addition, Vimochana's reliance on the monetary support of groups like the Christian Children's Fund (CCF) makes them vulnerable to the forces of international donor profiles and annual program preferences. This is painfully clear in Patil's response to an interviewer's question about the potential cessation of CCF funding: "If they stop I'll go insane" (ibid., 11).

In another interview Patil discusses the roles of deep-seated religious faith and poverty, and the hold this combination has on many *Devadasi* women's decisions to dedicate their daughters. In his words:

> It was very difficult to convince the women of their plight. Here strong deep roots in religion and faith in the Goddess along with poverty and illiteracy made people bow to legend. Every girl child was a potential bread winner if she could be dedicated and sold into prostitution. (Menon 1997, 2)

Although Patil identifies the religious, economic, and gender-related push-pull factors behind the *Devadasi* system, by sponsoring short-lived, demoralizing, and often useless petty programs the organization may be exacerbating the women's economic dependence on sex work. Furthermore, he does so with absolutely no consideration of the cultural and religious importance that the system still has in many women's lives.

The "blame the victim" idea and piecemeal economic approach of this particular organization is no different than the broader discourse and activities of *Devadasi* reform in Karnataka today. This was clear during interviews we conducted with project officers of the Devadasi Rehabilitation Project (DRP), which works through the Karnataka State Women's Development Corporation (KSWDC) that was established in 1991. The DRP's main objectives are to stop *Devadasi* initiations and abolish the system altogether, but their central activities are health and "awareness camps." The health camps are intended to monitor the women's health status and are conducted at the primary health clinics in each district. When asked for more details about the awareness camps, one officer said they are designed to inform the women that "the tradition is bad and that they should lead a normal life." When asked what "bad" referred to, three "superstitions" were mentioned: dedication, dreadlocks (*jati*), and begging in the name of the Goddess. The women view *jati* as an embodiment of the Goddess and an especially powerful call to service within the *Devadasi* system, but reformers have constructed it as a fungus or infection that is the result of poor hygiene and improper grooming, thus reinforcing the medical-moral ideology within reformist discourse. These same reformers have also taken part in statewide hair-cutting campaigns, forcefully removing the *jatis* from the heads of *Devadasi* women, a severe violation of both human rights and ritual status (Ramberg 2006).

Additional examples of the neo-Social Purity beliefs that define the DRP emerged during discussions about the procedures *Devadasis* have to undergo prior to being approved for a loan, which is the organization's chief means of helping women become rehabilitated. The women told us that when they apply for a loan a program staff member takes them to a local hospital for a checkup, which involves a urine test and some kind of blood test. They also have to make a "self-declaration," which they described as similar to swearing an oath to tell the truth in a court of law. Placing their hand upon a sacred Hindu text, they must swear that they will quit doing sex work once they participate in a loan scheme under the DRP. Only when they pass the medical exam and make their declaration, which has to be on bond paper, can they be considered for a loan.

Five kinds of loans are offered by the DRP. The first is a housing loan, which is only available to *Devadasis* who have a plot of land in their name and can prove this claim with the appropriate legal certificates. The second loan program pertains to small industry and training, and involves the sum of Rs 10,000 (U.S.$ 2360), of which Rs 4,000 (U.S.$950) has to be repaid within a year. Cattle loans are the third type, and these usually entail a 60 percent subsidy on Rs 12,000 (U.S.$2,832). A fourth kind of loan has to do with vegetable farming and operate along the same lines as the small industry and training loan (60 percent subsidy on Rs 10,000 [U.S.$240]). The last loan type is for sweater knitting and includes nine months of training and the donation of sewing machines. The number of *Devadasis* per village and the number of loans available in each category also bear on the distribution of support. In 2000–2001, a total of three hundred housing loans were approved.

A consistent refrain we heard from *Devadasi* women about DRP or other government programs was that they were not useful and did not provide enough of a return to allow them to stop doing sex work. Common assertions during one interview included the following: "they are there and others have used them, but I don't use them because I can't return the money from the loan"; "no, because if we take a loan we can't return the money and the interest grows, we don't make anything from it"; and "what's the use of getting a cow if you can't make any money from it?"[1] During another interview, we learned that a group of women who had been struggling for the past eleven years to get DRP loans were swindled by men who promised them support through the state organization. Similar experiences are described by Menon (1997) in her article about *Devadasis* involved with the DRP. She found that the houses they received have almost all been defective and cannot withstand the constant shuttling of the heavy looms provided under the sewing program. Women Menon interviewed also admitted that because of the dismal economic return through the loan programs they continue working as prostitutes. Like many of the *Devadasis* with whom we spoke, those featured in this article feared the loss of their income, property, and status as a result of their participation social reform programs.

Since they were clearly aware of the insufficiency of the loan schemes, we asked the women what they thought about rehabilitation generally. Some said that it has raised awareness about the *Devadasi* tradition and helped them become more educated, which was explained as a collective realization that they do not "need" to initiate young girls into the system. Many of these same women have adopted the language of reform, which was evident when they talked about *jati* as a disease and the result of improper care of the hair. However, those who continue to view the dreadlock hairstyle as a strong link with the deity resent the medical approach taken by the DRP. When describing her feelings about this issue, one older woman shook her head, looked up to the ceiling, and raised her arms, illustrating with her body both her resistance to reform and her enduring bond with the Goddess above. Whether or not they adopt reform rhetoric, virtually all *Devadasis* who receive loans use the income to supplement, not supplant, the income they receive from sex work, which is impossible to quit given the major economic burdens most women assume within their household (e.g., financing weddings, medical care, and basic amenities). Still others are totally unaware of the government offering any reform activities.

Bottom's Up: Collectivization as an Alternative to State-Run, Top-Down HIV Interventions

Prostitute-run collectives have existed throughout the world since the 1970s, when they were part of the women's struggles against police harassment and state abuse, and for the decriminalization of sex work (Bell 1994; Kempadoo 1998). As part of "second-wave" feminism, these groups experienced both support and controversy in the wider domain of women's political protests over issues such as reproductive rights, child care, wage parity with men, gender and racial discrimination, and sexual freedom. Although groups like COYOTE (Call Off Your Old Tired Ethics) in San Francisco and CORP (Canadian Organization for Prostitute's Rights) in Toronto, Canada, were able to mobilize various sex worker communities and politicize the issue of sex work, their achievements applied mainly to women in "First World" countries.

Indian sex workers have also been coming together in small groups since the 1970s to assert themselves and fight for safer working conditions, mainly in large urban centers in the northern part of the country. In 1972 a group of sex workers and women previously involved in the trade formed a registered organization called Nari Kalyan Samiti in Calcutta (Sleightholme and Sinha 1997). The women mobilized out of their shared frustration with the violence and morally degrading abuses directed toward them by a local political figure, who almost killed one of the group's leaders (ibid.). Although they were successful in having the man arrested, the organization dissolved as a result of the members' differing political views. In 1980, again in Calcutta, several women joined forces to set up the Mahila Sangha (Women's Organization) and focused on exposing and prosecuting a local criminal who extorted money from them (ibid.). Several years later, in 1992, the Abahelit Mahila Samiti was established by former leaders of the dissolved Nari Kalyan Samiti, who now work to secure educational access for the children of sex workers as well as better legal protection and social support for women selling sex (ibid.).

Based in Sonagachi, Calcutta's oldest and largest red light area, the STD/ HIV Intervention Programme (SHIP) is the best-known sex worker project in India. Launched in 1992 by the All-India Institute of Hygiene and Public Health along with community-based organizations and local NGOs, SHIP's main objectives are to provide health-care services, HIV/STD education and awareness, and condom promotion (Jana et al. 1999, 58). Working against the traditional medical- and state-intervention models of "rescuing" or "rehabilitating" the women, SHIP concentrates instead on promoting peer education as the principle means to develop an empowering environment, help the women achieve a sense of self-definition, and establish sustainable programs (Jana 1999; Jana et al. 1999). The "three Rs" approach—Respect, Reliance, and Recognition—has worked remarkably well, and rates of STDs and HIV among the women have dropped significantly and condom use rose from 27 percent in 1992 to 86 percent in 2001 (Jana et al. 1999). Their commitment to involving clients, police, and other local players in sex trade-related interventions is another important component of their success, especially because the initiative was seen as a partner in helping the women remain healthy and work longer, rather than as an obstacle or competitor to the established sex trade system.

As noted above, our research team worked with the Belgaum Integrated Rural Development Society, an NGO that began as an agricultural cooperative. BIRDS began doing their HIV-related work in 1996, and in 1997 a sex worker collective, or *sangha*, was formed in the district of Belgaum. The organization's efforts in the area of sex work began in 1996–1997, when BIRDS was selected as a model NGO collective for sex workers, based in part on the organization's successes in cooperative activism at the grass-roots level. HIV/AIDS prevention is one of their prime objectives, and they have established the peer-education system to train and educate the women. Peers are selected by and from the women, in collaboration with BIRDS representatives. The representatives help with technical coordination and the development of appropriate training strategies to educate the women about HIV/ AIDS, condoms, collectivization, legal advice, and other health issues.

Belgaum, the first collective (*sangha*) to be established, is based in the city of Gokak and at the time of my research had 135 members, representing all the women in northern Karnataka. The group in Bijapur district soon separated, however, followed by the group in the town of Mudhol (Bagalkote district). These fissions were not the result of interpersonal problems but of natural geographic and logistic practicalities. Each collective has eleven board members who are elected annually and meet weekly to discuss developments in the field and the women's concerns, and to receive condoms. All the *sanghas* have two bank accounts: one is held jointly by the elected president and secretary and is the source of the wages for peer educators, and the other is a self-help group account that BIRDS initiated which consists of weekly donations from the women. Sometimes these donations are collected at the end of the month and are available as a loan for a woman in particular need. As of 2006 fourteen collectives were registered throughout the state, and several more are in the process of being established (Halli et al. 2006).

Despite the dedicated work of BIRDS organizers and counselors and of peer-educators, a number of issues appear to be impeding the NGO's ability to go beyond its central activity of condom distribution. The topics raised below are based on data gleaned from notes taken during *sangha* meetings, BIRDS workshops, and observations in the field. I include them here because they expose some of the structural factors contributing to the continuation of certain socio-sexual and health inequalities among *Devadasis* and other sex workers who receive assistance from BIRDS.

In a spring 2002 meeting it was revealed that some clients still do not want to wear *nirodhs* (condoms), claiming that they will not be sexually satisfied, and this is causing the *Devadasis* to lose clients and money. This is not unexpected, but that women have received condom distribution for more than five years in this area speaks to the persistent difficulties they experience when trying to enforce their use with clients. This is troubling because, in their interviews, the women and girls described a different picture: they all said that they *always* used condoms, particularly with non-regular clients, that they did not have problems getting clients to wear them, and if they ever encountered problems they would just "send them off." Clearly, after five years of intensive condom distribution and education, this is not the case, and, unfortunately, it is a common experience among sex workers in various settings (Campbell 2000).

Going beyond condom distribution is important, especially with respect to gaining political presence and strength for the collectives. What is impeding the *sanghas*, and what is the impact on *Devadasis*? Four interrelated factors appear to be at play in preventing the *sanghas* from moving beyond condom distribution toward broader and more self-sustaining programs. First, BIRDS is a male-run organization. Although the *sanghas* operate largely through networks of women, their funding, training, supplies, and direction all stem from the parent NGO, which was founded and run by men. This contrasts sharply with the female-directed and feminist/human rights ideologies guiding the DMSC in Calcutta and other similar organizations, many of which insist that no men are involved after incidents of unwanted sexual advances and disruptive affairs between women and male staff members. The second factor is the limited experience of BIRDS organizers and counselors with women in prostitution. Groups of sex workers in Calcutta have existed since the early 1970s, whereas BIRDS has been in the field of sex work and HIV prevention for a relatively short time. This point is not intended to belittle the organization's influential work but to draw attention to the challenges involved in becoming well equipped to deal with the population(s) and issues in question, especially given their extended areas of focus from agriculture to sex work and HIV/AIDS.

The third issue is the lack of broader programs that could reach several of the other populations that the women deal with at work and in their personal lives (i.e., clients and *khiams*, or long-term lovers). Initiatives such as literacy and leadership training, housing programs that actually work (versus those under the DRP), and the development of alternative employment opportunities could reduce the women's socioeconomic dependency on sex work. This is a daunting task, however, given that BIRDS has to work under the constraints of a mainly foreign-funded program that does not want to provide funds for general social welfare programs but wants, instead, to fund programs with the specific aim of achieving high rates of condom use and distribution (Orchard 2002).

The final factor relates to the ideological and programmatic influences that have impacted BIRDS. As the name Belgaum Integrated Rural Development Society implies, this NGO borrows heavily from the program structures implemented under the national Integrated Rural Development Programs (IRDP) introduced in the late 1970s and the 1980s (Mendelsohn and Vicziany 1998). Although it differed from other antipoverty schemes by envisioning tangible assets (e.g., cows and sewing machines) that its beneficiaries could use to make a better living, the implementation of the IRDP has been "little short of a nightmare" because the government assumed that thousands of habitually poor, usually illiterate people could become mini-entrepreneurs (Mendelsohn and Vicziany 1998, 162). Although BIRDS is trying to establish more effective strategies for development and empowerment among the women than offering cows or sewing machines, it has not yet been able to transform its organizational structure and implement programs to help this become a reality.

Discussion

This chapter has examined some of the historical and contemporary impacts of social reform on *Devadasi* women and girls, demonstrating the largely moral-medical and individualistic discourse operating within both approaches to providing services for *Devadasis*. We have seen how state and NGO reliance on these tactics, far from helping the women and girls to any great extent, may in fact lead to new forms of inequalities in socioeconomic, health, gender, political and sexual spheres. Alternatives to these top-down tactics have developed, such as the formation of sex worker collectives organized by peers within the women's communities to fight the spread of HIV and cope with other pressing socioeconomic and sexual issues.

Two fundamental ideas that have defined *Devadasis* within reform movements are that prostitution is a necessary evil and that the women and girls who participate in this system are victims of barbaric traditions and patriarchy, or they are marginalized in a presumably powerless status as "Third World" sex workers (Doezema 1998, 2001; Whitehead 1998). Since the mid-nineteenth century, several shifts occurred in how these women have been represented and regulated, many of which involved far-reaching extensions of state power through legislation and broader political objectives geared toward presenting India as a modern nation. For instance, the International Social Purity campaigns and the rising rates of venereal disease among British nationals stationed in India combined to produce an image of prostitutes as degraded, dangerous, and a threat to national health and security because of their "natural" tendencies to spread sexual disease. *Devadasis* were not "just prostitutes," however, and their complex association with religious traditions and practices, not to mention their relatively powerful status compared to other Hindu women, presented the colonial project in India with particular challenges over issues of sexuality, culture, and administrative control. Rising to these challenges involved not only sweeping social reforms and legislation but also a radical transformation of Indian beliefs and ideas about the *Devadasi* system. In many ways this significant shift can be viewed as resulting from the process of internal colonization, which perceived the institution as a tarnished remnant of a more uncivilized time and the women themselves as impediments of modernity.

Many current social reform efforts operate through tropes similar to those of the past, including "rescue" and "rehabilitation," but newer concerns, including child prostitution and HIV/AIDS, have added fuel to what is now termed a "burning issue" (Orchard 2007), and now these concerns often exacerbate the women's already disadvantaged socioeconomic, religious, and sexual status. Moreover, the state's alternative to sex work is little more than the classic strategy of blaming the victim, while a medical-moral discourse and short-term loans often lead to greater economic dependency on insufficient government handouts and a deep sense of betrayal among the women regarding the displacement of their beliefs, practices, and identity, both at the individual level and in the collective realm.

In response to these top-down, state-run programs, some NGOs have assisted sex workers, including *Devadasis,* in establishing their own collective organizations through which they educate one another about HIV, distribute condoms, obtain legal advice, and help to mobilize the community. Despite such efforts, however, structural factors that include gender, police brutality, and predominantly individualistic models of development hamper the NGOs' ability to achieve "real" empowerment; sometimes the NGOs may even replicate some of the existing socioeconomic, gender, sexual, and health inequalities that work to marginalize *Devadasi* women and girls.

This chapter has explored contemporary techniques of social reform in the context of the current neoliberal period, highlighting the implications of the state's strategies for exercising power over *Devadasi* women and girls and their families. As Ramberg (2006, 126) has asserted in her account of ethics, kinship, and ritual among modern *Devadasis*, contemporary social reforms produce new kinds of subjects and new relations to the state. These new relations are partially the product of a particular historical relationship that has long existed between *Devadasis* and certain power structures, including the state and temple administration, and are partially the result of new forms of resistance to government programs and state intervention, primarily through the establishment of collectives. Today many *Devadasis* in Karnataka are engaged in collective mobilization efforts through which they hope to make socioeconomic and political improvements in their lives. Although these endeavors are not always easy or without their own inequalities, in the process and contrary to associations with a backward tradition, the *Devadasis* have shown themselves to be adept, creative, and most certainly modern citizens of India.

NOTE

1. For a similar example, see Ramberg 2006, 125.

14

Moral Panic

Sex Tourism, Trafficking, and the Limits
of Transnational Mobility in Bahia

ERICA LORRAINE WILLIAMS

The opportunities for transnational mobility available to socially and economically disadvantaged Brazilian women often arise through their intimate encounters with foreigners, but sensational media stories frequently depict such instances where foreign tourists facilitate trips to the tourists' home countries as criminal cases of "trafficking." The experiences of the Brazilian women Ivete and Fabiana illustrate how this problem typically may occur, for the underlying assumption is that the women will be forced into prostitution.

When I visited the home of Pérola, a black woman who was an active member of the Association of Prostitutes of Bahia (APROSBA), she showed me a picture of her friend Ivete, a brown-skinned woman in her late thirties who had just returned from Germany. Ivete had gone to visit a "gringo" she met doing *programas* (commercial sexual exchange) in Salvador de Bahia. After a month in Germany, she returned to Salvador and shared with her friends news, pictures, and memories of her positive experience overseas. In contrast to Ivete's rewarding trip, Fabiana, the president of APROSBA, expressed anxiety over the risks of transnational mobility and migration for sex workers. She once had a foreign client-turned-boyfriend who wanted to marry her and take her to Europe. Instead of eagerly taking advantage of the opportunity to travel abroad, Fabiana was cautious about putting herself in a potentially precarious situation and she declined his offer: "I'm afraid to leave Brazil. I'm afraid of the cold . . . of not having money to return."

My point in juxtaposing Fabiana's fear of overseas travel with Ivete's positive experience of foreign travel is not necessarily to question the extent to which sensationalized horror stories of trafficking are true or not. Rather, my critique is that campaigns against sex tourism and trafficking often unwittingly fall into the trap of constructing any and all situations in which "vulnerable" women travel abroad with the help of foreigners as potential cases of trafficking.

This chapter analyzes public debates surrounding sex tourism, as well as the effects and limitations of anti–sex tourism campaigns in Salvador de Bahia, Brazil, mounted by the state and civil society. Although sex tourism and trafficking are separate issues, they are often conflated in the official policies of national and international agencies. What are the divergent ways in which governmental and nongovernmental agents understand sex tourism and trafficking, and how do these understandings shape their efforts? How do campaigns against sex tourism and trafficking risk reaffirming patriarchal values and placing further restrictions upon (specific) women's mobility, especially women of African descent. In this way we can see how anti-trafficking discourse in Brazil is informed by fears and beliefs about race. In analyzing the work of CHAME (Humanitarian Center for the Support of Women), a nongovernmental organization (NGO) that raises awareness about sex tourism and trafficking, I offer a critique of how their well-intentioned campaigns often reproduce stereotypical images and sensationalized stories that contribute to a "moral panic" (Carby 1992; Cohen 1972; Herdt 2009) over interracial sex and transnational border crossings. At the same time I suggest that a more effective approach to improve sex workers' lives can be found in the work of Associação das Prostitutas da Bahia (APROSBA).

CHAME

CHAME is the only NGO engaged in campaigns to raise public awareness about sex tourism and trafficking in Brazil. Founded in 1994 by Jacqueline Leite, CHAME became an independent NGO in 2001. The mission of CHAME is to:

> alert society to the risks of exploitation of young and adult women in the different forms of migration and recruitment for forced labor (sexual, domestic, and other modalities of slavery, usually linked to physical or psychological violence), respecting her freedom of choice. (CHAME pamphlet, n.d.)

Though terms such as "slavery," "forced labor," and "exploitation" parallel the vocabulary of abolitionist organizations, the use of the phrase "freedom

other purposes such as sweatshop labor, adoption, and domestic work. That there seems to be a greater deal of mobilization and outcry about trafficking for sex work belies two assumptions: that sexual labor is more pernicious and devastating than other forms of labor and that the state has a vested interest in maintaining other forms of exploitative labor (Chang 2004).

CHAME's Perspectives on Sex Tourism and Trafficking

CHAME understands trafficking not only as a problem of morality, migration, and organized crime but also as a violation of fundamental human rights and "one of the most perverse forms of violence against women" (CHAME pamphlet 1, n.d.). CHAME identifies eight contributing factors to trafficking: (1) social and economic inequality, (2) unemployment, (3) social exclusion, (4) sex tourism, (5) gender discrimination, (6) laws and politics about migration and migrant work, (7) corruption of authorities, and (8) organized crime. CHAME conflates sex tourism and trafficking by referring to sex tourism as the "gateway" or "tip of the iceberg" to trafficking (Ana Paula, interview, 2005; CHAME materials). I was told by Reginaldo Serra, an officer of the specialized police force that deals with tourist issues (Delegation for the Protection of Tourists—Deltur):

> It's a very serious problem . . . They [foreign men] take women over there [abroad] . . . [with] the proposal to live in Europe . . . [but] it's nothing like they thought it would be. They're held hostage by elements of the mafia and can't return home again. Sex tourism is really ambiguous, but it's criminal. The tourist comes seeking people to take back with him. (Interview, 2006)

For Officer Serra, sex tourism and trafficking are virtually indistinguishable. Officer Serra conflates sex tourists with *mafiosos* and traffickers, and assumes that the goal of sex tourists is to find women to "bring back" to their home countries.

Discourses of sex tourism and trafficking construct "victims" in particular ways. Categories such as gender, race, age, and sexuality inform which group is seen as in need (read: *worthy*) of intervention, protection, and rescue from the state and civil society (Alexander 1991; Agustín 2007). As sociologist Laura Agustín (2007, 39) argues, in treating "perpetrator" and "victim" as identities rather than temporary conditions, the violence against women framework situates "victims" as "passive receptacles and mute sufferers who must be saved." Brazilian Gabriela Leite, a sex workers' rights activist, claimed that when the concept of trafficking is confused with sex tourism, it is automatically assumed that a woman traveling with her own money is a "victim of trafficking." As Leite explained in a presentation I attended (Central Unica dos Trabalhadores 2005), "If a prostitute is caught in Europe, of course [she is] going to say [she was] trafficked!" Similarly, as Adriana Piscitelli (2008) points out in her research on Brazilian women who migrate to Italy and Spain to marry or work in the sex industry, the danger of illegality often encourages migrant sex workers to say they were trafficked in order to escape persecution.

Although CHAME respects women's freedom of choice to travel, much of the educational materials it produces use scare tactics that risk limiting the possibilities of mobility for women who are deemed "vulnerable." In the critical work they do to raise awareness of the dangers of sex tourism and trafficking, CHAME advocates for women's rights to have transnational aspirations but simultaneously highlights the risks involved in the *means* through which many women have access to transnational mobility, for example, through people they meet in the touristscape of Salvador de Bahia. It is important to realize, however, that the kinds of access that Bahians have to transnational connections and mobility are profoundly affected by disparities of race and class. For instance, a working-class black woman in Bahia, regardless of her educational level, is less likely to have opportunities to travel abroad unless it is through her romantic, friendly, or familial connections with foreigners. Jafari Sinclaire Allen (2007) and Denise Brennan (2004) and others have also discussed this in the context of Cuba and the Dominican Republic, respectively. I had numerous conversations with Bahians about this unequal access to travel. Young black Brazilian students, activists, hip-hop artists, and dancers were stuck in place, unable to travel abroad, while at home in Bahia they constantly encountered young students, researchers, and volunteers visiting from North America and Europe.

CHAME's Campaign Materials: An "Archive of Racialized Sexuality"

CHAME's campaign materials constitute an "archive of racialized sexuality" (Reddy 2005) that reflects global perspectives about black Brazilian women, foreign (European) men, and the possibilities of sex, intimacy, migration, love, marriage, and exploitation. Chandan Reddy defines such an archive as an "active technique by which sexual, racial, gendered, and national differences . . . are suppressed, frozen, and redirected" (115).

The CHAME materials use stock images depicting Brazilian women of African descent as naïve, ignorant, and willing to do anything for the opportunity to migrate to Europe. In one of CHAME's pamphlets, for example, there is a cartoon image on the front of a blond, muscular European man standing in an open door superimposed on a land mass labeled "Europa." The European man is smiling and reaching out his hand to someone. Upon opening the pamphlet, another image depicts a large white hand holding a postcard of a curvaceous black woman wearing a miniscule bikini. The woman makes a "thumbs-up" sign with one of her hands, while seductively yet playfully pointing the other hand down toward her pubic area. Upon closing the pamphlet, the front image is now complete; we see that the European man is reaching out to this black Bahian woman. She is superimposed on a land mass marked "Brasil." In high heels, short shorts, and a tank top revealing a bare midriff, she stands with her knees slightly bent and her arms outstretched, as if ready to leap into the man's arms. Lips puckered and eyes wide and bright, the three hearts circling her head suggest she is smitten. This final image evokes hopefulness, eagerness, and desire. But its location in a brochure warning about the dangers of trafficking leaves the reader with the unsettling feeling that things may not turn out the way the Bahian woman hopes.

Conversely, in these campaign materials, European men are generally cast as evil and sinister perpetrators who always have ulterior motives. In the brochure titled "Travel Is a Dream? Sometimes a Nightmare!" drawn by Mario Brito, the front cover features a black woman and a blond-haired, blue-eyed, European man embracing. The woman's eyes are closed, and a circle of hearts flutters above her head. She imagines this man as a smiling prince with a crown, an angelic halo, and a big heart. She cannot see his face, however, which is contorted into a sinister snarl, as he imagines her as a domestic worker holding a broom while dressed in sexy lingerie with a ball and chain tied to her ankle.

The comic strip tells the tragic (love) story of this couple who met during Carnaval. As the woman puts the finishing touches on her makeup, she says to herself with a conniving grin, "Who knows, maybe I'll hook up [arrumo] with a gringo in the streets." Next we see two blond male tourists enjoying Carnaval and conversing about how "easy" [oferecidas] Bahian women are, so different from the "civilized white women" of Europe. One of the men says, "We're going to get the most out of these [women] . . . they fall easily for our game and even think we're rich." At that moment, they spot the black woman dancing seductively by herself. After this encounter in the street, the story quickly shifts to one of the men sitting with the woman at a table full of empty beer bottles and cans, and then her accompanying him back to his hotel; finally, we see them in bed, the sheets rumpled. The man promptly asks her if she would like to go to his country with him, and she responds, "That's all I've ever wanted. It's like a dream!" The seamlessness of this narrative is not only striking but is obviously oversimplified to ensure the brevity and clarity of the brochure's message.

Things quickly deteriorate when she travels to his (unidentified European) country. The Brazilian woman is pictured alone in an empty, rundown room with four locks on the door. Pregnant and crying, she laments about how she feels used and vulnerable in a foreign country far from her family. She continues, "He keeps me in prison and doesn't let me leave . . . I thought I was smart . . . that I would marry him. I want to go back, but the jerk hid my travel documents. I don't have any money." Thus the Bahian woman was tricked by the man she thought was her "prince charming."

Finally, the last frame zooms in on the woman's face and pregnant belly as she screams: "The dream turned into a nightmare!!! I want to go home!!!" She is repentant for her naïveté, for her eagerness to trust this foreigner and put her fate into his hands in the hope of a better future. The notion that the "prince charming" turns into a "frog" once the Brazilian woman is in Europe reflects consistent themes in how CHAME represents the "dangers of sex tourism and trafficking," particularly regarding the naïveté and unrealistic expectations of Brazilian women of African descent. Is this woman's situation intended to be seen as an example of trafficking or simply as a transnational romance and migration gone awry? If the purpose of trafficking is to exploit some kind of labor, what kind of labor is she expected or forced to perform?

The representational strategy of cartoons unwittingly reproduces stereotypes both of Brazilian women of African descent and European men. The graphic images imitate the ways in which postcards from Brazil eroticize black women's sexuality as a tourist attraction. The women are often pictured alone, as if inviting the foreign tourist to an isolated beach where he will find single, available women. The comic strips and testimonies in CHAME's educational materials differ from touristic postcards in that they rely almost exclusively on the use of "terrifying" life narratives of trafficked persons.

Upon asking Jacqueline how the idea to use cartoon images emerged as a significant tool in their educational and awareness-raising campaign efforts, she explained that the organization did not want to use photos that "could link anyone directly to crime or criminal connotation" (personal communication, 2009). She also stated that they thought cartoons would appeal to young people and that the images would not directly connect women or youth to any specific community of Salvador. Despite their best intentions, however, CHAME's campaigns unwittingly fall into the use of sensational methods to get the message across. The sensational images of the CHAME educational materials contradict Leite's critique of government campaigns against sex tourism as being xenophobic and creating "hysteria" in Brazil around sex tourism, in which "any foreigner in Salvador is seen as if he were a sex tourist."

Moral Panic

Even while espousing their rights to travel abroad if they so choose, CHAME's campaign materials nonetheless construct an image of Brazilian women of color as naïve, vulnerable, innocent victims of unscrupulous foreign men. The images, as well as the unparalleled attention garnered by sex tourism and trafficking, indicate that a "moral panic" has emerged around questions of interracial sex and sexuality, national image, and transnational tourism and mobility (Herdt 2009; Cohen 1972). Although the travels and travails of European men are the *source* of this panic, their effects are shifted to the bodies of women of African descent. This raises a crucial question: Who is *allowed* to enjoy the privileges of transnational mobility?

As vulnerable subjects and targets of a moral panic, black women and sex workers (neither synonymous nor mutually exclusive categories) are constructed in a way that places their right to be transnationally mobile into question. In other words, the specter of sex tourism has created a situation in which Brazilian women of African descent who want to move beyond national borders are not only discouraged because of the "risks and dangers" of trafficking but are also automatically seen as "suspect." In referring to the "specter of sex tourism," I am suggesting that not only sex workers or sex tourists feel the effects of discourses surrounding sex tourism. These discourses also profoundly impact the interactions between foreign tourists and locals and what they think about each other's motivations and intentions, particularly regarding sex and intimacy.

Moral panic occurs when "a condition, episode, person or group of persons emerges to become defined as a threat to societal values and interests" (Cohen 1972, 9). Moral panic creates a flurry of mass-media activity, where the object of the panic is presented in "stylized and stereotypical fashion," and experts propose solutions and develop coping strategies for the problem (ibid.). Moral panic provokes new techniques for governing the self and others, and "produce[s] state and non-state stigma, ostracism, and social exclusion" (Herdt 2009, 3). In articulating the concept of "moral panic," I draw from Hazel Carby's (1992) essay, in which she argues that the migration of black women to northern cities in the United States in the early twentieth century generated a moral panic associated with the construction of black female migrants as both "sexually degenerate and socially dangerous" (739), and in need of protection as they are "at risk" or "vulnerable" to falling into prostitution (741).

This idea resonates with the Brazilian campaigns against sex tourism and trafficking that depict Brazilian women of African descent as not only naïve but also eager to use their transnational ties to foreigners as a "get-rich-quick" scheme. The underlying implication might be that, lacking the necessary skills and qualifications to succeed and acquire a higher standard of living in Brazil, these women seek out opportunities to try their luck abroad. They see transnational romance and marriage or job opportunities as the best and most efficient strategy to achieve upward mobility. Their dreams of transnational mobility, however, violate a moral and social order in which they are always already poor, marginalized, and unable to move. Like M. Jacqui Alexander's (2005) concept of the "queer fetishized native," they are discursively stuck in place, never allowed to move or travel. Ironically, although black women have long been situated at the bottom of a racial/gender hierarchy, they are overwhelmingly sought out by foreign tourists who travel to Brazil in search of erotic adventures with "exotic Others." Thus a major disruption of the racial social order occurs when a Brazilian woman of African descent successfully travels abroad.

The fears provoked by the migration of black women to northern U.S. cities in the early 1900s and those aroused by black women's mobility in contemporary Bahia raise questions about the gendered aspects of travel. Paulla Ebron (1997) points out that women travelers are often portrayed as morally distasteful and sexually promiscuous, whereas men's travels are seen as "stories of masculine agency" (225). Moreover, as Laura Agustín (2007) asks: Why should the travels of people from less wealthy countries be understood as fundamentally different from those of Europeans? Although many seem to think that the term "cosmopolitan" should be reserved for "elite, urbane globetrotters," Agustin contends that there is no reason poorer travelers should be disqualified from cosmopolitanism (44).

Conclusion: APROSBA as an Alternative Model

APROSBA's depiction of sex workers as dignified subjects with the power to control their destinies rather than as vulnerable victims is perhaps a more fruitful response to untangling the sex work–trafficking conflation. Founded in 1997, APROSBA is the only organization in Bahia run by and for prostitutes. That adult prostitution is legal in Brazil has not ameliorated its stigmatization. Prostitutes in Salvador must therefore negotiate their agency in a society that stigmatizes their trade, a police system that often abuses and criminalizes them rather than protecting them, and a health system that perceives them as "vectors of disease." APROSBA mobilizes for prostitutes' rights, recognition, and the full benefits of citizenship. In the words of the organization's co-founder, Fabiana: "We want to show that prostitutes are also dignified people who exercise a profession like any other" (cited in Francisco 2006). The activities of APROSBA include weekly meetings for members, safe sex workshops, group activities, and the distribution of condoms and educational materials. APROSBA also refers members to lawyers and health centers, offers support in cases of sexual and physical abuse, and contacts local media outlets when organizing protests.

APROSBA is integrated into regional, national, and international networks of sex workers' associations. Not only is it a member of the Rede Brasileira de Prostitutas (Brazilian Network of Prostitutes), established in 1987 by Gabriela Leite, but it was selected by the Rede to organize the Projeto Sem Vergonha (Without Shame Project) in May 2007, which consisted of a weeklong training program that brought together fifteen sex worker activists from various organizations in the northeastern region. In March 2006 APROSBA became the first prostitutes' association in the world to launch its own radio station. Funded by the Ministry of Culture, Radio Zona was envisioned as a way to reach out to prostitutes and transform society's dominant views of prostitution by discussing issues such as human rights, sexual abuse, social issues, HIV/AIDS prevention, and racism (Francisco 2006).

In examining the circulation of discourses around "sex tourism" and "trafficking" in Brazil, this chapter has illustrated how even the most well-intended efforts can reproduce stereotypical images that confine people to their respective places. The "specter of vulnerability" creates a moral panic in which already marginalized people are stigmatized even further. The ways in which moral panic affects even women who are not engaged in sex work is exemplified in the following case from my fieldwork.

Sean is an African American gay man who has lived for a long time in Salvador, where he is a member of the Afro-Brazilian religion of candomblé. Iya Taís, his *mãe de santo* (godmother in the candomblé house where he lives), is an attractive Afro-Brazilian woman who looks significantly younger than her years would suggest. When Iya Taís wanted to travel to the United States to visit Sean for Thanksgiving, she made the trip to the nearest U.S. consulate in Recife, Pernambuco, armed with all the necessary supporting documents from Sean. To both her and Sean's dismay, neither the carefully prepared documents nor her responsibilities as a mother, grandmother, wife, and *mãe de santo* that tied her to Salvador were sufficient to convince the consular agent that she was not a migration risk. The agent promptly denied Iya Taís a U.S. visa simply because she did not believe her story.

In this case, the consular agent apparently could not imagine a young-looking, attractive, black woman traveling to the United States for any legitimate reason that did not involve transnational intimacies or the risk of illegal migration. This story underlines the message of this chapter, that the specter of sex tourism has created a situation in Bahia in which black Brazilian women who wish to move beyond their borders are seen as suspicious and discouraged because of the "risks and dangers" of trafficking. As such, limiting and limited transnational mobility is yet another extension of the multiple forces of institutional racism, discrimination, policing, and violence that black Brazilians suffer daily. The denial of Iya Taís's visa is a sad but vivid illustration of how state policy and nongovernmental projects surrounding sexual labor, informed by cultural beliefs about sex, race, and class, and citizenship more generally, further marginalize black Brazilian women, whether they are sex workers or not.

References

Abel, Gillian, Lisa Fitzgerald, and Cheryl Brunton. 2009. "The Impact of Decriminalization on the Number of Sex Workers in New Zealand." *Journal of Social Policy* 38:1–17.

Abel, Gillian, Lisa Fitzgerald, and Catherine Healey, eds. 2010. *Taking the Crime out of Sex Work: New Zealand Sex Workers' Fight for Decriminalization.* Bristol, UK: Policy.

Abrahams, Naeema, Rachel Jewkes, and Ria Laubsher. 1999. "'I Do Not Believe in Democracy in the Home': Men's Relationships and Abuse of Women." Cape Town: Medical Research Council Report. Retrieved October 13, 2010, from http://www.mrc.ac.za/gender/nodemocracy.pdf.

Abreu, Maurício de. 1997 [1979]. *A Evolução Urbana do Rio de Janeiro.* Rio de Janeiro: IPLANRIO.

Adler, Amy. 2007. "Symptomatic Cases: Hysteria in the Supreme Court's Nude Dancing Decisions." *American Imago* 64 (3): 297–316.

Agarwal, Sheela. 2006. "Social Exclusion at English Seaside Resorts." *Tourism Management* 27:351–372.

Aggleton, Peter, ed. 1999. *Men Who Sell Sex: International Perspectives on Male Prostitution and HIV/AIDS.* Philadelphia: Temple University Press.

Agustín, Laura Maria. 2007. *Sex at the Margins: Migration, Labor Markets, and the Rescue Industry.* London: Zed Books.

AIDS in Brazil. 2008. "A Portrait in Red." *The Economist Online,* March 13. Retrieved from http://www.tiny.cc/hvvov.

Alexander, M. Jacqui. 1991. "Redrafting Morality: The Postcolonial State and the Sexual Offences Bill of Trinidad and Tobago." In *Third World Women and the Politics of Feminism,* ed. Chandra T. Mohanty, Ann Russo, and Lourdes Torres, 63–100. Bloomington: Indiana University Press.

———. 2005. *Pedagogies of the Crossing: Meditations on Feminism, Sexual Politics, Memory, and the Sacred.* Durham, NC: Duke University Press.

Allen, Jafari Sinclaire. 2007. "Means of Desire's Production: Male Sex Labor in Cuba." *Identities: Global Studies in Culture and Power* 14: 183–202.

Altink, Sietske. 1995. *Stolen Lives: Trading Women into Sex and Slavery.* London: Scarlet.

Altink, Sietske, and Sylvia Bokelman. 2006. *Rechten van Prostituees* (Rights of Prostitutes). Amsterdam: Rode Draad.

Alves, José Eustáquio Diniz, and Sônia Corrêa. 2009. "As Interfaces de Gênero no Cairo +15." Text presented at the "Brasil, 15 anos após a Conferência do Cairo," Belo Horizonte, Brazil, August 11.

Amar, Paul. 2009. "Operation Princess in Rio de Janeiro: Policing 'Sex Trafficking,' Strengthening Worker Citizenship, and the Urban Geopolitics of Security in Brazil." *Security Dialogue* 4–5 (40): 513–541.

Amnesty International. 1997. *Breaking the Silence: Human Rights Violations Based on Sexual Orientation.* London: Amnesty International.

Arnold, David. 1993. *Colonizing the Body: State Medicine and Epidemic Disease in Nineteenth-Century India.* Berkeley: University of California Press.

Asia Watch. 1993. *A Modern Form of Slavery: Trafficking of Burmese Women and Girls into Brothels in Thailand.* New York: Human Rights Watch.

Bandura, Albert. 2000. "Exercise of Human Agency through Collective Efficacy" *Current Directions in Psychological Science* 9: 75–78.

———. 2001. "Social Cognitive Theory: An Agentic Perspective." *Annual Review of Psychology* 52:1–26.

Barkin, David. 2000. Social Tourism in Rural Communities: An Instrument for Promoting Sustainable Resource Management. Paper presented at the Meeting of the Latin American Studies Association, Miami, FL, March 16.

———. 2002. "Globalization: Love It or Leave It." *Latin American Perspectives* 29 (6): 132–135.

Barry, Kathleen. 1996 [1986]. *The Prostitution of Sexuality: The Global Exploitation of Women.* New York: New York University Press.

Basi, J. K. Tina. 2009. *Women, Identity, and India's Call Center Industry: Close Calls and Hang Ups.* London: Routledge.

Beck, F. 1969. "Colour and Heat in South Indian Ritual." *Man* 4:553–72.

Becker, Howard, and Anselm Strauss. 1956. "Careers, Personality, and Adult Socialization." *Journal of American Sociology* 3 (62): 254–263.

Bedford v. Canada, ONSC 4264, Ontario Superior Court of Justice. September 28, 2010.

Bell, Holly, Lacey Sloan, and Chris Strickling. 1998. "Exploiter or Exploited: Topless Dancers Reflect on Their Experiences." *Journal of Women and Social Work* 13 (3): 352–368.

Bell, Shannon. 1994. *Reading, Writing, and Rewriting the Prostitute Body.* Bloomington: Indiana University Press.

Belliveau, Jeannette. 2006 *Romance on the Road: Travelling Women Who Love Foreign Men.* Baltimore, MD: Beau Monde.

Bernstein, Elizabeth. 2007a. *Temporarily Yours: Intimacy, Authenticity, and the Commerce of Sex.* Chicago: University of Chicago Press.

———. 2007b. "Sex Work for the Middle Classes." *Sexualities* 10 (4): 473–488.

Black, Maggie. 1994. "Home Truths." *New Internationalist* (February): 11–13.

Blanchard, J., J. O'Neil, B. M. Ramesh, P. Bhattacharjee, T. Orchard, and S. Moses. 2005. "Understanding the Social and Cultural Context of Female Sex Workers in Karnataka, India: Implications for Prevention of HIV Infection." *Journal of Infectious Disease* 191 (Suppl. 1): S 139–146.

Blanchette, Thaddeus Gregory. 2001. *Gringos.* Master's diss. Rio de Janeiro: PPGAS/MN/UFRJ.

Blanchette, Thaddeus Gregory, and Ana Paula da Silva. 2005. "'Nossa Senhora da Help': sexo, turismo e deslocamento transnacional em Copacabana." *Cadernos Pagu* 25: 249–280.

———. 2008. "Mulheres Vulneráveis e Meninas Más." 4th place article, 1st Libertas Prize competition. Brasília, Ministério da Justiça.

———. 2009 "Sexual Tourism and Social Panics: Research and Intervention in Rio de Janeiro." *Souls* 11 (2): 203–212.

Bliss, Katherine. 2001. *Compromised Positions: Prostitution, Public Health, and Gender Politics in Revolutionary Mexico City*. University Park: Pennsylvania State University Press.

Boonchalaksi, Wathinee, and Philip Guest. 1994. *Prostitution in Thailand*. Mahidol University, Bangkok: Institute for Population and Social Research.

Bradburd, Daniel. 1998. *Being There: The Necessity of Fieldwork*. Washington, DC: Smithsonian Institution.

Brants, Chrisje. 1998. "The Fine Art of Regulated Tolerance: Prostitution in Amsterdam." *Journal of Law and Society* 25: 621–635.

Brennan, Denise. 2004. *What's Love Got to Do with It? Transnational Desires and Sex Tourism in the Dominican Republic*. Durham, NC: Duke University Press.

Brents, Barbara, and Kathryn Hausbeck. 2005. "Violence and Legalized Brothel Prostitution in Nevada: Examining Safety, Risk, and Prostitution Policy." *Journal of Interpersonal Violence* 20 (3): 270–295.

Brents, Barbara, Crystal Jackson, and Kathryn Hausbeck. 2009. *The State of Sex: Tourism, Sex, and Sin in the New American Heartland*. New York: Routledge.

Brooks, Ethel. 2007. *Unravelling the Garment Industry: Transnational Organizing and Women's Work*. Minneapolis: University of Minnesota Press.

Brownell, Susan. 1995. *Training the Body for China: Sports in the Moral Order of the People's Republic*. Chicago: University of Chicago Press.

Bujra, Janet. 1975. "Women Entrepreneurs of Early Nairobi." *Canadian Journal of African Studies* 9 (2): 213–234

Bureau of Democracy, Human Rights, and Labor. 2008. *Human Rights Report: Thailand*. Washington, DC: Country Reports on Human Rights Practices. Retrieved November 25, 2009, from http://www/state.gov/g/drl/rls/hrrpt/2008/eap/119058.htm.

Cabezas, Amalia. 2009. *Economies of Desire: Sex and Tourism in Cuba and the Dominican Republic*. Durham, NC: Duke University Press.

Campbell, Catherine. 2000. "Selling Sex in the Time of AIDS: The Psycho-Social Context of Condom Use by Southern African Sex Workers." *Social Science and Medicine* 50:479–494.

Canadian HIV/AIDS Legal Network. 2005. "New Zealand and Sweden: Two Models for Reform." *Sex, Work, Rights: Reforming Canadian Criminal Laws on Prostitution*, Information Sheet No. 9.

Carrillo, Héctor 2002. *The Night Is Young: Sexuality in Mexico in the Time of AIDS*. Chicago: University of Chicago Press.

"Castro Mwangi, Killer of Prostitute, Goes Home Free." 2004. *The Mirror,* September 4, p. 22.

Caulfield, Sueann. 1997. "The Birth of Mangue: Race, Nation, and the Politics of Prostitution in Rio de Janeiro." In *Sex and Sexuality in Latin America: An Interdisciplinary Reader,* ed. D. Balderston and D. J. Guy, 86–100. New York: New York University Press.

Central Unica dos Trabalhadores (Central Workers Union). 2005. "Transforming the Relationship between Labor and Citizenship: Production, Reproduction, and Sexuality." August 11, Salvador, Brazil.

Centro de Informacíon y Análisis de Chiapas (CIACH), Coordinación de Organismos No Gubermentales Por La Paz (CONPAZ), y Servicios Informativos Procesados (SIPRO). 1997. *Para Entender Chiapas: Chiapas en Cifras.* Mexico City: CIACH, CONPAZ, SIPRO.

Chacham, Alessandra S., et al. 2007. "Sexual and Reproductive Health Needs of Sex Workers: Two Feminist Projects in Brazil." *Reproductive Health Matters* 15 (29): 108–118.

Chakraborthy, Kakolee. 2000. *Women as Devadasis: Origin and Growth of the Devadasi Profession.* New Delhi: Deep & Deep.

Chakravarti, Uma. 1989. "What Happened to the Vedic *Dasi*? Orientalism, Nationalism, and a Script for the Past." In *Recasting Women: Essays in Colonial History,* ed. Kumkum Sangari and Sudesh Vaid, 27–87. New Delhi: Kali For Women.

CHAME. 1998. *What's Up in Bahia? The Other Side of Tourism in Salvador.* Salvador: CHAME.

———. n.d. *Sumário. Women's International Migration: Causes and Consequences.* Salvador, Brazil: CHAME.

Chang, Grace. 2004. Paper presented in the Transnational Political Economies panel. Con/Vergences: Critical Interventions in the Politics of Race and Gender. Berkeley: University of California Press.

Chant, Sylvia H. 1985. "Family Composition, and Housing Consolidation: The Case of Queretaro, Mexico." DPU Gender and Planning Working Paper 2. London: Development Planning Unit, Bartlett School of Architecture and Planning, University College.

———. 1991. *Women and Survival in Mexican Cities: Perspectives on Gender, Labour Markets, and Low-Income Households.* New York: St. Martin's.

Chapkis, Wendy. 1997. *Live Sex Acts: Women Performing Erotic Labor.* New York: Routledge.

Chawla, Anil. 2002. *Devadasis—Sinners or Sinned Against. An Attempt to Look at the Myth and Reality of History and Present Status of Devadasis.* Internet document available at http://www.samarthbharat.com.

Chetwynd, Jane. 1996. "'The Prostitutes' Collective: A Uniquely New Zealand Institution." In *Intimate Details and Vital Statistics: AIDS, Sexuality, and the Social Order in New Zealand,* ed. P. Davis, 136–149. Auckland: Auckland University Press.

"Child Molester Flees Thailand." 1995. *Bangkok Post,* January 31.

Chiñas, Beverly. 1991. *The Isthmus Zapotecs: A Matrifocal Culture of Mexico.* Case Studies in Cultural Anthropology Series. Fort Worth, TX: Harcourt Brace College.

Clausen, Victor. 2007. "An Assessment of Gunilla Ekberg's Account of Swedish Prostitution Policy." Unpublished paper.

Clayton, Jonathan. 2005. "Where Sex Crime Is 'Just a Bit of a Game.'" *The Times,* August 12. Retrieved October 13, 2010, from http://www.timesonline.co.uk/tol/news/uk/article554402.ece.

Cobb, William Jelani. 2006. "Blame It on Rio." *Essence,* August.

Cohen, Stanley. 2002 [1972]. *Folk Devils and Moral Panics: The Creation of the Mods and Rockers.* London: Routledge.

Commonwealth Secretariat, London. 2003. Report of the expert group on strategies for combatting the trafficking of women and children.

"Copacabana também vai ser obra de arte em museu na orla." 2009. *O Dia Online,* November 11. Retrieved from http://odia.terra.com/br/portal/rio/html/2009/8/copacabana_tambem_vai_ser_obra_de_arte_em_museu_na_orla_28750.html.

Crago, Anna-Louise. 2008. *Our Lives Matter: Sex Workers Unite for Health and Rights.* New York: Open Society Institute.

Cressy, Paul Goalby. 2008 [1932]. *The Taxi Dance Hall*. Chicago: University of Chicago Press.

Criminal Law (Sexual Offences and Related Matters) Amendment Act, No 32. 2007.

Croce-Galis, Melanie, ed. 2008. *Strategies for Change: Breaking Barriers to HIV Prevention, Treatment, and Care for Women*. New York: Open Society Institute.

Daalder, A. L. 2004. *Lifting the Ban on Brothels*. The Hague: Ministry of Justice.

———. 2007. *Prostitution in the Netherlands since the Lifting of the Brothel Ban*. The Hague: Ministry of Justice.

Datar, Chhaya. 1992. "Reform or New Form of Patriarchy? Devadasis in the Border Region of Maharashtra and Karnataka." *Indian Journal of Social Work* 53 (1): 81–91.

Davis, Eric St. A. 1939. "Some Problems Arising from the Housing Conditions and Employment of Natives in Nairobi." Rhodes House Manuscripts (Africat.13). Rhodes House, Oxford University.

Day, Sophie. 2007. *On the Game: Women and Sex Work*. London: Pluto.

Delacoste, Frédérique, and Priscilla Alexander, eds. 1987. *Sex Work: Writings by Women in the Sex Industry*. Pittsburgh: Cleiss.

Delius, Peter, and Glaser, Clive. 2002. "Sexual Socialisation in South Africa: A Historical Perspective." *African Studies* 61: 27–54.

Dewey, Susan. 2008. *Hollow Bodies: Institutional Responses to Sex Trafficking in Armenia, Bosnia, and India*. Sterling, VA: Kumarian.

———. 2011. *Neon Wasteland: On Love, Motherhood, and Sex Work in a Rust Belt Town*. Berkeley: University of California Press.

Dodillet, Susanne. 2004. "Cultural Clash on Prostitution: Debates in Germany and Sweden in the 1990s." Paper presented at the Conference on Sex and Sexuality, Salzburg, October 14.

———. 2009. *Är Sex Arbete? Svensk Och Tysk Prostitutionspolitik Sedan 1970-talet* ("Is Sex Work? Swedish and German Prostitution Policy since the 1970s"). Ph.D. diss., University of Gothenburg.

Doezema, Jo. 1998. "Forced to Choose: Beyond the Voluntary v. Forced Prostitution Dichotomy." In *Global Sex Workers: Rights, Resistance, and Redefinition*, ed. Kamala Kempadoo and Jo Doezema, 34–50. New York: Routledge.

———. 2001. "Ouch! Western Feminists' 'Wounded Attachment' to the 'Third World Prostitute.'" *Feminist Review* 67: 16–38.

Douglas, Mary. 2000 [1966]. *Purity and Danger: An Analysis of the Concepts of Pollution and Taboo*. New York: Routledge.

Drummond, Andrew, and Andrew Chant. 1994. "'Child Sex' Britons Freed with Bribes." *London, Evening Standard*, March 7.

Duffy, Lori. 1995. "Adult Theater Workers Face Prostitution Charges." *Post-Standard*, September 22, p. C1.

Dworkin, Andrea. 2006 [1986]. *Intercourse*. New York: Basic Books.

Ebron, Paulla. 1997. "Traffic in Men." In *Gendered Encounters: Challenging Cultural Boundaries and Social Hierarchies in Africa*, ed. Maria Grosz-Ngate and Omari Kokole. New York: Routledge.

Edin, Kathryn and Maria Kefalas. 2005. *Promises I Can Keep: Why Poor Women Put Motherhood Before Marriage*. Berkeley: University of California Press.

Ehrlich, Richard. 1994. "Disneyland for Pedophiles." *Freedom Review* 25 (2): 1–2.

Ekberg, Gunilla. 2004. "The Swedish Law That Prohibits the Purchase of Sexual Services." *Violence against Women* 10: 1187–1218.

Elmore-Meegan, Michael, Ronan Conroy, and Bernard Agala. 2004. "Sex Workers in Kenya, Numbers of Clients and Associated Risks: An Exploratory Survey." *Reproductive Health Matters* 12 (23): 50–57.

Emirbayer, Mustafa, and Ann Mische. 1998. "What Is Agency?" *American Journal of Sociology* 103 (4): 962–1023

Engels, Friedrich. 1975 [1884]. *The Origin of the Family, Private Property, and the State: In the Light of the Researches of Lewis H. Morgan.* New York: International.

Ennew, Judith. 1986. *The Sexual Exploitation of Children.* Cambridge: Polity.

Epp, Linda. 1997. "Violating the Sacred? The Social Reform of Devadasis among Dalits in Karnataka, India." Ph.D. diss., York University.

Fabian, Cosi. 1997. "The Holy Whore: A Woman's Gateway to Power." In *Whores and Other Feminists,* ed. Jill Nagle, 44–54. New York: Routledge.

Farley, Melissa. 2004. "Bad for the Body, Bad for the Heart: Prostitution Harms Women Even If Legalized or Decriminalized." *Violence against Women* 10 (10): 32–40.

Farmer, Paul. 2003. *Pathologies of Power: Health, Human Rights, and the New War on the Poor.* Berkeley: University of California Press.

Farrer, James. 2000. "Dancing through the Market Transition." In *The Consumer Revolution in Urban China,* ed. Deborah Davis. Berkeley: University of California Press.

Farthing, Linda. 1995. "Bolivia: The New Underground." In *Free Trade and Economic Restructuring in Latin America,* ed. Fred Rosen and Deidre McFadden, 141–150. New York: Monthly Review Press

Federation of Women Lawyers (FIDA). 2008. *Documenting Human Rights Violations of Sex Workers in Kenya: A Study Conducted in Nairobi, Kisumu, Busia, Nanyuki, Mombasa, and Malindi.* Kenya, Nairobi: FIDA.

Fick, Nicolé. 2005. *Coping with Stigma, Discrimination, and Violence: Sex Workers Talk about Their Experiences.* Cape Town: Sex Workers Education and Advocacy Task Force Report. Retrieved October 13, 2010, from http://www.sweat.org/za/docs/coping.pdf.

Fondo Nacional de Fomento al Turismo (FONATUR). 2009. *Proyectos y Desarrollo.* Retrieved from http://fonatur.gob.mx/es/index_desarrollos.asp?sec=HUA.

Forbes, Geraldine. 1996. *Women in Modern India.* Cambridge: Cambridge University Press.

Fordham, Graham. 2005. *A New Look at Thai AIDS: Perspectives from the Margin.* Oxford: Berghahn.

Fosado, Gisela. 2004. *The Exchange of Sex for Money in Contemporary Cuba: Masculinity, Ambiguity, and Love.* Ann Arbor: University of Michigan Press.

Foucault, Michel. 1982. "The Subject and Power." *Critical Inquiry* 8 (4): 777–795.

———. 1990 [1977]. *Discipline and Punish: The Birth of the Prison.* New York: Pantheon.

Francisco, Luiz. 2006. "Prostitutas vão administrar radio FM em Salvador." Folha Online—Agencia Folha, March 8. Retrieved May 13, 2009, from http://www1.folha.uol.com.br/folha/cotidiano/ult95u11947.shtml.

Freeman, Carla. 2000. *High Tech and High Heels in the Global Economy: Women, Work, and Pink Collar Identities in the Caribbean.* Durham, NC: Duke University Press.

French, W. 1992. "Prostitutes and Guardian Angels: Women, Work, and the Family in Porfirian Mexico." *Hispanic American Historical Review* 72 (4): 529–553.

Freyre, Gilberto. 1948. *Ingleses no Brasil.* Rio de Janeiro: Livraria José Olympio Editora.

Fussy, P. 2008. "Brasil 2014 combate esgoto a céu aberto e turismo sexual." Exclusive interview with Marta Suplicy. Retrieved from http://esportes.terra.com.br/futebol/brasil2014/interna/0,,OI2787228-EI10545,00.html.

Gaspar, Maria Dulce. 1984. *Garotas de Programa. Prostituição em Copacabana e Identidade Social.* Rio de Janeiro: Jorge Zahar.

Giddens, Anthony. 1986. *The Constitution of Society: Outline of the Theory of Structuration.* Cambridge: Polity.

Gill, Lesley. 2009. The Limits of Solidarity: Labor and Transnational Organizing against Coca-Cola. *American Ethnologist* 36 (4): 667–680.

Giri, V. Mohini. 1999. *Kanya: Exploitation of Little Angels.* New Delhi: Gyan.

Global Alliance Against Trafficking in Women (GAATW). 2000. *Human Rights and Trafficking in Persons: A Handbook.* Bangkok: GAATW.

Gmelch, George. 2003. *Behind the Smile: The Working Lives of Caribbean Tourism.* Bloomington: Indiana University Press.

Goes, Felipe. 2010. "Projeto Porto Maravilha." Instituto Nacional de Altos Estudos (INAE).

Goffman, Erving. 1963. *Stigma: Notes on the Management of Spoiled Identity.* Englewood Cliffs, NJ: Prentice Hall.

Goldman, Jay. 1981. "Agent Raps Court's Topless Bar Ruling." *Syracuse Herald-Journal,* June 24, pp. C4.

Gonzalez de la Rocha, Mercedes. 1994. *The Resources of Poverty: Women and Survival in a Mexican City.* Studies in Urban and Social Change. Cambridge, MA: Blackwell.

———. 2000. "Private Adjustments: Household Responses to the Erosion of Work." Conference Paper Series 6. New York: Social Development and Poverty Elimination Division, Bureau for Development Policy, United Nations Development Program.

———. 2002. "The Erosion of a Survival Model: Urban Household Responses to Persistent Poverty." *Papers on Latin America* 47. New York: Columbia University, Institute of Latin American Studies.

Goodyear, Michael. 2007. "Public Health Policy Must Be Based on Sound Evidence, Not Opinion." *British Medical Journal* 334: 863–864.

Gould, Arthur. 2001. "The Criminalization of Buying Sex: The Politics of Prostitution in Sweden." *Journal of Social Policy* 30: 437–456.

Gould, Chandré, in collaboration with Nicolé Fick. 2008. *Selling Sex in Cape Town: Sex Work and Human Trafficking in a South African City.* Pretoria: Institute for Security Studies.

"Government Gets Tough on Sex Trade." 2008. *The Local,* July 16.

Government of South Africa. Sexual Offences Act, No. 23. 1957. Pretoria, South Africa.

Green, James N. 1999. *Beyond Carnival: Male Homosexuality in Twentieth-Century Brazil.* Chicago: University of Chicago Press.

Greenhouse, Linda. 1981. Court Upholds Ban on Topless Dancing in Bars. *Syracuse Herald-Journal,* June 23, pp. A–2.

Grupo Davida. 2005. "Prostitutas, 'Traficadas' e Pânicos Morais: Uma Análise da Produção de Fatos em Pesquisassobre o 'Tráfico de Seres Humanos.'" *Cadernos Pagu* 25.

Gullette, Gregory. 2004. "Tourists, Immigrants, and Family Units Analysis of Tourism Development and Migration Patterns in and from the Bays of Huatulco, Mexico." Ph.D. diss., University of Georgia.

Hairong, Yan. 2003. "Neoliberal Governmentality and Neohumanism: Organizing Suzhi/ Value Flow through Labor Recruitment Networks." *Cultural Anthropology* 18 (4): 493–523.

———. 2007. "Migration and Tourism Development in Huatulco, Oaxaca." *Current Anthropology* 48 (4): 603–611.

Hall, Oswald. 1948. "The Stages of a Medical Career." *Journal of American Sociology* 5 (53).

Hallgrimsdottir, Helga Kristin, Rachel Phillips, and Cecilia Benoit. 2006. "Fallen Women and Rescued Girls: Social Stigma and Media Narratives of the Sex Industry in Victoria, B.C., from 1980 to 2005." *Canadian Review of Sociology & Anthropology* 43 (3): 265-80.

Halli, S., B. M. Ramesh, J. O'Neil, S. Moses, and J. Blanchard. 2006. "The Role of Collectives in STI and HIV/AIDS Prevention among Female Sex Workers in Karnataka, India." *AIDS Care* 18 (7): 729–749.

Hantrakul, Sukanya. 1983. "Prostitution in Thailand." Paper presented at the Women in Asia Workshop, Monash University, Melbourne.

Harre, Rom. 1986. "The Step to Social Constructionism." In *Children of Social Worlds: Development in a Social Context*, ed. M. Richards and P. Light, 287–296. Cambridge: Polity.

Harting, Don. 1990. "Just Keep Your Shirts On: New Topless Bar in Clay Raises Neighborhood's Ire." *Post-Standard*, October 25, p. 3.

Harvey, David. 2005. *A Brief History of Neoliberalism*. Oxford: Oxford University Press.

Healy, Catherine, and Anna Reed. 1994. "The Healthy Hooker." *New Internationalist* 252: 16–17.

Hejjegalu: A Collection of Articles. 2001. Athani: Vimochana.

Held, David, Anthony McGrew, David Goldblatt, and Jonathan Perraton. 1999. *Global Transformations: Politics, Economics, and Culture*. Cambridge: Polity.

Heng, Geraldine, and Janadas Devan. 1997. "State Fatherhood: The Politics of Nationalism, Sexuality, and Race in Singapore." In *The Gender Sexuality Reader*, ed. Roger Lancaster and Micaela Di Leonardo, 107–121. New York: Routledge.

Herdt, Gilbert, ed. 2009. *Moral Panics, Sex Panics: Fear and the Fight over Sexual Rights*. New York: New York University Press.

Hirsch, Jennifer S. 2003. *A Courtship after Marriage: Sexuality and Love in Mexican Transnational Families*. Berkeley: University of California Press.

Hirst, Michael. 2003. *Jurisdiction and the Ambit of the Criminal Law*. Oxford: Oxford University Press.

Hochschild, Arlie. 1983. *The Managed Heart: Commercialization of Human Feeling*. Berkeley: University of California Press.

Holmstrom, Charlotta, and May-Len Skilbrei. 2009. *Prostitution in the Nordic Countries*. Copenhagen: Nordic Council of Ministers.

Hornblower, Margot. 1993. "The Sex Trade." *Time*, June 21.

Huisman, Wim, and Hans Nelen. 2007. "Gotham Unbound Dutch Style: The Administrative Approach to Organized Crime in Amsterdam." *Crime, Law, and Social Change* 48: 87–103.

Hunter, Mark. 2002. "The Materiality of Everyday Sex: Thinking beyond 'Prostitution.'" *African Studies* 61: 99–120.

Instituto Nacional de Estadística y Geografía (INEGI). 1985. Censo General de Población y Vivienda. Mexico City, Mexico.

———. 2000. Censo General de Población y Vivienda. Mexico City, Mexico.

Izugbara, Chimaraoke. 2007. "Constituting the Unsafe: Nigerian Sex Workers' Notions of Unsafe Sexual Conduct." *African Studies Review* 50 (3): 29–49.

"Jail Men Who Pay for Sex." 2008. *The Local,* April 8.

Jana, Smarajit. 1999. "Intervention through Peer-based Approach: A Lesson from Sonagachi." *AIDS Research and Review* 2 (2): 58–63.

Jana, Smarajit, Nandinee Bandyopadhyay, Amitrajit Saha, and Mrinal Kanti Dutta. 1999. "Creating an Enabling Environment. Lessons Learnt from the Sonagachi Project, India." *Research for Sex Work* 2: 4.

Jeffreys, Sheila. 2008. *The Industrial Vagina: The Political Economy of the Global Sex Trade.* London: Spinifex.

Jewkes, Rachel, and Naeema Abrahams. 2008. *Violence against Women in South Africa: Rape and Sexual Coercion.* Pretoria, South Africa: Crime Prevention Resources Centre Report.

Jewkes, Rachel, Loveday Penn-Kekana, Jonathan Levin, Matsie Ratsaka, and Margaret Schrieber. 1999. "'He Must Give Me Money, He Mustn't Beat Me': Violence against Women in Three South African Provinces." Pretoria: Medical Research Council Report, Retrieved October 13, 2010, from http://www.mrc.ac.za/gender/violence.pdf.

Jolin, Annette. 1994. "On the Backs of Working Prostitutes: Feminist Theory and Prostitution Policy." *Crime and Delinquency* 40 (1): 69–83.

Jordan, Jan. 1991. *Working Girls: Women in the New Zealand Sex Industry Talk to Jan Jordan.* Auckland: Penguin.

Jordan, Kay. 1993. "Devadasi Reform: Driving the Priestess or the Prostitutes out of Hindu Temples?" In *Religion and Law in Independent India,* ed. Robert D. Baird, 257–277. New Delhi: Manohar.

Kannabiran, Kalpana. 1995. "Judiciary, Social Reform, and Debate on 'Religious Prostitution' in Colonial India." *Economic and Political Weekly* (October 28): WS59–69.

Kantola, Johanna, and Judith Squires. 2004. "Discourses Surrounding Prostitution Policies in the UK." *European Journal of Women's Studies* 11:77–101.

Katsulis, Yasmina. 2008. *Sex Work and the City: The Social Geography of Health and Safety in Tijuana, Mexico.* Austin: University of Texas Press.

Kaye, Kerwin. 2007 "Sex and the Unspoken in Male Street Prostitution." *Journal of Homosexuality* 53 (1): 37–73.

Kelly, Patty. 2008. *Lydia's Open Door: Inside Mexico's Most Modern Brothel.* Berkeley: University of California Press.

Kempadoo, Kamala. 1998. "Introduction: Globalizing Sex Workers' Rights." In *Global Sex Workers: Rights, Resistance, and Redefinition,* ed. Kamala Kempadoo and Jo Doezema, 1–28. New York: Routledge.

Kersenboom, Saskia. 1987. *Nityasumangali: Devadasi Tradition in South India.* Delhi: Motilal Banarsidass.

Kitzinger, Jenny. 1984. "Who Are You Kidding? Children, Power, and the Struggle against Sexual Abuse." In *Constructing and Reconstructing Childhood: Contemporary Issues in the Sociological Study of Childhood,* ed. Allison James and Alan Prout, 7–34. London: Falmer.

Kokken, Juline, David Bimbi, and Jeffrey Parsons. 2010. "Male and Female Escorts: A Comparative Analysis." In *Sex for Sale: Prostitution, Pornography and the Sex Industry,* ed. Ron Weitzer, 205–232. New York: Routledge.

Kong, Travis S. K. 2006. "What It Feels Like for a Whore: The Body Politics of Women Performing Erotic Labour in Hong Kong." *Gender, Work & Organization* 13 (5): 409–434.

Kulick, Don. 1996. "Causing a Commotion: Scandal as Resistance among Brazilian Travesti Prostitutes." *Anthropology Today* 12 (6): 3–7.

Kuo, Lenore. 2002. *Prostitution Policy: Revolutionizing Practice through a Gendered Perspective*. New York: New York University Press.

Kuosmanen, Jari. 2010. "Attitudes and Perceptions about Legislation Prohibiting the Purchase of Sexual Services in Sweden." *European Journal of Social Work* 4: 1–17.

Larvie, Patrick. 1997. "Homophobia and the Ethnoscape of Sex Work in Rio De Janeiro." In *Sexual Cultures and Migration in the Era of AIDS: Anthropological and Demographic Perspectives*, ed. Gilbert Herdt, 143–166. New York: Oxford University Press.

———. 1999. "Natural Born Targets: Male Hustlers and AIDS Prevention in Urban Brazil." In *Men Who Sell Sex: International Perspectives on Male Prostitution and HIV/AIDS*, ed. Peter Aggleton, 159–177. Philadelphia: Temple University Press.

Leander, Karen. 2006. "Reflections on Sweden's Measures against Men's Violence against Women." *Social Policy and Society* 5: 115–125.

Leclerc-Madlala, Suzanne. 2003. "Transactional Sex and the Pursuit of Modernity." *Social Dynamics* 29 (2): 213–233.

Lee, Nick. 2001. *Childhood and Society: Growing Up in an Age of Uncertainty*. Philadelphia: Open University Press.

Leggett, Ted. 2001. *Rainbow Vice: The Drugs and Sex Industries in the New South Africa*. Cape Town: David Philip.

Leite, Gabriela. 2009. *Filha, Mãe, Avó e Puta*. Rio de Janeiro: Objetiva.

Leite, Juçara Luzia. 1993. "A República do Mangue: Controle Policial e Prostituição no Rio de Janeiro, 1954–1974." Master's diss., Universidade Federal Fluminense, Rio de Janeiro.

Lewis, Jacqueline. 2000. "Controlling Lap Dancing: Law, Morality, and Sex Work." In *Sex for Sale: Prostitution, Pornography and the Sex Industry*, ed. Ronald Weitzer, 203–216. New York: Routledge.

Lichtenstein, Bronwen. 1999. "Reframing 'Eve' in the AIDS Era: The Pursuit of Legitimacy by New Zealand Sex Workers." *Sexuality and Culture* 2: 37–59.

Lomnitz, Larissa Adler de. 1974. *Cómo Sobreviven Los Marginados. Sociología y Política*. Mexico, DF: Siglo Veintiuno Editores.

Long, Veronica Hope. 1990. "Resident Reaction to Mitigation of Social Impacts of Tourism Development: Santa Cruz Huatulco, Oaxaca, Mexico." Ph.D. diss., California State University, Chico.

Longo, Paulo H. 1998a. *Michê*. Rio de Janeiro: Planeta Gay Books.

———. 1998b. "The Pegação Program: Information, Prevention, and Empowerment of Young Male Sex Workers in Rio De Janeiro." In *Global Sex Workers: Rights, Resistance, and Redefinition*, ed. Kamala Kempadoo and Jo Doezema, 231–239. New York: Routledge.

Lucas, Ann. 2005. "The Work of Sex Work: Elite Prostitutes' Vocational Orientations and Experiences." *Deviant Behavior* 26 (6): 513–546.

Luiz, John M., and Leonn Roets. 2000. "On Prostitution, STDs, and the Law in South Africa: The State as Pimp." *Journal of Contemporary African Studies* 18: 21–38.

Macleod, Donald. 2004. *Tourism and Cultural Change: An Island Community Perspective*. Toronto: Channel View.

Maddux, James. 1995. *Self-Efficacy, Adaptation, and Adjustment: Theory, Research, and Application.* New York: Plenum

Madsen Camacho, Michelle. 1996. "Dissenting Workers and Social Control." *Human Organization* 55 (1): 33–40.

Marcus, T., K. Oellermann, and N. Levin. 1995. "AIDS and the Highways: Sex Workers and Truck Drivers in KwaZulu-Natal." *Indicator South Africa* 13: 80–84.

Marglin, Frederique Apffel. 1985. *Wives of the God-King: The Rituals of the Devadasis of Puri.* Delhi: Oxford University Press.

Marx, Karl. 1977 [1867]. *Das Capital.* Vol. 1. New York: Vintage Books.

Mauss, Marcel. 1990 [1924]. *The Gift.* New York: Norton.

McClintock, Anne. 1991 "The Scandal of the Whorecracy: Prostitution in Colonial Nairobi." *Transition* 52: 92–99.

———. 1993. "Sex and Sex Workers." *Social Text* 11 (4): 1–10.

McKinley, James C., Jr. 2005. "A New Law in Tijuana Regulates the Oldest Profession." *New York Times,* December 13. Retrieved December 18, 2005, from http://www.nytimes.com/2005/12/13/international/americas/13prostitutes.html.

Meekers, Dominique. 2000. "Going Underground and Going After Women: Trends in Sexual Risk Behaviour among Gold Miners in South Africa." *International Journal of STD & AIDS* 11: 21–26.

Mendelsohn, Oliver, and Marika Vicziany. 1998. *The Untouchables: Subordination, Poverty, and the State in Modern India.* Cambridge: Cambridge University Press.

Menon, Meena. 1997. "INDIA-AIDS: An NGO Gets Sex Workers to Enforce Condom Use." InterPress News Service, August 20.

Messing, Ulrika. 1998. Statement in the Riksdag, May 2. Retrieved December 18, 2008, from http://www.riksdagen.se/Webbnav/index.asp?nid=101&bet=1997/98: 114.

Mies, Maria. 1986. *Patriarchy and Accumulation on a World Scale: Women in the International Division of Labor.* London: Zed Books.

Migot-Adhola, Shem E. 1982. *Study of Tourism in Kenya with Emphasis on the Attitudes of the Residents of the Coast.* Institute for Development Studies Consultancy, Report No. 7, Nairobi University.

Mimiaga, M. J., S. L. Reisner, J. P. Tinsley, K. H. Mayer, and S. A. Safren. 2009. "Street Workers and Internet Escorts: Contextual and Psychosocial Factors Surrounding HIV Risk Behavior among Men Who Engage in Sex Work with Other Men." *Journal of Urban Health* 86 (1): 54–66.

Minca, Claudio, and Tim Oakes, eds. 2006. *Travels in Paradox: Remapping Tourism.* Oxford: Roman and Littlefield.

Ministry of Industry, Employment, and Communications. 2005. Fact Sheet, "Prostitution and Trafficking in Human Beings." Stockholm, April.

Ministry of Integration and Gender Equality. 2008. *Action Plan against Prostitution and Human Trafficking for Sexual Purposes.* Stockholm.

Moffett, Helen. 2006. "These Women, They Force Us to Rape Them": Rape as Narrative of Social Control in Post-Apartheid South Africa." *Journal of Southern African Studies* 32: 129–144.

Montgomery, Heather. 2001a. *Modern Babylon? Prostituting Children in Thailand.* Oxford: Berghahn.

———. 2001b. "Motherhood, Fertility, and Ambivalence among Young Prostitutes in Thailand." In *Managing Reproductive Life: Cross Cultural Themes in Sexuality and Fertility*, ed. Soraya Tremayne. Oxford: Berghahn.

———. 2007. "Working with Child Prostitutes in Thailand: Problems of Practice and Interpretation." *Childhood* 14 (4): 415–430.

———. 2008 "Buying Innocence: Child Sex Tourists in Thailand." *Third World Quarterly* 29 (5): 903–917.

———. 2010. "Child Sex Tourism: Is Extra-Territorial Legislation the Answer?" In *Tourism and Crime*, ed. David Botterill and Trevor Jones, 69–78. Oxford: Goodfellow.

Morgan, Lewis Henry. 1985 [1877]. *Ancient Society: Or, Researches in the Line of Human Progress from Savagery through Barbarism to Civilization*. Tucson: University of Arizona Press.

Mossman, Elaine, and Pat Mayhew. 2007a. *Central Government Aims and Local Government Responses: The Prostitution Reform Act 2003*. Wellington, New Zealand: Ministry of Justice,

———. 2007b. *Key Informant Interviews Review of the Prostitution Reform Act 2003*. Wellington, New Zealand: Ministry of Justice.

Mott, Luiz, and Marcelo Ferreira de Cerqueira. 2003. *Matei porque odeio gay*. Salvador, Brasil: Editora Grupo Gay da Bahia.

Muecke, Marjorie. 1992. "Mother Sold Food, Daughter Sells Her Body—The Cultural Continuity of Prostitution." *Social Science and Medicine* 35 (7): 891–901.

Muñoz, José Esteban. 1999. *Disidentifications: Queers of Color and the Performance of Politics*. Minneapolis: University of Minnesota Press.

Murphy, Kathleen. 1998. *Single Mothers and Double-Voiced Words: Popular and Political Discourse in Guadalajara, 1993-1995* (Doctoral dissertation). Retrieved from ProQuest Dissertations and Theses Database. 9838060.

Murray, Alison. 2006. "Tourism." In *Encyclopedia of Prostitution and Sex Work*, ed. Melissa Hope Ditmore, 488–490. Westport, CT: Greenwood Press.

Nader, Laura. 1972. "Up the Anthropologist: Perspectives Gained from Studying Up." In *Reinventing Anthropology*, ed. Dell Hymes, 284–311. New York: Pantheon.

Newman, Katherine. 2000. *No Shame in my Game: The Working Poor in the Inner City*. New York: Vintage.

———. 2008. *Chutes and Ladders: Navigating the Low-Wage Labor Market*. Cambridge, MA: Harvard University Press.

New York State Department of Labor. 2009. "Independent Contractors." Retrieved from http://www.labor.state.ny.us/ui/dande/ic.shtm.

New York State Office of General Counsel. 2003. "Legal Memorandum LU03, Municipal Regulations of Adult Uses." Retrieved from http://www.dos.state.ny.us/cnsl/lu03.htm.

New York State Penal Code. 1965. "Article 235, Obscenity, Definitions of." Retrieved from http://public.leginfo.state.ny.us/menugetf.cgi?COMMONQUERY=LAWS.

O'Connell Davidson, Julia. 2005. *Children in the Global Sex Trade*. Cambridge: Polity.

O'Connell Davidson, Julia, and Jacqueline Sanchez Taylor. 1996. *Child Prostitution and Sex Tourism: South Africa*. Bangkok: ECPAT.

Oehmichen Bazán, Cristina. 2005. *Identidad, Género y Relaciones Interétnicas: Mazahuas en la Ciudad de México*. Mexico, DF: Universidad Nacional Autónoma de México.

O'Flaherty, Wendy Doniger. 1980. *Women, Androgynes, and Other Mythical Beasts*. Chicago: University of Chicago Press.

O'Grady, Ron.1992. *The Child and the Tourist*. Bangkok: ECPAT.

O'Hara, Jim. 1995. "Dirty Dancing Draws Arrests." *Syracuse Herald-Journal*, September 22, p. B3.

Okal, Jerry. 2009. "Sexual and Physical Violence against Female Sex Workers in Kenya: A Qualitative Enquiry." Unpublished essay, Nairobi, Kenya.

Olsson, Niclas. 2010. "Handlar det om Val? Sexhandeln via Community, Chatt Och Portal." Malmö, Sweden: Kompetenscenter Prostitution.

Omondi, Rose K. 2003. "Gender and the Political Economy of Sex Tourism in Kenya's Coastal Resorts." Paper presented at the International Symposium on Feminist Perspectives on Global Economic and Political Systems and Women's Struggles for Global Justice. Tromso, Norway, September 24–26.

O'Neil, J., T. Orchard, R.C. Swarankar, J. Blanchard, K. Gurav, B. K. Barlaya, R. M. Patil, C. G. Hussain Khan, and S. Moses. 2004. "Dhanda, Dharma and Disease: Traditional Sex Work and HIV/AIDS in Rural India." *Social Science and Medicine* 59 (4): 851–860.

Orchard, Treena. 2002. "Strategies for Sustainability among HIV/AIDS–Related NGOs in Canada and India." *Practicing Anthropology* 24 (2): 19–22.

———. 2007. "Girl, Woman, Lover, Mother: Towards a New Understanding of Child Prostitution among Young *Devadasi* Sex Workers in Rural Karnataka, India." *Social Science & Medicine* 64 (12): 2379–2390.

Orr, Leslie. 2000. *Donors, Devotees, and Daughters of God: Temple Women in Medieval Tamilnadu*. New York: Oxford University Press.

Otero, Gerard. 1996. "Neoliberal Reform and Politics in Mexico: An Overview." In *Neoliberalism Revisited: Economic Restructuring and Mexico's Political Future*, ed. Gerardo Otero, 1–26. Boulder, CO: Westview.

———, ed. 2004. *Mexico in Transition: Neoliberal Globalism, the State, and Civil Society*. London: Zed Books.

Outshoorn, Joyce. 2001. "Debating Prostitution in Parliament: A Feminist Analysis." *European Journal of Women's Studies* 8: 472–490.

———. 2004. "Pragmatism in the Polder: Changing Prostitution Policy in the Netherlands." *Journal of Contemporary European Studies* 12: 165–76.

Padilla, Mark. 2007. *Caribbean Pleasure Industry: Tourism, Sexuality, and AIDS in the Dominican Republic*. Chicago: University of Chicago Press.

"Paes se diz contra a legalização da prostituição." 2008. *O Globo*, October 20.

Pankonien, Dawn. 2008. "She Sells Seashells: Women and Mollusks in Huatulco, Oaxaca, Mexico." In *Gender, Households, and Society: Unraveling the Threads of the Past and the Present*, ed. C. Robin and E. M. Brumfiel, 102–114. Arlington, VA: Archaeology Division, American Anthropological Association (Archaeological Papers #18).

———. 2009. "Smart Sex in the Neoliberal Present: Tourism Development, Sexual Commodification, and Single-Parent Families." Presentation at the 108th Annual Meeting of the American Anthropological Association, Philadelphia, 4 December.

Park, Robert E., and Ernest Burgess. 1984 [1925]. *The City: Suggestions for the Investigation of Human Behavior in the Urban Environment*. Chicago: University of Chicago Press.

Parker, Richard. 1999. *Beneath the Equator: Cultures of Desire, Male Homosexuality, and Emerging Gay Communities in Brazil*. New York: Routledge.

Parreñas, Rhacel Salazar. 2001. *Servants of Globalization: Women, Migration, and Domestic Work*. Stanford: Stanford University Press.

Parsons, Jeffrey T., Juline A. Koken, and David S. Bimbi. 2007. "Looking Beyond HIV: Eliciting Individual and Community Needs of Male Internet Escorts." *Journal of Homosexuality* 53 (1): 219–40.

Pasini, Eliane. 2005. "Sexo para quase todos: a prostituição feminina na Vila Mimosa." *Cadernos Pagu* 25 (December): 185–216.

Pauw, Ilse, and Loren Brenner. 2003 "'You are Just Whores—You Can't be Raped': Barriers to Safer Sex among Women Street Sex Workers in Cape Town." *Culture, Health & Sexuality* 5: 465–481.

"Pedophiles Slip through Net Despite Sex Laws." 2005. *The Local,* July 20.

Phillips, Michael M. 2005. "Brazil Refuses U.S. AIDS Funds, Rejects Conditions," *Wall Street Journal,* May 2.

Phongpaichit, Pasuk. 1982. *From Peasant Girls to Bangkok Masseuses.* Geneva: International Labour Organization.

Pierce, Frederic. 2000. "Council Regroups on Adult Businesses." *Syracuse Herald-Journal,* January 20, p. B3.

Pierce, Frederic, and Mike McAndrew. 1999. "City Puts Sex Trade on Notice." *Post Standard,* June 13, p. A 1, A14.

Piscitelli, Adriana. 2008. "Looking for New Worlds: Brazilian Women as International Migrants." *Signs: Journal of Women in Culture and Society* 33 (4): 784–793.

"Poll Steels Anti-Prostitution Resolve." 2003. *New Zealand Herald,* May 14.

Prostitution Law Reform Committee (PLRC). 2003. *An Evaluation Framework for the Review of the Prostitution Reform Act.* Wellington, New Zealand: Ministry of Justice.

———. 2005. *The Nature and Extent of the Sex Industry in New Zealand.* Wellington, New Zealand: Ministry of Justice.

———. 2008. *Report of the Prostitution Law Review Committee on the Operation of the Prostitution Reform Act.* Wellington, New Zealand: Ministry of Justice.

Raghuramaiah, K. 1991. *Night Birds: Indian Prostitutes from Devadasis to Call Girls.* New Delhi: Chanakya.

Raj, M. Sundara. 1993. *Prostitution in Madras. A Study in Historical Perspective.* New Delhi: Konark.

Ramberg, Lucinda. 2006. "Given to the Goddess: South Indian Devadasis, Ethics, Kinship." Ph.D. diss., University of California, Berkeley.

Ramjee, Gita, and Eleanor Gouws. 2002. "Prevalence of HIV among Truck Drivers Visiting Sex Workers in KwaZulu-Natal, South Africa." *Sexually Transmitted Diseases* 29: 44–49.

Raphael, Jody. 2004. *Listening to Olivia: Violence, Poverty, and Prostitution.* Boston: Northeastern University Press.

Rattachumpoth, Rakkit. 1994. "The Economics of Sex." *The Nation,* February 3.

Reddy, Chandan. 2005. "Asian Diasporas, Neoliberalism, and Family: Reviewing the Case for Homosexual Asylum in the Context of Family Rights." *Social Text* 23 (3–4): 101–119.

Republic of South Africa, Criminal Law (Sexual Offences and Related Matters) Amendment Act, No. 32. 2007. Pretoria, South Africa.

Revista Terra. 2009. "Help! Tradicional reduto da prostituição carioca, a pista quente da Help fecha as portas em breve." *Revista Terra.com.br,* November 13. Retrieved July 12, 2010, from http://newhost.revistatpm.com.br/revista/93/reportagens/help.html.

Reynolds, Holly. 1980. "The Auspicious Married Woman." In *The Powers of Tamil Women*, ed. Susan Wadley, 35–60. Syracuse, NY: Maxwell School of Citizenship and Public Affairs.

Ribeiro, Miguel Angelo. 2002. *Território e Prostituição na Metrópole Carioca*. Rio de Janeiro: Ecomuseu Fluminense.

Richards, Francesca Elizabeth. 2005. "*La Vida Loca* (The Crazy Life): An Exploration of Street Kids' Agency in Relation to the Risk of HIV/AIDS and Governmental and Non-Governmental Interventions in Latin America." Master's thesis, University of Sussex.

Rivera, George, Jr., Hugo Vicente-Ralde, and Aileen F. Lucero 1992. "Knowledge about AIDS among Mexican Prostitutes." *Sociology and Social Research* 76 (2): 74–80.

Rohter, Larry. 2005. "Prostitution Puts U.S. and Brazil at Odds on AIDS Policy." *New York Times*, July 24.

Rojas Wiesner, Martha Luz, and Esperanza Tuñón Pablos. 2001. "Situación demográfica y ocupacional de las mujeres del estado de Chiapas en los años noventa." In *Mujeres en las Fronteras: Trabajo, Salud, y Migración*, ed. Esperanza Tuñón Pablos, 77–120. Mexico City: ECOSUR-COLSON-COLEF.

Sakboon, Mukdawan. 1993. "A Silver Lining on Longman's Stormy Cloud." *The Nation*, July 18.

Sakhon, Samut. 1994. "Two Burn to Death in Brothel Fire." *Bangkok Post*, June 13.

Sanders, Teela. 2004. "Controllable Laughter: Managing Sex Work through Humor." *Sociology* 38: 273–291.

———. 2005. "'It's Just Acting': Sex Workers' Strategies for Capitalizing on Sexuality." *Gender, Work & Organization* 12 (4): 319–342.

"Sanpei xiaojie de Falu Baohu Wenti" (Legal protection of hostesses). 2002. *Shenzhen Fazhi bao* (Shenzhen Law Newspaper), June 25.

Saunders, Penelope. 2005. "How 'Child prostitution' became 'CSEC.'" In *Regulating Sex: The Politics of Intimacy and Identity*, ed. Elizabeth Bernstein and Laurie Schaffner. London: Routledge.

Schwarzer, Ralf. 1992. *Self-Efficacy: Thought Control of Action*. Washington, DC: Hemisphere.

Scott, James C. 1985. *Weapons of the Weak: Everyday Forms of Peasant Resistance*. New Haven, CT: Yale University Press.

———. 1998. *Seeing Like a State: How Certain Schemes to Improve the Human Condition Have Failed*. New Haven, CT: Yale University Press.

Scott, Joseph E. 1991. "What is Obscene? Social Science and the Contemporary Community Standard Test of Obscenity." *International Journal of Law and Psychiatry* 14:29–45.

Scoular, Jane. 2004. "Criminalizing 'Punters': Evaluating the Swedish Position on Prostitution." *Journal of Social Welfare and Family Law* 26:195–210.

Servicios Coordinados de Salud Pública en el Estado de Chiapas. 1989. Archivo Municipal de Tuxtla Gutiérrez, Expediente Zona Galáctica.

Shankar, Jogan. 1990. *Devadasi Cult: A Sociological Analysis*. New Delhi: Ashish.

Shteir, Rachel. 2005. *Striptease: The Untold History of the Girlie Show*. Oxford: Oxford University Press.

Simões, Soraya. 2010. *Vila Mimosa: Etnografia da cidade Cenografia da Prostituição Carioca*. Niteroi: EdUFF.

Sinha, Mrinali. 1998. *Selections from Mother India*. New Delhi: Kali for Women.

Siu, Helen. 1989. "Socialist Peddlers and Princes in a Chinese Market Town." *American Anthropologist* 16:195–212.

———. 1993. "The Reconstitution of Brideprice and Dowry in South China." In *Chinese Families in the Post-Mao Era*, ed. Deborah Davis and Steven Harrell. Berkeley: University of California Press.

Skarhed, Anna. 2010. *A Prohibition of the Purchase of Sexual Services: An Evaluation 1999–2008.* Statens offentliga utredningar [SOU] 49, July 2.

Sleightholme, Carolyn, and Indrani Sinha. 1997. *Guilty without Trial: Women in the Sex Trade in Calcutta.* New Brunswick, NJ: Rutgers University Press.

Sloan, Lacey, and Stephanie Wahab. 2004. "Four Categories of Women who Work as Topless Dancers." *Sexuality and Culture* 8 (1): 18–43.

Smith, David. 2009. "Quarter of Men in South Africa Admit Rape, Survey Finds." *The Guardian*, June 17. Retrieved October 17, 2010, from http://www.guardian.co.uk/world/2009/jun/17/south-africa-rape-survey.

Smith, Keith. 2005. *The Status of Cape Town: Development Overview.* Cape Town: Isandla Institute.

Smith, Michael D., Christian Grov, and David Seal. 2008. "Agency-Based Male Sex Work: A Descriptive Focus on Physical, Personal, and Social Space." *Journal of Men's Studies* 16 (2): 193–210.

Socialstyrelsen. 2001. *Social Rapport 2001.* [South Africa] Criminal Law (Sexual Offences and Related Matters) Amendment Act, No 32 of 2007.

Spar, Debora. 2006. *The Baby Business: How Money, Science, and Politics Drive the Commerce of Conception.* Cambridge, MA: Harvard University Press.

Srinivasan, Amrit. 1985. "Reform and Revival: The Devadasi and Her Dance." *Economic and Political Weekly* 20 (44): 1869–1876.

Stacey, Judith. 1997. The Neo-Family-Values Campaign. In *The Gender Sexuality Reader*, ed. Roger Lancaster and Micaela di Leonardo, 453–470. New York: Routledge.

Statens offentliga utredningar (SOU). 1981. *Prostitutionen i Sverige 71.*

Stephen, Lynn. 2005 [1991]. *Zapotec Women: Gender, Class, and Ethnicity in a Globalized Oaxaca.* Durham, NC: Duke University Press.

———. 2002. *Zapata Lives! Histories and Cultural Politics in Southern Mexico.* Berkeley: University of California Press.

Sullivan, Tom. 2009. "Sweden Revisits Prostitution Law." *Christian Science Monitor*, June 28.

Sun, Shaoguang. "Dalian e mo ba xiaojie fenshi shiyi kuai" (A man in Dalian divided a hostess's dead body into eleven pieces). 2003. *Dongbei xinwen wang* (Northeastern News Net), December 12.

Sundara, Raj M. 1993. *Prostitution in Madras: A Study in Historical Perspective.* New Delhi: Konark.

Svanström, Yvonne. 2004. "Criminalizing the John: A Swedish Gender Model?" In *The Politics of Prostitution*, ed. J. Outshoorn. Cambridge: Cambridge University Press,

Swedish Crime Barometer. 2008. *Brottsförebyggande Rådet.*

"Swedish Prostitution: Gone or Just Hidden?" 2008. *The Local*, January 10.

Sydsvenskan. 2007. "Dags att Koppla av." July 26.

Tait, Robert, and Noushin Hoseiny. 2008. "Eight Women and a Man Face Stoning in Iran for Adultery." *The Guardian*, July 21, p. 17.

Tantiwiramanond, Darunee, and Shashi Ranjan Pandey. 1987. "The Status and Role of Women in the Pre-Modern Period: A Historical and Cultural Perspective." *Sojourn* 2 (1): 125–147.

Tarachand, K. C. 1991. *Devadasi Custom: Rural Social Structure and Flesh Markets.* New Delhi: Reliance.

Teichman, Judith. 1996. "Economic Restructuring, State-Labor Relations, and the Transformation of Mexican Corporatism." In *Neoliberalism Revisited: Economic Restructuring and Mexico's Political Future,* ed. Gerardo Otero, 149–166. Boulder, CO: Westview.

Tomura, Miyuki. 2009. "A Prostitute's Lived Experiences of Stigma." *Journal of Phenomenological Psychology* 40: 51–84.

"Tourists Pay Dearly for Underage Sex." 1993. *Bangkok Post,* October 6.

"Tráfico prostitui menores." 2009. *O Globo,* April 5.

Trotter, Henry. 2007. "The Women of Durban's Dockside Sex Industry" In *Undressing Durban,* ed. Rob Pattman and Sultan Khan, 441–452. Durban: Madiba.

———. 2008. *Sugar Girls and Seamen: A Journey into the World of Dockside Prostitution in South Africa.* Johannesburg: Jacana Media.

———. 2009. "Soliciting Sailors: The Temporal Dynamics of Dockside Prostitution in South Africa." *Journal of Southern African Studies* 35 (3): 699–713.

———. 2011. *Sugar Girls and Seamen: A Journey into the World of Dockside Prostitution in South Africa.* Athens: Ohio University Press.

Tullio, G., and M. Ronci. 1996. "Brazilian Inflation from 1980 to 1993: Causes, Consequences, and Dynamics." *Journal of Latin American Studies* 28 (3): 635–666.

UOL Esportes. 2009. "Rio de Janeiro terá sistema implantando por Giuliani em Nova York." *UOL Esporte,* 3 December. Retrieved April 5, 2010, from http://esporte.uol.com.br/rio-2016/ultimas-noticias/2009/12/03/ult8508u22.jhtm.

Uribe, Patricia, Laura Elena de Caso, Victor Aguirre, and Mauricio Hernández. 1998. "Prostitución en México." In *Mujer: Sexualidad y Salud Reproductiva en México,* ed. Ana Langer and Kathryn Tolbert. New York: The Population Council.

U.S. Department of State. 2004. Trafficking in Persons Report. U.S. Department of State Publication, 11150. Office of the Under Secretary for Global Affairs.

Vainfas, Magali Engels. 1985. *Meretrizes e Doutores: O Saber Médico e a Prostituição na Cidade do Rio de Janeiro, 1845–1890.* Master's diss., Universidade Federal Fluminense, Rio de Janeiro.

Valadares, Lícia. 2005. *A Invenção da Favela: do Mito de Origem a Favela.* Rio de Janeiro: Fundação Getulio Vargas.

Valverde, Mariana. 1987. "Too Much Heat, Not Enough Light." In *Good Girls/Bad Girls: Sex Trade Workers and Feminists Face to Face,* ed. Laurie Bell, 27–33. Toronto: Women's Press.

van der Fort, Fouzia. 2010. "Fewer Accidents, Drunks on the Road: Naming and Shaming Works, Says Traffic Chief." *Cape Argus,* October 11.

Varga, Christine A. 1997. "The Condom Conundrum: Barriers to Condom Use among Commercial Sex Workers in Durban, South Africa." *African Journal of Reproductive Health* 1: 74–88.

Velho, Gilberto. 1994. *Projeto e Metamorfose: antropologia das sociedades complexas.* Rio de Janeiro: Jorge Zahar Editores.

"Vila Mimosa no caminho do trem." 2010. *O Dia Online*, May 16. Retrieved from http://odia.terra.com.br/portal/rio/html/2010/5/vila_mimosa_no_caminho_do_trem_81476.html. Accessed on 5.17.10.

Waddell, Charles. 1996. "HIV and the Social World of Female Commercial Sex Workers." *Medical Anthropology Quarterly* 10 (1): 75-82.

Wadley, Susan. 1988. "Women and the Hindu Tradition." In *Women in Indian Society: A Reader*, ed. R. Ghadially, 23–43. New Delhi: Sage.

Wagenaar, Hendrik. 2006. "Democracy and Prostitution: Deliberating the Legalization of Brothels in the Netherlands." *Administration and Society* 28: 198–235.

Wagner, David. 1997. *The New Temperance: The American Obsession with Sin and Vice*. Boulder, CO: Westview.

Wang, Gan. 1999. "Conspicuous Consumption, Business Networks, and State Power in a Chinese City." Ph.D. diss., Yale University.

Weber, Max. 1964 [1913]. "The Definitions of Sociology and of Social Action." *The Theory of Social and Economic Organization*. New York: Free Press.

Weismantel, Mary J. 2001. *Cholas and Pishtacos: Stories of Race and Sex in the Andes*. Chicago: University of Chicago Press.

Weitzer, Ronald. 2009a. "Legalizing Prostitution: Morality Politics in Western Australia." *British Journal of Criminology* 49: 88–105.

———. 2009b. "Sociology of Sex Work." *Annual Review of Sociology* 35:213–234.

———. 2010a. "Sex Work: Paradigms and Policies." In *Sex for Sale: Prostitution, Pornography, and the Sex Industry*, ed. R. Weitzer. 2nd ed. New York: Routledge.

———. 2010b. "The Mythology of Prostitution: Advocacy Research and Public Policy." *Sexuality Research and Social Policy* 7: 15–29.

White, Luise. 1986. Prostitution, Identity, and Class Consciousness in Nairobi during World War II. *Signs: Journal of Women in Culture and Society* 11 (2): 255–273.

———. 1990 *The Comforts of Home: Prostitution in Colonial Nairobi*. Chicago: University of Chicago Press.

Whitehead, Judy. 1998. "Community Honor/Sexual Boundaries: A Discursive Analysis of *Devadasi* Criminalization in Madras, India, 1920–1947." In *Prostitution: On Whores, Hustlers, and Johns*, ed. James Elias, Vern Bullough, Veronica Elias, and Gwen Brewer, 91–106. New York: Prometheus Books.

Wijers, Marjan. 2010. "Komt er een Pasjeswet Voor Sekswerkers?" *De Rode Lantaarn*. Amsterdam: Prostitution Information Center.

Wiley, Lauren. 1996. "Topless Dancing in DeWitt Draws Ire." *Syracuse Herald-Journal*, March 27, p. B4.

Willis, Katie. 1993. "Women's Work and Social Network Use in Oaxaca City, Mexico." *Bulletin of Latin American Research* 12 (1): 65–82.

———. 1994. *Women's Work and Social Network Use in Oaxaca City, Mexico: An Analysis of Class Differences*. Oxford: Oxford University Press.

Wilson, William Julius. 1997. *When Work Disappears: The World of the New Urban Poor*. New York: Vintage Books.

Wojcicki, Janet Maia. 2002. "'She Drank His Money': Survival Sex and the Problem of Violence in Taverns in Gauteng Province, South Africa." *Medical Anthropology Quarterly* 16: 267–293.

Wojcicki, Janet Maia, and Josephine Malala. 2001. "Condom Use, Power, and HIV/AIDS Risk: Sex-workers Bargain for Survival in Hillbrow/Joubert Park/Berea, Johannesburg." *Social Science & Medicine* 53: 99–121.

Wolfenden Report. 1957. *Report of the Departmental Committee on Homosexual Offenses and Prostitution.* London: Her Majesty's Stationery Office.

Wood, Katherine, and Rachel Jewkes. 1996. *Sex, Violence and Constructions of Love among Xhosa Adolescents: Putting Violence on the Sexuality Agenda.* Cape Town: Medical Research Council Report, Retrieved October 15, 2010, from http://www.mrc.ac.za/gender/sexviolence.pdf.

———. 1998. "Love is a Dangerous Thing": Micro-dynamics of Violence in Sexual Relationships of Young People in Umtata, Pretoria: Medical Research Council Report, Retrieved October 13, 2010, from http://www.mrc.ac.za/gender/finallove.pdf.

Wonders, Nancy A. and Raymond Michalowski. 2001. "Bodies, Borders, and Sex Tourism in a Globalized World: A Tale of Two Cities—Amsterdam and Havana." *Social Problems* 48: 545–571.

World Tourism Organisation. n.d. "Protection of Children in Tourism—Legislation." Retrieved November 25, 2009, from http://www.unwto.org/protect_children/campaign/en/legislation.php?op=1&subop=7.

World Values Survey. Various years. Retrieved October 15, 2010, from http://www.wvsevsdb.com/wvs/.

Wright, Gloria. 1993. "Guy Denies Crusading against Nudie Club." *Post-Standard*, February 4, p. B2.

Zelizer, Viviana. 2007. *The Purchase of Intimacy.* Princeton, NJ: Princeton University Press.

Zhang, Li. 2001. *Strangers in the City: Reconfigurations of Space, Power, and Social Networks within China's Floating Population.* Stanford: Stanford University Press.

Zheng, Tiantian. 2006. "Cool Masculinity: Male Clients' Sex Consumption and Business Alliance in Urban China's Sex Industry." *Journal of Contemporary China* 15 (46): 161–182.

———. 2009a. *Red Lights: The Lives of Sex Workers in Postsocialist China.* Minneapolis: University of Minnesota Press.

———. 2009b. *Ethnographies of Prostitution in Contemporary China: Gender Relations, HIV/AIDS, and Nationalism.* New York: Palgrave Macmillan.

About the Contributors

THADDEUS GREGORY BLANCHETTE is Professor of Anthropology at the Federal University of Rio de Janeiro.

ZOSA DE SAS KROPIWNICKI is currently working as a consultant in Sub-Saharan Africa and has a Ph.D. in International Development Studies from the University of Oxford.

SUSAN DEWEY is Assistant Professor of Gender and Women's Studies and adjunct in International Studies at the University of Wyoming. She is the author of *Neon Wasteland: On Love, Motherhood, and Sex Work in a Rust Belt Town, Hollow Bodies: Institutional Responses to Sex Trafficking in Armenia, Bosnia, and India,* and *Making Miss India Miss World: Constructing Gender, Power, and the Nation in Postliberalization India.*

MICHAEL GOODYEAR is Assistant Professor of Medicine at Dalhousie University in Halifax, Nova Scotia, and the Coordinator of the Centres for Sex Work Research and Policy.

CHIMARAOKE IZUGBARA, Nigerian social anthropologist, is currently a research scientist at the African Population and Health Research Center (APHRC), in Nairobi, Kenya. He is lecturer-at-large at the University of Uyo, Nigeria, as well as an Honorary Associate Professor, School of Public Health, University of Witwatersrand, South Africa. He is also lead editor of *Old Wineskins, New Wine: Readings in Sexuality in Sub-Saharan Africa* (2010).

PATTY KELLY is Assistant Research Professor of Anthropology at George Washington University in Washington, DC. She is the author of *Lydia's Open Door: Inside Mexico's Most Modern Brothel.*

GREGORY MITCHELL is a Mellon Graduate Fellow in Gender Studies and a Ph.D. Candidate in Performance Studies at Northwestern University.

HEATHER MONTGOMERY is Senior Lecturer in Childhood Studies at Open University in the United Kingdom. She is the author of *Modern Babylon? Prostituting Children in Thailand* and *An Introduction to Childhood: Anthropological Perspectives on Children's Lives.*

TREENA ORCHARD is Assistant Professor in the School of Health Studies at the University of Western Ontario.

DAWN PANKONIEN is a Ph.D. Candidate in Anthropology at Northwestern University.

ANA PAULA DA SILVA is a Postdoctoral Fellow in Anthropology at the University of São Paulo.

HENRY TROTTER is a Ph.D. Candidate in African History at Yale University and the author of *Sugar Girls & Seamen: A Journey into the World of Dockside Prostitution in South Africa.*

RONALD WEITZER is Professor of Sociology at George Washington University. He is the editor of *Sex for Sale: Prostitution, Pornography, and the Sex Industry,* and author of *Legalizing Prostitution: From Illicit Vice to Lawful Business.*

ERICA LORRAINE WILLIAMS is Assistant Professor in the Department of Sociology and Anthropology at Spelman College in Atlanta, Georgia.

TIANTIAN ZHENG is Professor of Anthropology at the State University of New York, Cortland. She is the author of *Red Lights: The Lives of Sex Workers in Postsocialist China, Ethnographies of Prostitution in Contemporary China: Gender Relations, HIV/AIDS, and Nationalism, HIV/AIDS through an Anthropological Lens,* and *Sex-Trafficking, Human Rights, and Social Justice.*

Index

brothels: in Brazil, 130–132, 138, 143, 147, 161; in China, 8, 45; in Europe, 16–20; in Mexico, 1–2, 12, 32, 36, 39–40; in Nevada, 5, 76, 121; in New Zealand, 25, 27; in Sub-Saharan Africa, 86, 89–90, 92, 96; in Thailand, 147–148, 149–150, 155
bureaucracy, 5, 170
Bush, President George W., 159–160

cabines, 130, 162–63
call girls, 131–132, 137, 144
Canada, 28, 78, 183
Cape Town, 87, 98, 100–101, 105, 109, 111, 113
capitalism, 3, 48, 60–61, 71, 76
caregiving work, 85, 168
carioca, 130, 135, 136, 140, 142, 144
Carnaval, 195
casas. See brothels
cash, 76, 118, 126, 156, 170
Catholicism, 34, 44, 143
cell phone. *See* mobile phone
CHAME, 190–191, 193–197
charity, 149, 153, 180
Chiapas, 8, 32, 35–36, 37–38, 41, 43
children: responsibilities for, 39, 59, 63–64, 66, 68, 108, 169; sex work among, 2–3, 13, 100, 132, 146, 149–151, 153–156. *See also* pedophiles; South Africa; Thailand
China: abolitionist policy, 46, 48; economic reform in, 46–48; migration 8, 55
choice, 9, 11, 40, 46, 62, 66, 100, 103, 115, 136, 155, 190, 194. *See also* agency
church, 36, 81, 128, 169. *See also* Catholicism
city council, 116, 122–123
class. *See* social class
clientele: choice of, 9, 64, 77, 89–90, 104–105, 119, 161; competition for, 41, 107; criminalization of, 17, 20–21, 157; potential for abuse by, 1, 12–13, 31, 53, 55, 86, 111; spending by, 47–48, 56, 79, 131, 156, 162, 172–73. *See also* masculinity; regulars
coercion, 17, 19, 26, 40, 86, 96, 111, 113, 173
cohabitation. *See* housing

colonialism, 8, 101, 117, 119, 172, 174, 176, 187
computer, 66, 170. *See also* Internet
condoms: distribution and availability, 7, 42, 132, 183, 184–85, 199; factors impacting use, 11–12, 43, 90, 115, 125, 161, 163
consent, 5, 86, 89
consumer spending, 64, 71, 118
"contemporary community standard," 77–78
control. *See* regulations, legal and municipal
Copacabana, 132, 134, 136–137, 139–140, 142
correctional facilities. *See* prison
corruption, 2, 49, 50, 116, 121, 123, 151, 157, 172, 178–179, 193
cost of living, 60, 118
countryside. *See* rural
court, 24, 27, 78–81, 119, 123–124, 126, 152, 181
crackdown, 32, 49–51
criminal: elements, 17–18, 54, 86, 110, 183; law, 26–27, 48, 81, 119
criminalization, 5–7, 12, 16, 20–21, 23, 25, 88, 93–94, 116, 121–123, 147, 199

Dalian. *See* China
dance, 46–47, 49, 76–80, 87, 92, 96, 162, 172
danger, 9, 73–74, 79–80, 93, 97, 104, 127, 132, 166, 176, 191. *See also* risks
Daspu, 160
debt, 55, 71, 153, 192
deindustrialization, 12, 75–76
demand, 25, 50, 52, 95, 106
development, 34–35, 47, 50, 60–62, 67, 71, 147, 150–151, 159, 180, 188
deviance, 32–33, 46, 49, 83, 173
Diaz, Porfirio, 33–34, 43
discotheque, 130–131, 135, 142
discourse(s): competing, regarding sex work, 3, 7, 17, 21, 24, 28, 77, 81, 175; moral medical, 8, 11, 37, 137, 187; racialized, 9, 105; trafficking, 10, 56–57, 190, 193, 197, 199 discretion, 87, 91, 94, 96, 124
disease, *See* Sexually Transmitted Infections (STIs)
disorder, 32, 37, 79–81

homosexuality, 25, 120, 167

hostility, 39, 125, 170. *See also* hierarchies; stigma; violence

hotels, 32, 34, 47, 52, 61, 86, 91, 131

housing, 51, 55, 65, 70, 102, 109, 117–118, 156, 181–182

human rights, 26, 32, 48, 102, 116, 151, 157, 160, 165, 181, 192

human trafficking. *See* sex trafficking

husbands, 41, 43, 68, 124, 128, 134, 173

hustle, 162, 164

hygiene, 8, 12, 33–35, 170, 177, 181, 183

illegality. *See* regulations, legal and municipal

illiteracy, 41, 180, 186,

immigration. *See* migration

immoral, 5, 26, 28, 40, 70, 83, 119, 177

imprisonment. *See* prison

income. *See* earnings

independence: political, 8, 118, 172; sex work and, 10, 54–55

India: *devadasi* origins and reform movement, 8, 172–173; precolonial period, 174; independence in, 176, 179; sex workers' rights movements in, 183–185

indigenous, 60, 66–68, 147, 151

industrial area, 81–82. *See also* zoning

industrialization, 33, 71, 75, 79–80, 82, 118, 136, 147

infants, *See* baby; children

innocence, 5, 18, 45, 100, 149, 151, 197

International Social Purity Campaigns, 174, 187

Internet, 19, 23–24, 64–66, 70, 88, 91, 132, 136–137, 144

intimacy, 4, 82, 91, 98, 192. 194, 197

intimate partner violence. *See* violence

investment, 23, 26, 33, 55, 61, 66, 75, 154

Ipanema, 132, 137, 139

jail, 24, 40, 111, 178

Japan, 47, 49, 55, 88

jobs, 8, 40, 51, 54, 62–63, 68, 70, 75, 103, 118, 133–135, 147, 155, 166, 168–169

judgment, 78, 89, 123–124

karaoke, 45–47, 87

Karnataka, 172, 175–176, 179–180, 184, 188

Kenya: colonial, 7, 117–118; sex work regulations in, 5, 120–122; social factors impacting sex work in, 119–120, 125–128

kinship. *See* family; fictive kinship

Kvinnofrid (Peace for Women), 21–22

labor: conditions, 45, 54, 93, 103, 159, 168; Labor Party, 25–26; practices, 9–10, 37, 68, 71, 74–75, 136; rights, 16, 133, 160, 190–191

labor unions, 9, 47, 75–76, 191

Latin America, 6, 191. *See also* Brazil; Mexico

law enforcement, 1, 88, 94, 116, 119–120, 122–123, 126–127, 129, 146, 151–152. *See also* police

laws. *See* regulations, legal and municipal

lawyers, 103, 116, 120, 123, 179, 199

legal issues. *See* regulations, legal and municipal

Leite, Gabriela, 140, 144, 160, 190–91

liberalization, 16–17, 19, 118. *See also* neoliberalism

licensing, 18, 80–81, 84

life improvement. *See* social mobility

literacy, 41, 170, 180, 186

living arrangements. *See* housing

loans, 35, 170, 179, 181–182, 184, 187

loitering, 16, 97, 117, 120

love: clients and, 45, 155–156, 186, 195; romantic partners and, 111, 156

machismo, 11, 160. *See also* masculinity

madams, 51, 53, 133, 136

management, 53, 73, 79, 92, 130, 142, 162

marginalization: processes of, 6, 13, 18, 25, 34, 79, 82–83, 116, 165, 172; sex workers and, 4–5, 41, 74, 152, 198–199

markets: legal status of sex work and, 18–19, 22, 29, 88, 96, 132, 179; labor, relationship to sex work, 32, 37, 46, 54, 75, 133, 140, 147, 161

marriage, 59–60, 62, 67–69, 72, 117, 133–15, 172–173, 178, 192, 194, 198. *See also* husbands

surveillance, 22, 32–34, 40, 73–74, 82–83, 92–93, 96

sweatshop, 8, 57, 193

Sweden, 7, 16, 20–25, 28–29, 94, 105, 152

syphilis, 5, 33, 42

termas, 130, 132, 134–135, 138–139, 141, 144

Thailand: anti-child sex tourism campaigns in, 150–151, 157–158; economy, 148–149, 155; immigration policy in, 157; importance of tourism in, 146–148, 153

third parties, 14, 16, 18–19, 48, 86–87, 90, 92–93, 96–97, 112, 119, 136–137, 144

tips, 53, 68, 84, 121

tolerance zones, 5–6, 38. *See also* Galactic Zone

topless dancers. *See* dance

tourism, 11, 60–61, 64, 68–71, 118, 141, 143–144, 147, 153. *See also* sex tourism

trafficking. *See* sex trafficking

travestis, 36–37

truck drivers, 86, 88–90, 96–97, 132

Tuxtla Gutierrez (Mexico), 32, 35–38, 41, 43

unemployment, 60, 69, 193

unions. *See* labor unions

United Kingdom, 148, 152

United States, 43, 68, 71, 83, 85, 147, 159, 192, 198, 200

unskilled work, 45 ,103

Upstate New York. *See* Rust Belt

venereal infections. *See* sexually transmitted infections

victimization. *See* violence

violence: descriptions of, 39, 53, 104–105, 108–109, 112–113, 121; intimate partner, 102–103; risk of, 7, 12, 23–24, 52, 73, 86, 88–92, 101, 110, 119; sex work as a form of, 6, 17, 21–22, 48, 193; structural, 85, 113. *See also* abuse of sex workers; risks

virginity, 108, 173

visa, 26, 55, 200

vocational training, 40, 179

wages. *See* earnings

weddings, 56, 182

welfare, 2, 20, 23, 26, 43, 91, 157, 186

widows, 60, 62, 119

youth. *See* children

Zapatista, 36–37, 39

zoning, 12, 27, 74, 79–80, 82, 141